German Graphic Narratives and Trauma

Studies in German Literature, Linguistics, and Culture

German Graphic Narratives and Trauma

Edited by Elisabeth Krimmer and
Maureen Burdock

Rochester, New York

Copyright © 2025 Editors and Contributors

All Rights Reserved. Except as permitted under current legislation, no part of this work may be photocopied, stored in a retrieval system, published, performed in public, adapted, broadcast, transmitted, recorded, or reproduced in any form or by any means, without the prior permission of the copyright owner.

First published 2025
by Camden House

Camden House is an imprint of Boydell & Brewer Inc.
668 Mt. Hope Avenue, Rochester, NY 14620, USA
and of Boydell & Brewer Limited
PO Box 9, Woodbridge, Suffolk IP12 3DF, UK
www.boydellandbrewer.com

Our Authorised Representative for product safety in the EU is Easy Access System Europe - Mustamäe tee 50, 10621 Tallinn, Estonia, gpsr.requests@easproject.com

ISBN-13: 978-1-64014-202-2

Library of Congress Cataloging-in-Publication Data
CIP data is available from the Library of Congress.

The publisher has no responsibility for the continued existence or accuracy of URLs for external or third-party internet websites referred to in this book, and does not guarantee that any content on such websites is, or will remain, accurate or appropriate.

Contents

Introduction: Graphic Narratives and Trauma   1
Elisabeth Krimmer

Part I: Traversing Spaces and Species

1: Landscapes of Trauma: Relational Aesthetics and Politics in Contemporary Transnational German Comics   21
Katja Herges

2: Going Home: East German Trauma in Olivia Vieweg's Graphic Novels   41
Evelyn Preuss

3: Olivia Vieweg's *Endzeit*: The Trauma of Climate Change, Disease, and Plants Run Amok   60
Heather I. Sullivan

Part II: Rethinking Race

4: Born into Trauma? The Interplay of Biologism and Social Paradigms in Trauma Theory and Graphic Novels   81
Aylin Bademsoy

5: Birgit Weyhe's *Rude Girl* (2022): Comics, Blackness, and Transnational Dialogue: A Conversation with Priscilla Layne, Birgit Weyhe, and Elizabeth "Biz" Nijdam   102
Elizabeth "Biz" Nijdam

Part III: Countering Violence

6: On the Making of *But I Live:* A Conversation between Miriam Libicki, Gilad Seliktar, and Barbara Yelin   119
Charlotte Schallié

7: Portrait of the Artist as a Young Man: Perpetrators, Postmemory, and Implicated Subjects in Volker Reiche's *Kiesgrubennacht*   140
Christina Kraenzle

8: Comics on Display: Conceptual Remarks on *Gewalt erzählen: Eine Comic-Ausstellung / Narrating Violence: A Comic Exhibition* (Sigmund Freud Museum Vienna) 164
Marina Rauchenbacher

9. Disrupting the Counterculture: An Analysis of Rolf Dieter Brinkmann's Sampling of Comics 182
John D. Benjamin

Notes on Contributors 205

Index 209

Introduction: Graphic Narratives and Trauma

Elisabeth Krimmer

IN MANY WAYS, the emergence of comics as an internationally respected art form is intimately linked with the representation of traumatic experiences and with the genre of autobiography.[1] As comics scholar Andrew J. Kunka points out, "the autobiographical comics that get the most critical and scholarly attention often deal with trauma (the Holocaust, the Iran-Iraq War, a father's suicide)."[2] Similarly, in her study of graphic narratives by women, Hillary Chute notes that female creators of comics often focus on "retracing—materially reimagining trauma."[3] According to Chute, comics are "invested in the ethics of testimony."[4] Indeed, the most celebrated graphic narrative, Art Spiegelman's *Maus: A Survivor's Tale* (1986), is a case in point. *Maus*, which, along with Will Eisner's *A Contract with God and Other Tenement Stories* (1978), marked the birth of the contemporary "graphic novel" form, combines the memories of Spiegelman's father, who suffered persecution as a Jew in Nazi-occupied Poland and survived Auschwitz, with the artist's own experience of growing up in a family of survivors. Miriam Katin's *We Are on Our Own: A Memoir* (2006) and *Letting It Go* (2013) also deal with the Holocaust, while Joe Sacco's much-lauded *Palestine* (1993), *Footnotes in Gaza* (2009), and *Safe Area Goražde* (2000) portray war and occupation in the conflict zones of Israel-Palestine and Bosnia. Marjane Satrapi's

---

1   Anne Rothe extends this claim to the genre of memoir as such: "The triumph of the memoir was largely a result of its reorganization around trauma." Anne Rothe, *Popular Trauma Culture: Selling the Pain of Others in the Mass Media* (New Brunswick, NJ: Rutgers University Press, 2011), 87. Baetens and Frey note that the most celebrated graphic narratives favor "the autobiographical, documentaries, reportage, history." Jan Baetens and Hugo Frey, *The Graphic Novel: An Introduction* (Cambridge: Cambridge University Press, 2015), 12.

2   Andrew J. Kunka, *Autobiographical Comics* (London: Bloomsbury Academic, 2018), 2.

3   Hillary L. Chute, *Graphic Women: Life Narrative & Contemporary Comics* (New York: Columbia University Press, 2010), 2.

4   Chute, *Graphic Women*, 3.

international success *Persepolis* (2007) deals with the trauma of political persecution, religious extremism, war, and gender discrimination in Iran. Alison Bechdel's bestselling *Fun Home* (2006) gives form to the traumatic aftermath of a suicide, abusive relationships, family secrets, and closeted sexuality. Keiji Nakazawa's *I Saw It: A Survivor's True Story of the Atomic Bombing of Hiroshima* (1972) depicts both the day of the bombing and its aftermath and impact on survivors, including graphic representations of disfigured bodies. Aline Kominsky-Crumb's *Love that Bunch* (1990), Phoebe Gloeckner's *A Child's Life and Other Stories* (1998) and *The Diary of a Teenage Girl: An Account in Words and Pictures* (2002), Lynda Barry's *One! Hundred! Demons!* (2002), Craig Thompson's *Blankets* (2003), and David Small's *Stitches* (2009) all deal with various forms of sexual abuse, domestic violence, and family dysfunction.

The same focus on trauma that is evident in many of the most successful international comics also characterizes many of the most high-profile German graphic narratives. Olivia Vieweg's *Endzeit* (2012; *Ever After*, 2018), for example, features an apocalyptic world in which humans are attacked by zombies in the wake of a climate crisis. Simon Schwartz's *Packeis* (2012; *First Man: Reimagining Matthew Henson*, 2015) portrays the life of the black polar explorer Matt Henson who accompanied Commander Robert Peary on his expeditions to the North Pole. Schwartz highlights the daily injustices and brutal violence of racism. Birgit Weyhe's *Madgermanes* (2016; English 2021), which recounts the experiences of contract workers from Mozambique in East Germany, and her *Rude Girl* (2022; English 2024), which portrays the life of German scholar Priscilla Layne, also highlight racial discrimination. Ulli Lust's autobiographically inspired *Heute ist der letzte Tag vom Rest deines Lebens* (2008; *Today is the Last Day of the Rest of Your Life*, 2013) represents the young female protagonist's experiences of sexual harassment, sexual assault, and rape during a two-month trip to Italy. Barbara Yelin's *Irmina* (2014; English 2016) and *But I Live: Three Stories of Child Survivors of the Holocaust* (2022) both focus on the Second World War and the Holocaust, albeit from different perspectives: while *Irmina* is interested in the experiences of a bystander, *But I Live* recounts the stories of Jewish victims of the Nazis. Reinhard Kleist's *Der Boxer* (2011; *The Boxer*, 2014) also explores the Holocaust. Kleist portrays the life of Harry Haft, a Jewish boxer who survived Auschwitz. Olivier Kugler's *Dem Krieg entronnen: Begegnungen mit Syrern auf der Flucht* (2017; *Escaping Wars and Waves: Encounters with Syrian Refugees*, 2018) is based on his interviews with Syrian refugees. Other artists use comics to represent experiences tied to various illnesses, such as Daniela Schreiter's *Schattenspringer* (2014; *The World Beyond My Shadow: A Life with Autism*, 2016), which offers insights into how individuals cope with Asperger Syndrome, and Pirmin Beeler's *Hat man erst angefangen zu reden, kann alles Mögliche dabei herauskommen*

(2018; *Once You Start Talking, Pretty Much Anything Can Come Out*), which addresses mental health issues.

While there is a plethora of graphic narratives that focus on trauma, there are relatively few scholarly works on the topic and even fewer that deal with trauma in German-language comics.[5] With its nine original chapters, this edited volume seeks to contribute to the emerging scholarship on comics and trauma. To set the stage for this investigation, the introduction offers a survey of trauma research followed by some reflections on how comics use genre-specific qualities to represent traumatic experiences.

Definitions and Theories of Trauma

If one peruses scholarly works on trauma, one is struck with the centrality of the concept to our current times. Nancy K. Miller and Jason Tougaw open their edited volume *Extremities: Trauma, Testimony, and Community* with the comment that "if every age has its symptoms, ours appears to be the age of trauma."[6] Indeed, the use of the term "trauma" has become so common that critics are concerned that it might lose its explanatory force. In her book on *Comics, Trauma, and the New Art of War*, Harriet E. H. Earle cautions that the term "trauma" has become so ubiquitous that it now functions as "shorthand for negative experience."[7] Dominick LaCapra also notes the ubiquity of the term and warns against "the indiscriminate generalization of the category of survivor and the overall conflation of history or culture with trauma."[8] In light of such warnings, a study of comics and trauma would do well to avoid a concept of trauma that is vague and too broad. At the same time, there is a danger in advocating a concept of trauma that fails to accommodate a wide range

---

5 Scholarly works on the topic include *Documenting Trauma in Comics: Traumatic Pasts, Embodied Histories, and Graphic Reportage*, ed. Dominic Davies and Candida Rifkind (New York: Palgrave Macmillan, 2020); Andres Romero Jodar, *The Trauma Graphic Novel* (New York: Routledge, 2017); Kalina Kupczynska, "Unerzählbares erzählbar machen: Trauma-Narrative in der Graphic Novel," in *Der dokumentarische Comic: Reportage und Biografie*, ed. Dietrich Grünewald (Essen: Chr. A. Bachmann, 2013), 221–39; Brett E. Sterling, "The Intersection of Race, Gender, and Trauma in Ulli Lust's *Wie ich versuchte, ein guter Mensch zu sein*," *Journal of Austrian Studies* 55, no. 2 (2022): 65–99.

6 Nancy K. Miller and Jason Tougaw, "Introduction: Extremities," in *Extremities: Trauma, Testimony, and Community*, ed. Nancy K. Miller and Jason Tougaw (Urbana: University of Illinois Press, 2002), 1–21, here 1.

7 Harriet E. H. Earle, *Comics, Trauma, and the New Art of War* (Jackson: University of Mississippi Press, 2017), 9.

8 Dominick LaCapra, *Writing History, Writing Trauma* (Baltimore, MD and London: The Johns Hopkins University Press, 2001), xi.

of experiences. After all, traumatization has multiple causes. It includes trauma in the familial realm (incest, child abuse, domestic violence); it extends to the many manifestations of social injustice, ranging from victims of crimes to targets of structural racism and sexism; it can unfold in the public and political arena in both national and international contexts in the form of war, torture, mass rape, and genocide; it may be related to manmade natural disasters, including our current climate crisis; and it is, as Susan Merrill Squier and Irmela Marei Krüger-Fürhoff have pointed out, adjacent to experiences of illness, disability, grief, and pain.[9]

More often than not, these different types of trauma do not occur in isolation but rather are interlinked as personal experiences impact and are impacted by political structures and events: subjective experiences of racism may originate in structural injustices, personal loss may be caused by political decisions and developments, and individual pain and collective trauma meld into each other. In other words, no trauma unfolds in isolation, since "history, like trauma, is never simply one's own ... history is precisely the way we are implicated in each other's trauma."[10] In their response to traumatic events, individuals and groups try to resolve the crises of meaning, memory, and identity that trauma leaves in its wake.

Autobiographical narratives of trauma are inevitably dependent on the faculty of memory. Only those who recall the past—either cognitively or in bodily form—can experience trauma. While it is true, however, that there is no trauma without some form of memory, it is also true that the human memory is highly unreliable. Much has been written about the selectiveness of memory, and we are all aware of how memories fade over time, but these are but two of many sources of distortion. Daniel L. Schacter reminds us that memories may warp reality during multiple stages of the process of remembrance. To begin with, the act of encoding is not simply reproductive—"memories are never exact replicas of external reality ... incoming sensory information is not received passively"[11]—but rather is shaped by subjective predispositions, which, in turn, are influenced by social and political values and attitudes. Once formed, memories are not stable but are subject to alteration. Much evidence confirms that both post-event (mis)information and the retrieval environment can alter and distort memories. In other words, the act of retrieval does not resemble the opening of a

---

9 Susan Merrill Squier and Irmela Marei Krüger-Fürhoff, "Introduction," in *Narrative, Aesthetics, Contention, Community*, ed. Susan Merrill Squier and Irmela Marei Krüger-Fürhoff (University Park: Pennsylvania State University Press, 2020), 1–6, here 1.

10 Cathy Caruth, *Unclaimed Experience: Trauma, Narrative, and History* (Baltimore, MD: The Johns Hopkins Press, 1996), 24.

11 Gerald D. Fischbach and Joseph T. Coyle, "Preface," in *Memory Distortion: How Minds, Brains, and Societies Reconstruct the Past*, ed. Daniel L. Schacter (Cambridge, MA: Harvard University Press, 1995), ix–xi, here x.

computer file. Rather, every time we retrieve a memory, we create a new memory of an old experience, which may be altered according to the needs of the present, for example, to achieve greater coherence and conformity, or simply because it is conflated with extraneous reported or imagined events. Once faulty memories have taken hold, they are difficult to identify and eradicate, especially since the degree of confidence in a memory is in no way correlated to its accuracy. In short, we would do well to meet all our memories with some measure of mistrust.

While every type of memory formation is a fragile and fraught process, traumatic memories are characterized by a specific set of conditions. Many traumatic memories are not available to deliberate recall but rather appear spontaneously and often in intrusive form. At the same time, traumatic memories are often particularly vivid, and they have great staying power since high concentrations of stress hormones ensure the durability of memory. Importantly, traumatic memories tend to be fragmentary and do not necessarily present a complete picture since "emotional arousal typically enhances the accuracy of memory for the central aspects of an event and impairs memory for more peripheral details."[12] This feature of trauma may present problems in a court of law since what is perceived as central by a victim in the moment may not appear central to a judge. Victims of a mugging, for example, frequently remember the weapon that was directed at them with great detail but cannot describe the face of the aggressor. Trauma's elusive and fragmentary nature also presents problems with respect to narrativization, since the latter tends to favor coherence and structure.

In a fundamental sense, memories of trauma are characterized by disintegration or, in Cathy Caruth's words, by a "breach in the mind's experience of time, self, and the world."[13] They splinter reality into isolated units that often do not form a coherent whole, and they cannot easily be integrated into a victim's sense of self. Indeed, as the American psychiatrist David Spiegel explains, trauma erodes subjecthood and turns the self into an object: "Trauma can be understood as the experience of being made into an object, a thing, the victim of someone else's rage"; it may cause "feelings of unreality, automatic movements, lack of emotion, and a sense of detachment … Depersonalization and hyperalertness are prominent experiences during trauma."[14] In other words, trauma threatens to void the self as it severs the bonds between individual, community, and world.

The failure of integration that characterizes trauma may manifest in the form of intrusive memories, flashbacks, and nightmares, but also

---

12 Daniel L. Schacter, "Memory Distortion: History and Current Status," in *Memory Distortion*, ed. Schacter, 1–43, here 18.
13 Caruth, *Unclaimed Experience*, 4.
14 David Spiegel, "Hypnosis and Suggestion," in *Memory Distortion*, ed. Schacter, 129–49, here 135.

"hypersensitivity, hyperarousal, unprovoked violent outbursts, evasion of certain situations or sensations, irrational anger, emotional and psychological numbing."[15] Thus, trauma destroys the self's equilibrium and initiates a manic cycle of too much and not enough. Furthermore, trauma alters not only the functioning of one's sensory organs but also one's sense of time, for example, by collapsing past and present. As Judith Herman notes: "Long after the danger is past, traumatized people relive the event as though it were continually recurring in the present … It is as if time stops at the moment of trauma."[16] This disrupted sense of time can induce dissociative and fugue states as well as amnesia. Regardless of how specific forms of trauma manifest, however, they tend to define individuals in the most fundamental sense: "traumatic experiences are frequently focal experiences shaping the identity of traumatized individuals."[17] In other words, traumatic experiences are transformative: they change the self who undergoes them in such drastic ways that stability can be regained only once the new self has come to accept the changes effected by the traumatic rupture. On an individual level, such acceptance may need to be preceded by a period of mourning; in a national or political arena, it may require social restoration and reparative justice along with the formation of a new group identity.

Research on traumatic memories has relied on several problematic assumptions. For example, traumatic experiences have frequently been defined by the notion of suddenness, most prominently in the theories of Sigmund Freud and Cathy Caruth, who have both argued that traumatic experiences cannot be processed because they arrive suddenly and leave the self no time to prepare. According to Caruth, trauma is characterized by being "experienced too soon, too unexpectedly, to be fully known … [it] is therefore not available to consciousness until it imposes itself again, repeatedly, in the nightmares and repetitive actions of the survivor"; in other words, "what returns to haunt the victim … is not only the reality of the violent event but also the reality of the way that its violence has not yet been fully known."[18] While this assumption is much cited, one might object that the emphasis on the suddenness of trauma and a delayed, deferred response is unnecessarily restrictive. Why should we assume that the experience of torture is any easier if the victim has been warned that he or she will be tortured? Would a rape that is expected be

---

15 Earle, *Comics, Trauma, and the New Art of War*, 31.

16 Judith Lewis Herman, *Trauma and Recovery: The Aftermath of Violence from Domestic Abuse to Political Terror* (New York: Basic Books, 1992), 37.

17 John H. Krystal, Steven M. Southwick, and Dennis S. Charney, "Post Traumatic Stress Disorder: Psychological Mechanisms of Traumatic Remembrance," in *Memory Distortion*, ed. Schacter, 150–72, here 161.

18 Caruth, *Unclaimed Experience*, 4 and 6.

any easier to bear? Thus, rather than zero in on the temporal eruption of trauma, we might do well to highlight instead its imbrication in structures of power. After all, trauma is, as Judith Herman points out, an experience of profound powerlessness: "Traumatic reactions occur when action is of no avail. When neither resistance nor escape is possible."[19] Thus, trauma is defined not only by pain but by lack of control.

The second much-cited assumption of trauma theory concerns trauma's purported resistance to representation, its unspeakability. According to this dictum, trauma is defined as an unprocessed experience that resists verbal expression. In recent years, however, literary descriptions and visual representations of traumatic experiences, for example, in comics, have put pressure on this tenet while theorists of trauma have pointed to its logical inconsistency. Thomas Trezise, for example, notes astutely that there is "no conceivable subject position from which it is possible to know what supposedly remains, by definition, unknowable."[20] Importantly, Trezise argues that, quite frequently, it is not an inability to express traumatic experiences that foils communication but rather an unwillingness to listen or a failure to strike a proper balance between proximity and distance. Trezise insists that it is important to eschew "overidentification with survivors or the appropriation of their experience as our own," but it is also important not to take refuge in disidentification, estrangement, and othering.[21]

While Trezise highlights the victim-witness dynamic, Herman draws attention to the role of representation and expression in restoring justice. Silence, she notes, plays into the hands of perpetrators: "In order to escape accountability for his crimes, the perpetrator does everything in his power to promote forgetting. Secrecy and silence are the perpetrator's first line of defense."[22] Seen in this light, the assumption that trauma is unspeakable may unwittingly aid perpetrators. The literary scholar Michael Rothberg makes a similar point when he speaks of "the postmodern version of the bystander's lament whereby 'we didn't know' is transformed into 'we can't

---

19 Herman, *Trauma and Recovery*, 34.

20 Thomas Trezise, *Witnessing Witnessing: On the Reception of Holocaust Survivor Testimony* (New York: Fordham University Press, 2013), 46. Here, Trezise responds to Caruth's claim that "it is not so much the period of forgetting that occurs after the accident, but rather the fact that the victim of the crash was never fully conscious during the accident itself ... it is only in and through its inherent forgetting that it is first experienced at all." Caruth, *Unclaimed Experience*, 17. See also his comment that "Caruth confuses consciousness and assimilation: because the traumatic event cannot be readily integrated into a narrative or other symbolic framework, she mistakenly infers that it cannot have been consciously experienced or be consciously recalled." Trezise, *Witnessing Witnessing*, 52.

21 Trezise, *Witnessing Witnessing*, 224.

22 Herman, *Trauma and Recovery*, 8.

know.'"[23] Indeed, it seems crucial to defy the notion of trauma's unspeakability and to open up social spaces where traumatic experiences can be communicated, shared, and met with empathy. Such an approach is informed by a profound hope that, in telling their stories, survivors, and their audiences, will come to understand their experiences. Trezise maintains that narrating one's traumatic experiences may reintroduce a sense of wholeness and control as "the silenced victim becomes a storytelling survivor."[24] In contrast, others have argued that the notion of a whole and coherent self is itself a normative fiction. Earle, for example, proposes that we no longer regard "trauma as an 'unclaimed experience' that fragments psychic functioning and demands reintegration" but rather embrace "an understanding of 'healthy' mental operations that do not necessarily demand psychic unity."[25] Yet, while the notion of psychic unity may indeed be an all-too-optimistic fiction, it appears worthwhile to hold on to a hope of healing, of an integrated self, and of restorative justice in a community that commits itself to telling the truth. In such a framework, stories of trauma constitute a form of testimony that can be cathartic on both an individual, communal, and even national level: they confirm the reality of the narrated event both to the self and to society at large.

Comics and Trauma

Recent scholarship has posited an inherent affinity between comics and trauma. Comics scholars, such as Hillary Chute, have argued that the visual mode of graphic storytelling is structurally compatible with the non-verbal nature of traumatic experiences. Indeed, scholars of trauma confirm that "during traumatization, there is a shift away from verbal encoding toward encoding in emotional, pictorial, auditory, and other sensory-based memory systems."[26] In addition to comics' emphasis on pictorial encoding, Chute also remarks that the fragmented nature of the form of comics—the splintering into distinct panels separated by gutters—lends itself to the representation of traumatic experiences since memories of trauma are themselves characterized by fractures and discontinuities.[27]

---

23 Michael Rothberg, "Between the Extreme and the Everyday: Ruth Klüger's Traumatic Realism," in *Extremities*, ed. Miller and Tougaw, 55–70, here 67.
24 Trezise, *Witnessing Witnessing*, 16.
25 Earle, *Comics, Trauma, and the New Art of War*, 30. See also Chute who argues that female-authored graphic narratives tend to "unsettle ... selfsame subjectivity, presenting an unfixed, nonunitary, resolutely shifting female self." Chute, *Graphic Women*, 31.
26 Krystal, Southwick, and Charney, "Post Traumatic Stress Disorder," 158.
27 On the fragmented nature of comics, Thierry Groensteen writes: "the comics panel is fragmentary ... it never makes up the totality of the utterance but can and must be understood as a component in a larger apparatus." Thierry

And since comics represent temporal progressions through spatial design, they are able to "place pressure on traditional notions of chronology, linearity, and causality."[28] Similarly, it has been suggested that the technique of bleeding, of drawing beyond the borders of a panel, may be particularly serviceable for the representation of trauma since it visualizes trauma's transgressive nature, its refusal to be contained within clearly delimited boundaries, its capacity to collapse distinctions. In light of comics' structural reliance on the panel-gutter combination, bleeding is uniquely apt to depict trauma's ability to erode a person's sense of identity and wholeness, disrupt the flow of time, and destroy the bonds of community. The use of silent panels should also be noted in this context. In a comic that pairs word and image, the introduction of silent panels can serve to heighten an image's emotional impact on the reader.

While traumatic memories are often marked by lacunae, they can also be characterized by enhanced clarity. So-called flashbulb memories capture scenes, or aspects of scenes, in great detail. Here too comics provide a suitable medium since visualization allows for renditions that convey such enhanced attention to specific places, physical qualities, and sensory density. Comics can also accommodate the repetition compulsion that characterizes traumatic memories since they can challenge linear storytelling and allow for recursivity, for a return to the ever-same scene or image that marks the core of a traumatic experience. Finally, in addition to these structural affinities, the fact that trauma tends to manifest in the body also presents a point of contact with comics. As a visual form, comics depict, detail, and highlight bodies. Indeed, in comics, comics artist and theorist Will Eisner claims, "body posture and gesture occupy a position of primacy over text."[29]

Comics are frequently characterized as an interactive genre as the gutter—the void between panels—forces readers to take an active part in the creation of meaning: they must reconstruct what was left out and supply causal connections that are not explicitly given. Through the gutter, Victoria Aarons argues, comics create a "tension between the spoken and unspoken," which "mediates the representation of trauma."[30] Such interactive practices may instill feelings of connection and empathy in the reader. Similarly, Chute notes that the "handwritten marks on the

---

Groensteen, *The System of Comics*, trans. Bart Beaty and Nick Nguyen (Jackson: University Press of Mississippi, 2007), 5. See also Groensteen's statement that "comics is founded on reticence ... a story that is full of holes" (10).

28 Hillary Chute, *Disaster Drawn: Visual Witness, Comics, and Documentary Form* (Cambridge, MA: The Belknap Press of Harvard University Press, 2016), 4.

29 Will Eisner, *Comics and Sequential Art: Principles and Practices from the Legendary Cartoonist* (New York: W.W. Norton & Company, [1985] 2008), 106.

30 Victoria Aarons, *Holocaust Graphic Narratives: Generation, Trauma & Memory* (New Brunswick, NJ: Rutgers University Press, 2019), 4.

printed page" can convey a sense of intimacy.[31] Moreover, unlike film, comics do not define the temporal dimension of their consumption: readers determine the pace at which they absorb and digest the given story. As Eisner points out, readers of comics can linger over a panel, turn the page quickly if they wish, or "consider many images at the same time, or from different directions, a capability film lacks."[32] Precisely because they are multimodal and multilayered, Charles Hatfield suggests, comics can "nudg[e] us usefully out of accustomed habits of thought."[33] They may even invite their readers to choose their own reading path, just as they let readers decide whether they want to rest their gaze on an image or flip through the pages.[34] All these qualities encourage a sense of agency and connection that can counteract the feelings of powerlessness and isolation associated with trauma. Finally, it has often been pointed out that the dialogic nature of comics—its interplay of image and text, of narration and explanation, and of depictions of conversations between the creator's former and current self in autobiographical narratives—promotes self-reflectivity, which, in turn, may facilitate the integration of previously disconnected experiences. In combining images-in-sequence with texts, and in converting time into space, comics offer both the spatiality, physicality, and immediacy of the visual arts and the analytical depth and progressive trajectory of texts. They not only render snapshots of specific memories but self-reflexively visualize the process of remembrance itself.

In addition to allowing for agency, intimacy, and self-reflection, comics are defined by their handcrafted, subjective nature which may help to avoid or lessen the voyeuristic tendencies that are associated with photographic representations of traumatic suffering. Susan Sontag's warning against our easy consumption of images of pain is well known: "Perhaps the only people with the right to look at images of suffering of this extreme order are those who could do something to alleviate it … or those who could learn from it. The rest of us are voyeurs."[35] Sontag is particularly concerned with representations of bodies in pain, arguing that "all images that display the violation of an attractive body are, to a certain degree, pornographic."[36] To be sure, all representations of trauma run the risk of sensationalizing and/or aestheticizing experiences of pain and suffering, of, as Dominick Capra puts it, converting "trauma into

31   Chute, *Graphic Women*, 10.
32   Eisner, *Comics and Sequential Art*, 20.
33   Charles Hatfield, "Defining Comics in the Classroom; or, The Pros and Cons of Unfixability," in *Teaching the Graphic Novel*, ed. Stephen E. Tabachnick (New York: The Modern Language Association of America, 2009), 19–27, here 23.
34   See Jesse Cohn, "Mise-en-Page: A Vocabulary for Page Layouts," in *Teaching the Graphic Novel*, ed. Tabachnick, 44–57, here 52.
35   Susan Sontag, *Regarding the Pain of Others* (New York: Picador, 2003), 42.
36   Sontag, *Regarding the Pain of Others*, 95.

the occasion for sublimity."[37] They are also liable to impose meaning and order on existentially meaningless acts of sadistic brutality. And yet, one might argue that the hand-drawn lines of comics open up a stylistic repertoire that can skirt voyeurism and prurience.[38]

Clearly, many of the structural qualities of comics make them a suitable medium for the depiction of trauma. And yet, historically, comics have often been accused of inflicting trauma on their readers. All too often, mainstream comics, such as Hergé's *Tintin in the Congo* (1931), reproduced abhorrent racist or sexist stereotypes.[39] In the Marvel and DC comics universe, superhero-oriented comics tended to champion high-octane masculinity along with hypersexualized images of femininity.[40] In recent years, however, many comics artists have sought to draw attention to and counteract legacies of colonialism and genocide, histories of violence, dynamics of marginalization, and various forms of victimization and exclusion. To be sure, representations of trauma can have a traumatic effect on their readers—even if they take care to skirt voyeuristic renderings—but they can also counteract traumatization. Indeed, comics can, as Susan Merrill Squier and Irmela Marei Krüger-Fürhoff explain, contribute to healing because they make "public lived realities that often tend to be stigmatized, excluded, or disavowed by societies ... that cherish efficiency, health, and success."[41] In making these stories visible and public, comics can help to reintegrate individuals into communities and recreate social ties that were disrupted by traumatic experiences. They can also reestablish a sense of agency through the act of storytelling, which may involve pushing back against distortions, simplifications, and attempts to suppress and silence inconvenient and unwelcome narratives. In sum, graphic narratives can highlight the experience of marginalized

---

37 LaCapra, *Writing History, Writing Trauma*, 23.

38 The emphasis here is on *the potential* to resist sensationalizing images. There are certainly hand-drawn comics that exploit our worst instincts.

39 Will Eisner notes that such comics were not meant to be lasting works of art: "printed on low-grade newsprint [they were] never intended for long shelf life. The often-ancient presses utilized for printing comic books and Sunday strips could not even guarantee proper color registration or clarity of line." Eisner, *Comics and Sequential Art*, 1.

40 Yet, as Trina Robbins reminds us, "there was a time when more girls than boys read comics." Trina Robbins, *From Girls to Grrrlz: A History of Comics from Teens to Zines* (San Francisco, CA: Chronicle Books, 1999), 7. According to Robbins, "by the late 1940s, teen comics aimed at girls outnumbered crime comics, horror comics, and superhero comics" in the United States (38). It should also be noted that some of these comics were quite progressive and confronted "exploitative capitalists, deranged religious cults, and ecocatastrophes." Baetens and Frey, *The Graphic Novel: An Introduction*, 51.

41 Squier and Krüger-Fürhoff, "Introduction," 3.

and minoritized communities and may even serve as "another jurisdiction," as Leigh Gilmore has argued.[42]

In spite of their structural affinity to trauma, comics were long thought to lack the gravitas that the depiction of traumatic experiences requires. Historically, comics were associated with fantastic, made-up stories. Literary scholar Michael Chaney notes that autobiographies that rely exclusively on textual narratives—though often supplemented by photography—tend to lay claim to veracity and historical accuracy whereas autobiographical graphic narratives cannot but draw attention to their constructedness.[43] Comics are, as Chute puts it, "a conspicuously artificial form ... that is constantly aware of its own mediation."[44] Countering such arguments, artists, such as Art Spiegelman, have pointed out that, in many ways, the visuality of graphic narratives forces their authors to pay attention to a myriad of minutiae and thus to a form of factual accuracy that texts can easily elide. Consider, for example, Spiegelman's reflections on drawing the scene of his father Vladek's arrival at Auschwitz. Spiegelman notes that he had to make decisions about the exact gate where Vladek would arrive and about the direction from which he was coming. Thus, in some ways, graphic narratives can require a more stringent standard of accuracy than mere texts as creators need to make decisions about a plethora of details that are easily elided in a prose narrative—though, to be sure, not every graphic artist shares Spiegelman's investment in historical research or his stylistic preferences.

Moreover, in our digital age, in which photographs can easily be altered or even created wholesale by artificial intelligence, the indexical function of photographs has been destabilized. In comics, in contrast, the hand-drawn, personalized lines of the creator can be read to indicate the authenticity of the represented material. Comics are perceived as authentic precisely because the creator's subjective approach guarantees his or her investment in the story that is being told. Thus, beginning with the work of artists such as Spiegelman, graphic narratives reconnected with an "earlier function that drawing served before the camera—a kind of commemorating, witnessing, and recording of information."[45]

Many have welcomed the increased attention to trauma in graphic narratives since it can give voice to the experiences of marginalized communities and thus empower individuals while promoting social justice on

---

[42] Leigh Gilmore, *Tainted Witness: Why We Doubt What Women Say about Their Lives* (New York: Columbia University Press, 2017), 77. Throughout I use the term "graphic narratives" so as to avoid the problematic implication of fictional content associated with the term "graphic novel."

[43] Michael Chaney, ed., *Graphic Subjects: Critical Essays on Autobiography and Graphic Novels* (Madison: University of Wisconsin Press, 2011).

[44] Chute, *Disaster Drawn*, 17–18.

[45] Chute, *Disaster Drawn*, 28.

a communal or even societal level. As Aarons puts it, graphic narratives "reanimate[] the dead, giving voice to their memory"; they "create presence where there is absence. They create a whole out of fragments."[46] In doing so, they make sure that such irrecoverable losses are not also lost to commemoration. At the same time, a collective investment in trauma may also foster problematic trends. German scholar Anne Rothe warns against the dangers of kitschification and commodification attendant on selling the pain of others. Rothe is concerned that a focus on the commercial value of trauma narratives and their potential for voyeuristic media consumption in the form of entertainment may "remove these experiences of victimization and suffering from their socio-political contexts by reducing them to their smallest common denominator of a body in pain."[47] There is a danger that such narratives draw attention to spectacular, scandalous forms of trauma while ignoring "large-scale but covert victimization—through unemployment, poverty, and the exploitation of man and nature."[48] Rothe is also concerned that habituation to trauma narratives may obscure the difference between victims and perpetrators because it teaches us to conflate suffering and victimization: "While all victims suffer, not everyone who suffers is a victim."[49] In other words, the possibility of perpetrator trauma should not blind us to the crucial difference between victim and perpetrator. Conversely, victimization does not equal a permanent state of innocence. Finally, Rothe warns that the interest in autobiographical narratives of trauma might obviate the need for professional, analytical accounts, including those of historians and sociologists. The solution to the problems outlined by Rothe, however, is not to discourage or reduce narrativizations of trauma in comics, but rather to remain mindful of the fact that coping with traumatic experiences requires a multitude of discourses across different media and different genres. This volume seeks to contribute to these discourses.

Chapter Outline

This volume is divided into three sections: "Traversing Spaces and Species," "Rethinking Race," and "Countering Violence." The first section, "Traversing Spaces and Species," explores various forms of traumatization in the context of migration, neoliberalism, and neocolonialism. All chapters in this section are interested in restoring interrelationality and community both in the form of affective, interpersonal intimacy, as cross-species kinship, and as entanglements with non-human

46 Aarons, *Holocaust Graphic Narratives*, 69 and 8.
47 Rothe, *Popular Trauma Culture*, 5.
48 Rothe, *Popular Trauma Culture*, 24
49 Rothe, *Popular Trauma Culture*, 25.

environments. Katja Herges's "Landscapes of Trauma: Relational Aesthetics and Politics in Contemporary Transnational German Comics" reads Birgit Weyhe's *Madgermanes* (2016) and Pirmin Beeler's *Hat man erst angefangen zu reden, kann alles Mögliche dabei herauskommen* (2018) against the backdrop of global migration and mental health discourses. While *Madgermanes* documents histories of GDR labor migrants from Mozambique, Beeler engages with transnational family history in the context of psychiatric hospitalization and Turkish labor migration to Switzerland. Noting that both texts make extensive use of nature, landscape, and animal imagery, Herges argues that Weyhe and Beeler present a transnational, relational aesthetics that intervenes in representational politics and ethics of trauma in contemporary culture. Images of birds, trees, and landscapes touch deep emotional registers of subjectivity and thus facilitate an affective intimacy with traumatic memories of anxiety, loneliness, and foreignness that resist written and verbal forms of representation. Graphic visualizations evoke histories of colonialism and traumatic violence even as they highlight human entanglement with animals and landscapes. In rendering silenced memories visible and tying them to landscapes, they relocate individual trauma within culturally specific communal contexts, open up the possibility for social recognition and healing across cultures, and allow for affective and ethical engagements with the proximity of the Other across cultures.

While Herges explores a transnational, relational aesthetics, Evelyn Preuss's "Going Home: East German Trauma in Olivia Vieweg's Graphic Novels" situates Vieweg's *Endzeit* in the context of the post-1990 neoliberal transformation of East Germany. She argues that the graphic novel's protagonists can be read as stateless migrants who seek to gain their bearings amidst traumatic loss, disenfranchisement, lawlessness, and a sense of powerlessness in Germany's Wild East. Preuss conceives of post-unification East Germans as neocolonial subjects forced to cope with the de-solidarization of their society and the West's defamation and suppression of the East German legacy. Seen in this light, Vieweg's main characters are seekers intent on recuperating their subject positions and agency as they craft an alternative to Western society's extractive, exploitative, hierarchizing, and Othering relationship to the world. They mitigate homelessness through community and reestablish a sense of belonging through friendship, safe, affective communication, and mutual support. Evoking the historical layers that define the region around Weimar and Jena through visual references to the concentration camp Buchenwald and the region's GDR past, Vieweg refashions the East German landscape into a metaphoric place capable of projecting a utopian future and fostering communities that validate equality, social connectivity, and inclusivity.

Heather Sullivan's "Olivia Vieweg's *Endzeit*: The Trauma of Climate Change, Disease, and Plants Run Amok" also presents a reading of

Vieweg's *Endzeit*. However, while Preuss is primarily interested in the GDR context, Sullivan explores the text's representation of the climate crisis and of human-plant interdependencies. Sullivan reads Vieweg's graphic novel as a story of the reconquering of the world by plants and of multi-species entanglements. She argues that *Endzeit* is both a post-apocalyptic zombie story and a story about the trauma of climate change. Drawing on critical plant studies, eco-criticism, and eco-feminism, Sullivan argues that Vieweg's text creates an animated world of hybrid, vegetal-human multispecies life forms and cross-species kinship. Rather than presenting plants as passive matter, *Endzeit* makes us aware of our dependency on them. Rather than casting humans as rulers of nature, they share their bodies with vegetal life forms in a world dominated by plants. Throughout, *Endzeit* encourages a plant-focused perspective that points to the interdependence and entwinement of all life.

The second section, "Rethinking Race," deals with the problematic legacy of biologistic concepts of race, the violence of racism, and the fraught issue of cultural appropriation, but also considers the possibility of cross-racial empathy and interculturality. Aylin Bademsoy's "Born into Trauma? The Interplay of Biologism and Social Paradigms in Trauma Theory and Graphic Novels" explores how graphic narratives reinscribe or undermine biological reductionism and positivist discourses. Bademsoy notes that theories of intergenerational trauma highlight the role of the family in transmitting ancestral or parental traumata to the child. Since trauma is linked to the family and since the family is both a biological and social construct, concepts of trauma and trauma transmission are liable to reproduce biologistic reductionism and its conflation of social and biological elements. In a comparative reading of Art Spiegelman's *Maus* (1980–91) and Nora Krug's *Belonging: A German Reckons with History and Home* (2018), Bademsoy argues that Spiegelman counteracts essentialism by denaturalizing race and ethnicity, whereas Krug, in her effort to recuperate a positive concept of *Heimat*, reinforces the notion of an inherited and thus immobile identity. In *Maus*, the image of the mask is used to dismantle the purportedly biological nature of race; in *Belonging*, guilt is transmitted via nationality and ancestorial ties, thus collapsing history into biology.

While Bademsoy analyzes different conceptualizations of race, ethnicity, and nationality, "Birgit Weyhe's *Rude Girl* (2022): Comics, Blackness, and Transnational Dialogue: A Conversation with Priscilla Layne, Birgit Weyhe, and Elizabeth 'Biz' Nijdam" explores everyday realities of racism. The conversation offers insights into Weyhe and Layne's collaboration on the graphic novel *Rude Girl*, which was published in German in 2022. *Rude Girl* depicts Layne's experience as a child of Caribbean immigrants growing up in Chicago, her encounters with racism, and her interest and eventual career in German Studies. In her earlier graphic narrative *Madgermanes*, Weyhe, who spent her childhood in Uganda, Kenya, and the Seychelles, represented the lives of East German contract workers from Mozambique and was subsequently faced with accusations of cultural appropriation. *Rude Girl* engages with this discourse as Weyhe and Layne self-reflexively explore what it means for a white artist to represent Black lives, thus creating a comic about making comics. In their conversation, Weyhe offers reflections on the concept of home while Layne notes her desire to create a story that reflects the experiences of Black girls and that is invested in cross-racial empathy and interculturality. Both Weyhe and Layne point to the truly collaborative nature of the project that involved a constant process of back and forth as they pondered issues of multimediality, the selection of an appropriate title, and how to represent skin color. But they also note the inevitable fictionalization that occurs as an artist transforms memories into stories.

The third section, entitled "Countering Violence," is interested in questions surrounding the representation of violence, including the nexus of violence, spectacle, and voyeurism, the exploitation of suffering for the purpose of entertainment, and the role of remembrance in counteracting traumatization. The first chapter in this section, Charlotte Schallié's "On the Making of *But I Live*: A Conversation between Miriam Libicki, Gilad Seliktar, and Barbara Yelin," presents the artists' reflections on the creation of *"But I Live": Three Stories of Child Survivors of the Holocaust* (New Jewish Press, 2022), a collection of three graphic novellas that depict the experiences of four child survivors—Emmie Arbel (Kiryat Tiv'on, Israel), Nico and Rolf Kamp (Amsterdam, the Netherlands), and David Schaffer (Vancouver, Canada)—before, during, and after the Holocaust. Guided by Charlotte Schallié and supported by an arts-based participatory action research initiative, the project paired Holocaust survivors with graphic artists with the intent to co-create graphic narratives of their lives in the context of a comprehensive ethics of care framework. In their conversation, Libicki, Seliktar, and Yelin reflect on the intensely relational nature of their collaboration and of testimony in general, on working with and across different languages, on the difficulty of finding the right balance of distance and intimacy, on the fraught question of how to represent violence, on how their own family backgrounds affected their approach to the topic, on whether representations of violence have the potential to retraumatize survivors and traumatize artists, and on their artistic choices as they moved from recorded interviews to storyboarding to coloring.

Like Libicki, Seliktar, and Yelin's conversation, Christina Kraenzle's "Portrait of the Artist as a Young Man: Perpetrators, Postmemory, and Implicated Subjects in Volker Reiche's *Kiesgrubennacht*" also deals with the Holocaust, but, unlike the three artists, who explore the stories of four victims, Kraenzle is concerned with the perspective of perpetrators and their descendants. Kraenzle offers a reading of Volker Reiche's graphic memoir *Kiesgrubennacht* (Gravel Pit Night), in which Reiche recounts childhood memories of family conflict and violence. The text builds on a four-page comic published in 2003 in *Zebra*, entitled "Ein Tag in meinem Leben" (A Day in My Life) and on a six-page comic, created in 2008 as an autobiographical and self-reflective response to the German translation of a new edition of Art Spiegelman's *Breakdowns*. Like Spiegelman, Reiche works with dual timeframes, embedding memories from 1948 to 1973 in the contemporary context of 2012 and 2013, when he created the text. Unlike Spiegelman's text, however, which depicts victimization, Reiche's second-generation memories revolve around questions of guilt and his parents' support for the Nazi regime as the author contrasts his first-hand experience of domestic violence with his attempt to uncover the precise nature of his father's involvement in National Socialist atrocities. Kraenzle elucidates Reiche's reflections on the representation of violence and his own complicity in forms of entertainment that offer fantasies of violence, his thoughts on his ability to access memories and documents, and his exploration of his own artistic processes and his career in comics.

While Schallié and Kraenzle investigate processes of creation and issues of representation in graphic narratives, Marina Rauchenbacher's "Comics on Display: Conceptual Remarks on *Gewalt erzählen. Eine Comic-Ausstellung / Narrating Violence. A Comic Exhibition* (Sigmund Freud Museum Vienna)" reflects on Rauchenbacher's experience as curator of the exhibition *Narrating Violence. A Comic Exhibition*, which was on display in the Viennese Sigmund Freud Museum from October 22, 2023 to April 8, 2024. Unlike Schallié and Kraenzle, whose chapters deal primarily with the Second World War and the Holocaust, the exhibition curated by Rauchenbach explored a wide range of different manifestations of violence in the medium of comics, including physical, psychological, sexualized, gender-based, structural, and epistemic violence. Divided into four sections (sexualized and gender-based violence; coming of age; Shoah; and war, fleeing, and migration), *Narrating Violence* featured works by over thirty international artists, including Ulli Lust, Una, and Joe Sacco. In her chapter, Rauchenbacher parses the principles that guided her in the planning of the exhibit: contextualization designed to counteract a voyeuristic reception of the vulnerable bodies on display; self-reflectivity regarding both the medium of comics and the space of the museum itself along with its potential institutional involvement in practices of violence; and diversity of perspectives, topics, aesthetics, and styles. Rauchenbacher addresses the challenges involved in integrating the perspectives of both perpetrators and victims and reflects on the role of comics in remembrance and knowledge transfer. She also draws attention to insights into a comics' genesis afforded by the juxtaposition of originals and reproductions.

Like Rauchenbach's chapter, John D. Benjamin's "Normative Counterculture: Representational Injustice in Rolf Dieter Brinkmann's

Sampling of Comics," works with a wider definition of violence. Benjamin discusses two volumes of poetry by Rolf Dieter Brinkmann, *Die Piloten* (The Pilots, 1968) and *ACID: Neue amerikanische Szene* (ACID: New American Scene, 1969). Benjamin notes that the texts' formal innovations, their commitment to *sampling* and *archiving* of high and low culture, their investment in an aesthetics of the surface, their purportedly contentless *bricolage*, and their playful dialogue with 1960s American counterculture, in particular, the underground comix movement, have often been read as evidence of their norm-defying opposition to the conservative mainstream. Drawing on feminist and queer theory, Benjamin argues that this focus on formal innovation obscures modes of oppression conveyed in the content. Specifically, Benjamin points to Brinkmann's heteronormative and hypermasculine representations of women and women's bodies, which not only perpetuate gender stereotypes but remain beholden to consumer capitalism. In its recycling of oppressive gender roles and sexualized bodies, Brinkmann's postmodern *Popliteratur*, far from subversively undermining norms and hierarchies, perpetuates potentially trauma-inducing forms of social injustice and violence.

Throughout, the contributions ask how graphic narratives relate to visual archives of trauma, how they negotiate the aesthetics and ethics of trauma, and how they address issues of gender and race in representations of trauma. The contributors show how popular and non-mainstream graphic narratives give voice to individual, highly personal experiences of trauma and how they subtend notions of social justice. Indeed, Miller and Tougaw argue that there is an intimate link between private and collective healing: "In complex and often unexpected ways, the singular 'me' evolves into a plural 'us' and writing that bears witness to the extreme experiences of solitary individuals can sometimes begin to repair the tears in the collective social fabric."[50] At their best, graphic narratives can offer forms of "alternative jurisdiction" that contribute to processes of individual and collective healing as they "maneuver amid spaces of contradiction and extreme states of violent contestation."[51] Navigating the complex terrain of pain, memory, mourning, power, and violence, stories of individual, group, and national trauma help to restore the bonds between individual, community, and world.

---

50 Miller and Tougaw, "Introduction: Extremities," 3.
51 Gillian Whitlock, *Soft Weapons: Autobiography in Transit* (Chicago: University of Chicago Press, 2007), 194.

Part I

Traversing Spaces and Species

1: Landscapes of Trauma: Relational Aesthetics and Politics in Contemporary Transnational German Comics

Katja Herges

IN THE PAST decade, new subfields of German-language comics have been growing. This includes comics by German artists that attempt to capture the trauma of migrant experiences in Germany. Recent examples include works such as Paula Bulling's *Im Land der Frühaufsteher* (In the Country of Early Risers, 2012) and Reinhard Kleist's *Der Traum von Olympia: Die Geschichte von Samia Yusuf Omar* (2015; *An Olympic Dream: The Story of Samia Yusuf Omar,* 2016) and *Geschichten aus dem Grandhotel: Comic-Reportagen von Augsburger Design-Studierenden* (Stories from the Grand Hotel: Comic Reports by Augsburg Design Students, 2016). These comics are often rendered in documentary style and portray the artist's experiences with displaced persons. In addition, in line with the international rise of the field of Graphic Medicine, health-related comics, often about lived experiences of illness and disability, have emerged in Germany, ranging from Daniela Schreiter's *Schattenspringer* series (2014, 2015, 2018; *The World Beyond My Shadow,* 2016), which deals with autism, to Regina Hofer's *Blad* (2018; *Fat,* 2021), which portrays experiences related to eating disorders and body image. In the last decade, fictional comics about nature and climate crisis have gained prominence in the national and international comics scene and include works such as Frauke Berger's *Grün* (Green, 2018).

This essay will focus on two recent graphic narratives about traumatic experiences at the intersections of these trends, Birgit Weyhe's *Madgermanes* (2016; English 2021) and Pirmin Beeler's *Hat man erst angefangen zu reden, kann alles Mögliche dabei herauskommen* (Once you start talking, pretty much anything can come out, 2018). Both comics engage with experiences of migration, trauma, and health in uniquely transnational contexts. *Madgermanes* documents histories of Mozambican labor migrants who came to the GDR for professional training after the civil war against the Portuguese colonial power and Mozambique's independence in 1975, but experienced sexual violence, racism, financial exploitation, isolation, and (mental) health issues. In contrast, Beeler's comic engages with transnational family trauma in the context of psychiatric illness and long-term hospitalization, precarious marine labor, and sexual exploitation in the Global South, Turkish labor migrations to Switzerland, and Swiss migration to rural Turkey. While these two comics do not directly engage with environmental issues or the climate crisis, both make extensive use of animals, landscapes, and plants in their depiction of traumatic experiences of post-war labor migrations and mental health. *Madgermanes* and *Hat man erst* exemplify contemporary cultures of global migration, illness, trauma, and care for the more than human from partly autobiographical perspectives.

Both works are situated within the recent trends towards relational and transnational autobiography in life writing and comics. Traditional autobiography focused on celebrating the autonomous, often white male subject. However, as Nancy K. Miller has stated, all autobiographical writing is fundamentally relational; it is about "the web of entanglement in which we find ourselves."[1] This web includes not only individuals with whom the writer has shared life experiences, but also, importantly, the reader as imagined in the process of writing. Beyond the medium of writing, autobiographical comics and their specific narrative strategies produce multiple drawn versions of the narrator's own embodied identities while inviting the reader's active and affective participation in the creation of meaning.[2] While both the narratives examined here follow these trends in relational autobiographical comics—engaging readers in the co-construction of meaning and highlighting the relationality of the authors, narrators, characters, and images—both comics are unusual in their transnational focus beyond the Western world. In *Postcolonial Comics* (2015), Binita Mehta and Pia Mukherji claim that the medium of comics can foreground colonial legacies and reinscribe missing or misrepresented identities. Through both production and circulation, comics introduce new visual vocabularies and grammars that can challenge conventional "image-functions" and negotiate new identities.[3] At the same time, a transnational focus carries risks: comics by Western artists about "Others" have been complicit in reinforcing colonial power relations and reinscribing racialized stereotypes. For instance, Christina Kraenzle has

---

1 Nancy K. Miller, "The Entangled Self: Genre Bondage in the Age of the Memoir," *PMLA* 122, no. 2 (2007): 537–48, here 545.
2 Elisabeth El Refaie, *Autobiographical Comics: Life Writing in Pictures* (Jackson: University Press of Mississippi, 2012), 8–10.
3 Binita Mehta and Pia Mukherji, "Introduction," in *Postcolonial Comics: Texts, Events, Identities*, ed. Binita Mehta and Pia Mukherji (New York: Routledge, 2015), 1–22, here 3.

pointed out how, in the case of *Madgermanes*, Weyhe's fictionalization of testimonies of "Others" is problematic.[4] Priscilla Layne and others have further raised questions of cultural appropriation in Weyhe's comic, asking whether Weyhe has the right to tell these stories and to profit from them professionally while she only marginally acknowledges her privilege as a white German woman vis-à-vis the Mozambicans, particularly in the context of Germany's colonial past. However, Layne foregrounds how, in contrast to Weyhe's earlier works, Weyhe uses a feminist postcolonial approach to representation in *Madgermanes*, for instance through the aesthetic choice of a tricolor pattern for Black characters (rather than blackfacing or the colorblind avoidance of any color), anti-realist techniques, the complex interrelation of the stories, and her relational positioning in the narrative.[5]

In the following, I analyze how the comics' transnational and relational aesthetics that extends to the more-than-human intervenes in representational politics and ethics of trauma in contemporary culture. My essay intervenes in scholarship on comics studies and trauma studies. In the European tradition, trauma is often seen as a sudden piercing event, a "wound" inflicted on the mind that, according to Cathy Caruth, remains outside of narrative representation.[6] Scholarship on trauma, however, has challenged this view. Thomas Trezise, for instance, critiques the assumption that trauma is unspeakable; he notes that such a premise makes (Holocaust) testimonies generally suspect and might silence the voices of historical victims.[7] In postcolonial scholarship, Irene Visser highlights the continuous nature of (post)colonial trauma and its cultural dimensions, locating it in specific bodies, times, cultures, places, and narratives.[8]

---

4   Christina Kraenzle, "Risking Representation: Abstraction, Affect, and the Documentary Mode in Birgit Weyhe's *Madgermanes*," *Seminar* 56, no. 3–4 (2020): 212–34, here 214.

5   Priscilla Layne, "Diasporic Whiteness, Race and Representation in Birgit Weyhe's Graphic Novels," in *Zwischenräume: Geschlecht und Diversität in Comics*, ed. Christine Gundermann (Berlin: Bachmann, 2021), 101–24, here 118, 123. In her latest work, *Rude Girl* (2022), Weyhe engages with received critiques of the appropriation of Black narratives in *Madgermanes* and at the same time collaborates with Priscilla Layne, a Caribbean-born African American professor of German in the United States, to produce a dialogic graphic narrative of Layne's life that includes Layne's feedback on Weyhe's attempts to representat Blackness.

6   Cathy Caruth, *Unclaimed Experience: Trauma, Narrative and History* (Baltimore, MD: Johns Hopkins University Press, 1996), 3.

7   Thomas Trezise, *Witnessing Witnessing: On the Reception of Holocaust Survivor Testimony* (New York: Fordham University Press, 2013), 62.

8   Irene Visser, "Trauma Theory and Postcolonial Literary Studies," *Journal of Postcolonial Writing* 47, no. 3 (2011): 270–82, here 270.

Countering the notion of trauma's unspeakability, comic scholars have demonstrated the particular potential of the medium for representations of (postcolonial) trauma and its ability to encourage witnessing. Comics, Hillary Chute claims, are a suitable vehicle for traumatic memory: "Images in comics appear in fragments, just as they do in actual recollection; this fragmentation, in particular, is a prominent feature of traumatic memory."[9] Chute argues further that female authors of contemporary autobiographical comics, such as *Persepolis* (2000) or *Fun Home* (2006), "compellingly communicate and make sense of the challenges women face in relation to traumatic experiences."[10] Based on the suitability of the medium, Ebru Ustundag and Courtney Donovan make a case for the potential of comics to work through trauma and toward recognition and social justice. Comics demonstrates that "a combination of visual and textual narrative provides a more robust hybrid platform for documenting, describing and recognizing the experience of trauma as a foundation for claims to social justice."[11]

While trauma, particularly in its ethical and social dimensions, has been a prominent topic of comics scholarship, little attention has been paid to different material forms and functions of animal, vegetation, and landscape imagery in trauma representation, in particular in the postcolonial context. Cartoonists often invoke animals as metaphors that represent relationships between humans—Art Spiegelman's *Maus* (1991) is a prominent example. Discussing the autobiographical graphic novel more generally, Michael Chaney finds theorizations of the animal essential to sequential pictorial narratives of identity and otherness; here, the animal functions as a "ludic cipher of human otherness."[12] Moving beyond the use of animals as metaphors of otherness, Maureen Burdock has recently shown how comics about transgenerational and transnational trauma can re-establish material connections both with forebears and more-than-human others, allowing a relational ethics of trauma to emerge.[13]

Building on previous scholarship in comics studies, my article examines how comics strategies of relationality with the (more-than-human) Other expand the aesthetics and politics of trauma in transnational

---

9   Hillary Chute, *Graphic Women: Life Narrative and Contemporary Comics* (New York: Columbia University Press, 2010), 4.

10   Chute, *Graphic Women*, 2.

11   Ebru Ustundag and Courtney Donovan, "Graphic Narratives, Trauma and Social Justice," *Studies in Social Justice* 11, no. 2 (2017): 221–37, here 228.

12   Michel Chaney, "Animal Subjects of the Graphic Novel," *College Literature* 38, no. 3 (2011): 129–49, here 130.

13   Maureen Burdock, "Shapeshifters: Metamorphosing Transgenerational Trauma Through Comics," in *Contested Selves: Life Writing and German Culture*, ed. Katja Herges and Elisabeth Krimmer (Rochester, NY: Camden House, 2021), 229–47, here 246.

contexts. While Weyhe draws worlds of Mozambican and German plants, animals, and bodies that affectively recall histories of colonialism and traumatic violence, Beeler focuses on Swiss and Turkish rural landscapes and animals to give voice to silenced memories of psychiatric hospitalization, postcolonial exploitation, and political conflict. Both comics contribute to rethinking traumatic memories relationally, transnationally, and affectively. Both authors primarily visualize memories that are difficult to articulate in words alone, producing a nuanced and delicate form of testimony that opens up possibilities for social witnessing and healing.

Madgermanes: Relationality, Traumatic Memories, and Affect

Madgermanes starts with a brief self-referential prologue that establishes a relational framework for narrating different autobiographical experiences of migration. It introduces Weyhe's own memories of migrating from Germany to Uganda when she was a child and her continuous feelings of (un)belonging to East Africa as an adult who has moved back to Germany, where she has now lived for many years. The prologue connects her own experiences with the experiences of Mozambican migrant workers to Germany, who, mostly had to return to their country after 1990 and felt as "Fremde" (strangers) both in Germany and "im eigenen Land"[14] (in their own land). Second, the prologue explains the making of the comic as a work of collaboration and mediation between artist, interviewees, and readers. The panels illustrate how Weyhe, when she arrived for a visit in Mozambique—forty years after her move to Uganda—randomly met several men and women who had worked in the GDR in the past. In the following, she illustrates how she started to interview former workers in Mozambique and in Germany and combined and fictionalized their stories about migration and questions of identity into three narratives in the comic, of José, Basilio, and Anabella. As a gesture of relational life writing, Weyhe thanks the interviewees in the introduction and lists their names at the end of the work. For Paul John Eakin, the phenomenon of the "story of the story" is an important feature that marks the turn of autobiography away from a celebration of the autonomous subject to an acknowledgment of the interweaving of our lives with those of others in relational autobiographies.[15] At the same time, Weyhe does not link her childhood memories

---

14 Birgit Weyhe, *Madgermanes* (Berlin: Avant-Verlag, 2016), 15. All translations are taken from Birgit Wehye, *Madgermanes*, trans. Katy Derbyshire (Berlin: V&Q Books, 2021) with identical page numbers.

15 Paul John Eakins, *How Our Lives Become Stories: Making Selves* (Ithaca, NY: Cornell University Press, 1999), 56.

of attending a German school in Kampala and Nairobi to her white privilege and only marginally addresses her positioning as a white adult German woman in contemporary Mozambique.[16] Finally, the prologue introduces the motif of nature: Weyhe's portrayals of her arrivals in East Africa as a child and as an adult feature imagery of overwhelmingly sensory landscapes of heat, humidity, beauty, and noise which connects with the sensory and affective narratives of arrival of the three protagonists in Germany. In the following, I will analyze how the different nature motifs in each narrative open new relational and transnational modes of representing trauma.

The comparative scenes of arrival connect Weyhe's experiences of traumatic migration with the story of the first protagonist, José, and with the life of migratory birds. The images of Weyhe's arrivals in East Africa as a child and as an adult show macroscopic geographical maps of Africa, Uganda, and Mozambique, and microscopic images of the landscape, animals, and vegetation, surrounding the airport in Entebbe in Uganda and in Pemba in Northern Mozambique. The prologue further introduces an image of migratory birds that, like, Weyhe and the Madgermanes, return to their home country after long absences. In José's narrative of his arrival and life in Berlin, *Madgermanes* takes up the images of the magnified landscapes and the birds: José, who feels isolated and homesick in a housing complex for contract workers far outside of Berlin after his arrival from Maputo, is shown looking out through the window, watching a desolate German winter landscape with a raven sitting on a naked branch; the following panels present magnifications of the bird. In addition, the images of a bird in Berlin are juxtaposed with a splash page that features an image of a schematic ornamental bird on top of a cylindric African mask.[17] These images of (migratory) birds connect different traumatic memories of migration with anxiety, loneliness, and foreignness. In her analysis of the representation of birds in literature, Susana Vega Gonzales argues that,

---

16   Layne, "Diasporic Whiteness," 118.

17   Weyhe, *Madgermanes*, 30–31. Weyhe's use of African-style masks raises questions of appropriation of African art by a Western artist. Dennis Duerden shows how early twentieth-century modernist artists appropriated face-covering objects from the Congo-Niger region and used them in their own work. Thus, the terms "African art" and "mask" were generalized and removed from their specific geographical and ritual contexts, where they formed part of an entire costume, and linked to notions of "primitivity." See Dennis Duerden, "The 'Discovery' of the African Mask," *Research in African Literatures* 31, no.4 (2000): 29–47. However, Weyhe's mask is overlaid with strong golden brushstrokes that complicate the reader's perception of the mask. This artistic anti-realist technique suggests a distancing of Weyhe's style from claims of authenticity about African art.

because of their ability to fly and soar up in the air towards the sky, birds were considered messengers from heaven, possessors of occult secrets, or symbols of the sun and rebirth or of the flying souls that ascend to heaven after death. However, Vega Gonzales finds that in African American literature, for instance, in works by Toni Morrison, birds are often fraught with negative meaning; "of suffering, pain, humiliation, madness, and death, in keeping with the disruptive character of nature that is present in this author."[18] In José's narrative some images present birds as symbols of love (for example, in his love affair with another protagonist named Anabella) and of dreams of a hopeful future, but the magnified image of a lonely or anxious bird reappears in the narrative after his return to Mozambique. José, who settled in Wismar after his separation from Anabella, finally returns to Pemba (like Weyhe many years later) after the increasing racism of the "Wendezeit." However, in Mozambique he feels even more alone than in Germany; alienated from his family, frustrated over the loss of his quality of life in the GDR and his promised salary, traumatized by the death of his ill daughter, and isolated through his social marginalization as a "rich Westerner."

Beyond the affective implications of the bird metaphor, the bird panels in the prologue and in José's narrative use the visual and conceptual technique of scaling. According to Susan Merril Squier, scaling "unites the biological and the cultural, across a range of ascending scales from the microscopic to the macroscopic." Moving from one scale to the next, Squier argues, the viewer engages repeatedly in "scale framing," which she defines as "discursive practices that construct the scale at which a problem is experienced."[19] This allows us to take our perceptions beyond the "human-scale lens" and conceive the deep entanglement of our species with animals and landscapes. In *Madgermanes,* Weyhe scales experiences of trauma and migration from the biological to the geographical, cultural and political. The schematic bird on top of the mask with a long, sharp beak, a long neck, and stripes on top of the mask shares some resemblance with the saddle-billed stork, a bird resident of South Saharan Africa.[20] While the raven and the saddle-billed stork are resident birds that

18   Susana Vega Gonzales, "Broken Wings of Freedom: Bird Imagery in Toni Morrison's Novels," *Revista de Estudios Norteamericanos* 7 (2000): 75–84, here 82.

19   Susan Merrill Squier, "Scaling Graphic Medicine: The Porous Pathography, a New Kind of Illness Narrative," in *Pathographics: Narrative, Aesthetics, Contention and Community,* ed. Susan Merrill Squier and Irmela Marei Krüger-Fürhoff (University Park: Pennsylvania State University Press, 2020), 205–25, here 207.

20   Weyhe's schematic drawing, however, does not feature the stork's characteristic wattle under the beak or its long legs. Notably, the bird images connect to Weyhe's autobiographical interest in birds. In her autobiographical comic *Ich weiß*

tend to stay near their nesting grounds, many European birds migrate south to more temperate climates in winter. In contrast to the migrating birds, Weyhe and the protagonists migrated in opposite directions: While Weyhe moved to the global South and experienced an overwhelming sensory environment and political instability, José migrated north, where he faced a foreign climate with grey winter weather, and the racist political climate of East Germany. In his reading of *Madgermanes*, Johannes C. P. Schmid notes the links between animal and human experiences, arguing that "these metaphors from the domain of nature highlight how migration is not a human invention, but rather a larger aspect of the world."[21] By relating human and non-human scenes of arrival, residence and struggle, Weyhe's sensory and material environments point to the affective, transnational, and more-than-human experiences of traumatic migration.

In addition to landscapes and birds, *Madgermanes* draws on vegetation to extend the concept of traumatic memories of migration and isolation beyond the human and to express new complex feelings of belonging in the aftermath of trauma. The narration by the third protagonist, Anabella, focuses on vegetation in different locations. In contrast to the other protagonists, Anabella's narrative is one of recovery and transformation: it deals with experiences of family death in war, sexual violence, abortion, separation, mental health issues, and racism; yet she manages to stay in Germany, gets an education, and becomes a medical doctor. Despite these different trajectories, Anabella's and José's narratives are interrelated in complex ways: each narrative presents their relationship struggles, the fight over Anabella's pregnancy and abortion, and their sudden separation in different, at times contrasting perspectives, thereby highlighting the multi-perspectivism of traumatic experiences. Further, instead of presenting a simplified narrative of "integration" into German society, the images of gardens and flowers convey complex traumatic memories of belonging.

Madgermanes ends with Anabella's visit to the Parque municipal in Belo Horizonte in Brazil during a conference, where the lush local vegetation there reminds her of the local flora in Mozambique and by extension of the violent loss of her family and her home, and her feelings of

---

(*I know*, 2017) about her childhood in East Africa, Weyhe briefly touches upon her knowledge of African birds. During a trip to Tanzania in the Serengeti, she started reading *Birds of East Africa* in a mission library, an experience that turned her into an avid ornithologist, see Birgit Weyhe, *Ich weiß* (Berlin: Avant-Verlag, 2017), 184.

21 Johannes C. P. Schmid, "Framing and Translation in Weyhe's *Madgermanes*," in *Situated in Translations: Cultural Communities and Media Practices*, ed. Michaela Ott and Thomas Weber (Bielefeld: Transcript, 2019), 107–18, here 114.

unbelonging. In the following two-page spread, Annabella is shown sitting on a bench crying while surrounded by a variety of lush flowers and trees that are disproportionally large and cover almost the entire space.[22] The size of the vegetation acknowledges the affective load of migration, violence, and feelings of foreignness in Germany, together with the recognition that "Deutschland kann mir wohl nie meine Heimat ersetzen" (Germany will never take the place of my homeland, it seems).[23] While the motif of a lush garden can prompt nostalgic Western imagination of an exotic spectacle or a colonial enterprise,[24] Debbie-Ann Morrison finds that gardens are often evoked in contemporary Caribbean women's literature where repeated images are freighted with concerns about dislocation and relocation.[25] The harvestable garden has evoked visions of the forced transplantation of labor as well as peoples, plants, and animals, as well as physical and spiritual dislocation and domination. In addition to feelings of alienation and mourning, the time in Brazil also reveals Anabella's identification with German cultural traditions, such as punctuality, authenticity, and social security, acknowledging that "dort [in Mosambik] würde ich mich noch fremder fühlen" (I would feel even more foreign there).[26] The last page expresses these ambiguous feelings of belonging:

> Wie alle anderen Emigranten, die sich auf den Weg in ein neues Leben gemacht haben, gehöre ich weder zu dem einen noch dem anderen Land. Wir sind alle ohne Bindung, ohne Anker, schwebend zwischen den Kulturen. Egal ob wir zurückkehren oder bleiben.
>
> [Like all other emigrants, who have set out for a new life, I belong neither to one country nor the other. We are all without ties, unanchored, floating between cultures. No matter whether we go back or stay.][27]

22　Weyhe, *Madgermanes*, 232–33.
23　Weyhe, *Madgermanes*, 232.
24　The Parque municipal in Belo Horizonte is not of colonial origin but was created after Brazilian independence by French designer Paul Villon in 1897. Even so, as W. J. T. Mitchell explains, "like imperialism itself, landscape is an object of nostalgia in a postcolonial and postmodern era, reflecting a time when metropolitan cultures could imagine their destiny in an unbounded "prospect" of endless appropriation and conquest." W. J. T. Mitchell, "Imperial landscape," in *Landscape and Power*, ed. W. J. T. Mitchell (Chicago and London: University of Chicago Press, 1994), 5–34, here 20.
25　Debbie-Ann Morrison, "Ecowomanist Endeavors: Race, Gender, and Environmental Ethics in Contemporary Caribbean Women's Literature" (PhD diss., University of Miami, 2012), 16.
26　Weyhe, *Madgermanes*, 235.
27　Weyhe, *Madgermanes*, 236.

The text is situated in a two-page spread of magnified flowers, seeds, and pollen that float away, visualizing the complex and unstable experiences of belonging. Like the pollen and petals that change physical location and material shape, Anabella transforms through her experience of migration between cultures. Through the image of the transforming flower, Weyhe highlights the ambivalence of any migratory experience and identity, as fleeting and shifting, similar to what Gloria Anzaldúa calls "conciencia de la mestiza"[28] (consciousness of the Borderlands). Like Caribbean women's writing, *Madgermanes* simultaneously considers both the sociopolitical and the communal source of power in reclaiming the image of the garden and its physical space. The garden "becomes not only a source of pain and displacement, but also a symbol for and a physical site of aesthetic connection with the land, spiritual transcendence, and political empowerment."[29] In the context of African-German migration Weyhe draws the garden as a transnational site of female contemplation, post-traumatic mourning and creative re-connection across Mozambique, Brazil, and Germany.

Interestingly, the last image of the comic references the first page of Weyhe's prologue, which features flower petals in three consecutive, horizontally aligned panels. The panels show flowers and pollen in increasing magnitude like under a microscope: While the first panel shows dense black dots, the following two images zoom in on increasingly recognizable and detailed dandelions and their pollen that fly in different directions.[30] These images at different scales from microscopic abstraction to detailed macroscopic flowers and pollen together with the question "Woraus speist sich Erinnerung?" (What does memory feed on?)[31] suggest that memories, like pollen, are biological and sensual, fleeting and ever transforming, and can be viewed in different magnitudes and scales, like a scientific object of analysis. Through this series of images, Weyhe acknowledges her lingering childhood memories of belonging in Mozambique while linking her story to her characters' search for identity and traumatic memory in a gesture of relational life writing. In addition, the images of vegetation expand these traumatic memories to more than individual human experiences of loss, transformation, and creativity, connecting human and more-than-human, biological and cultural, microscopic and macroscopic, German and Mozambican.

Finally, in addition to visual metaphors of birds and vegetation, *Madgermanes* repeatedly relies on fantastical animals to express the

---

28 Gloria Anzaldúa, *Borderlands: La Frontera* (San Francisco, CA: Aunt Lute Books, 1987), 77–91.
29 Morrison, "Ecowomanist Endeavors," 16.
30 Weyhe, *Madgermanes*, 7.
31 Weyhe, *Madgermanes*, 7.

complex traumatic memories and experiences of the protagonists. In José's narrative, his pain about Anabella's abortion is expressed through a wild animal that attacks him. Similarly, in Basilio's case, his experience of a racist attack is translated into a scene with animals that resemble jackals, hyenas, or wild dogs. In both cases, the comic juxtaposes documentary and imaginary modes and styles. In the documentary panels of Basilio's story, he is forced to move from Berlin to Hoyerswerda in Saxony to work in the local brown coal mining industry. He witnesses daily racism, racist riots, and an arson attack on his asylum housing complex in 1991, when the police did not intervene to protect him and other immigrants.[32] In a spontaneous reaction to the attacks, he runs away from Hoyerswerda and his German partner without notice and never sees his child again. The documentary panel series of Hoyerswerda is juxtaposed with a one-page image in woodcut style that, in sharp contrast to the previous scenes, is situated in a savanna environment, where Basilio's avatar is hiding high up on branches of a tree and two wild fantastical animals underneath look up and clench their teeth.[33]

In her reading of *Madgermanes*, Christina Kraenzle explains how the comic combines complex visual languages that are not connected in simple ways. Rather, the comic oscillates between documentary style, objects of popular culture, traditional layout with multiple panels and gutters, and expressionist images that are reminiscent of woodcuts or ink wash painting and have symbolic value or express emotions. Through this referencing and juxtaposition of different aesthetic traditions (including German and African craft and design), the depictions create multiple associations, and the reader must work to make sense of the images in each panel transition. This experimentation with graphic documentary form, according to Kraenzle, allows Weyhe "to contrast various discourses and temporal layers of memory."[34] In doing so, Kraenzle continues, the comic reveals a forgotten or neglected aspect of Afro-German history and "bring[s] into view the often-suppressed history and legacies of colonialism in postwar Germany."[35]

In the scene referenced above, the juxtaposition invites different readings: Of course, the fantastical dangerous animals might symbolize German Neo-Nazis while the human figures hiding in the trees represent the attacked Mozambican workers. Such a metaphorical reading of animals in the context of National Socialism and its legacies is reminiscent of Spiegelman's *Maus*, in which Nazis are portrayed as cats and Jews as mice. Richard De Angelis argues that Spiegelman's visual mouse

---

32 Weyhe, *Madgermanes*, 140.
33 Weyhe, *Madgermanes*, 141.
34 Kraenzle, "Risking Representation," 226.
35 Kraenzle, "Risking Representation," 226.

metaphor serves to "expose the lie behind the artificial genetic hierarchy that Aryan anti-Semitism sought to establish within the human race."[36] In *Madgermanes*, the metaphor of the savage animal points at and subverts racialized imagery that constructs "Blackness" or "Africanness" as animality and savageness and as a threat to the white civilized settler.

In addition to a reading of the fantastical animal as a symbolic human other, the expressionist woodcut image can also be read as an archetypal childhood dream or nightmare. The two figures in the tree can be read as a surreal doubling of Basilio as a child (without the mustache of the adult Basilio), thus pointing at the dream quality of the scene, in which two fantastical, dangerous animals attack him. Such a scene is reminiscent of children's books, such as Maurice Sendak's *Where the Wild Things Are* (1963), in which a conflict between the main child character Max and his parents is transformed into a jungle scene with wild monsters. Similar to Sendak's work, Weyhe's *Ich weiß* (I know, 2017) draws extensively on biological and fantastical animals in the exploration of the author's childhood memories in East Africa, often to express ongoing political instability and violence. By drawing on African artistic traditions, the large size of the image and its highly affective style convey the intensity and unspeakability of existential fear in the past and present. The image of Basilio as a child is juxtaposed with the adult narrator's voice, acknowledging: "Zum ersten Mal in meinem Leben hatte ich wirklich Angst" (I was really scared for the first time in my life). Such a juxtaposition of adult and childhood self also relates to the prologue, in which Weyhe stages a visual dialogue between imagery of herself as a child sitting anxiously on a plane to Uganda, overwhelmed by the sensory landscape and the climate upon arrival, and the commentary of the adult narrator, who frames the images as the "prägendste meiner frühen Erinnerungen" (most formative of my childhood memories).[37] These juxtapositions of visual and verbal, past and present connect across different affective memories, of Germans and Mozambicans, and produce an entry point for the adult white Western reader to affectively connect to and engage with racist attacks from the perspective of the Other.[38]

At the same time, however, the juxtaposition of European and African traditions and the use of fantastic animals also carry risks since they open up problematic readings. The metaphorical reading of the wild animals as Neo-Nazis destabilizes established categories of "wild" African nature, while reifying an artificial hierarchy between humans and other species

---

36 Richard De Angelis, "Of Mice and Vermin: Animals as Absent Referent in Art Spiegelman's *Maus*," *International Journal of Comic Art* 7, no.1 (2005): 230–49, here 231.

37 Weyhe, *Madgermanes*, 8.

38 Weyhe, *Madgermanes*, 141.

and rendering the animal an invisible "absent referent."[39] In addition, the reading of the woodcut as a dream landscape could also suggest a colonialist fantasy in which Africans are portrayed as primitives who hide on trees. Nevertheless, this juxtaposition of panels about the same event but drawn in different scales and styles allows readers to participate in the process of meaning making across national and historical divides. Gillian Whitlock argues that comics free readers "to think and imagine and see differently" in engaging with the pain and suffering of others primarily through the particularities of the medium.[40] Gutters function as "blank spaces where new meanings can be generated, and a distinctive cross-cultural translation can occur."[41] This imaginative labor of reading and looking for closure is at the heart of how autographics shape affective and ethical engagements with the proximity of the Other across cultures. Through the juxtaposition of European and African visual styles, histories, and landscapes, and the use of affective fantasy animals, *Madgermanes* triggers the Western colonial gaze of the Other, but it also encourages the reader to question racialized imagery about "Africa" and "Africans." The comic allows the reader to translate and affectively relate to different temporal and emotional layers of trauma across cultures and to interrogate their own images of Otherness in various ways. *Madgermanes*' relational aesthetics juxtaposes European/African styles, Western/non-Western locations, human/non-human, biology/culture, past/present, word/image to envision a complex understanding of traumatic memories and experiences as transnational, affective, and relational.

Hat man erst angefangen zu reden: Visual Assemblages of Landscapes, Birds, Traumatic Memories, and Affects

While Weyhe situates herself in the comic and relates her own experiences of living in East Africa to the protagonists' experiences of migration, in Beeler's comic, the author does not appear as an explicit narrator. However, there is some resemblance between the author and the nameless narrator: The comic is dedicated to his mother, and in interviews Beeler acknowledges that the work fictionalizes his own mother's life and their relationship.[42] Like the narrator, Beeler explains that he works

39 De Angelis, "Of Mice and Vermin," 234.
40 Gillian Whitlock, "Autographics: The Seeing 'I' of the Comic," *Modern Fiction Studies* 52, no. 4 (2006): 965–79, here 967.
41 Whitlock, "Autographics," 978.
42 Cornelia Bisch, "Illustrator Pirmin Beeler über seine Lebensgeschichte: 'Erinnerungen sind unzuverlässig,'" *Luzerner Zeitung*, September 19, 2018, https://www.luzernerzeitung.ch/zentralschweiz/zug/

part-time as a psychiatric nurse. In addition to the autofictional character, Beeler's comic shares with *Madgermanes* a prologue as a framing device whose large images of landscapes introduce the transnational and relational setting of the narrative. The prologue starts with a phone call between the protagonist and narrator in Switzerland and his mother Anne in Southeastern Turkey, in which they discuss the son's upcoming visit to her and her partner Ali in a small Kurdish village. Within this transnational setting, the main narrative and the nature imagery connect the traumatic life narratives of all characters within their cultural and political contexts, ranging from violent Kurdish conflict, Kurdish-Swiss labor migration, and long-term psychiatric hospitalization in Switzerland, to childhood neglect, sexual exploitation, and marital conflict.

Like *Madgermanes*, *Hat man erst angefangen zu reden* starts with visual imagery of nature. During the son's visit to Turkey, a panel series shows large panoramic images of a rural landscape, featuring a small road surrounded by a dry empty landscape with some trees, hills, and a mountain in the background, and a large sky, all painted in light pastel watercolors. Rather than presenting a simplistic background or postcard imagery, the comic relates the subtly melancholic atmosphere of the rural Kurdish landscape to Ali's fragmented narratives of traumatic family histories, mythologies, and political conflicts. For instance, Ali mentions that Noah's Ark had landed in this area and that the ruins and the olive trees mark the former boundaries of the village and his parents' grave. This connection between family and local history is intensified in another scene in which the son and Ali watch a film about the armed Kurdish-Turkish conflict in the mountainous Kurdish landscape and and silently mourn the wounds and losses. Kurdish landscapes, political conflict, and family history are further linked to Swiss landscapes and migration: Against the background of a rural Switzerland, we learn how Ali migrated to Switzerland in the 1980s, worked on a farm, and met Anne, a cashier at a supermarket. In her discussion of Leslie Marmon Silko's novel *Ceremony* (1977), Michelle Satterlee examines aesthetic strategies of representations of traumatic memory and the role of landscape through the story of Tayo, who is a traumatized and initially silent World War II veteran of Laguna Pueblo and of Anglophone descent. The novel, Satterlee argues, does not suggest that trauma is an isolated event, but demonstrates how individual trauma is located within a cultural context and tied to landscapes and reflects the cultural trauma of an oppressed or displaced community. The landscape "functions within moments of remembering as a link between identity and

---

illustrator-pirmin-beeler-ueber-seine-lebensgeschichte-erinnerungen-sind-unzuverlaessig-ld.1054748.

memory, thus acting as both the place of trauma and the location of recovery."[43] Like *Ceremony*, the comic inscribes diverse landscapes with mourning, political conflict, and migration while painting these spaces as anchors for belonging and recovery for the similarly verbally silent Ali and his oppressed Kurdish community.. In contrast to the novel, Beeler makes further use of the comic form, which "mimics the procedure of memory"[44] through pauses, silences, and absences in and in between the landscape panels.

Rather than through rural landscapes, Anne's traumatic memories are expressed through oceanic waves. Like Ali, Anne is resistant to verbal narration about her past and the narrator draws on oceanic landscape images to fill memories of her past. After a failed attempt to talk about her past experiences to her son, he links her silence to emotional overflow: "Wenn Anne von sich erzählt, wird sie regelmäßig von ihren Gefühlen überrollt. Das war schon immer so. Als Kind habe ich sie oft weinen sehen und es nicht verstanden. Wenn ich gefragt habe, was los sei, hat sie sich die Tränen weggewischt und gelächelt" (When Anne talks about herself, she is regularly swept away by her own feelings. This has always been the case. As a child, I often saw her crying and didn't understand it. When I asked her what was going on, she wiped away her tears and smiled).[45] Rather than verbal expression, panels of ocean landscape with strong waves painted in watercolors of grey and brown with light touches of blue and a similarly colored large gloomy sky make Anne's emotional waves visible. In addition to atmospheric colors and imagery, the increasing and contrasting scale of the two ocean panels reinforces the enormity of the emotional load. The juxtaposition of verbal and visual, past and present, small and large scales allows the viewer to grasp the emotional gravity of the mother's experience, but also shows that the narrator's childhood was dominated by his mother's unspoken emotions. Through the juxtaposition of verbal silence and landscape imagery the comic communicates temporal, affective, and narrative layers of traumatic childhood memories. However, the comic also opens reflections on the authenticity of these memories through verbal-visual dialogues between different versions of the self. A panel series juxtaposes the narrator as a playing child at a family dinner with a large, dark landscape with a large, blackish, stormy sky over a mountain range and a lake. These visually charged childhood memories are

---

43 Michelle Satterlee, "Landscape Imagery and Memory in the Narrative of Trauma: A Closer Look at Leslie Marmon Silko's 'Ceremony,'" *Interdisciplinary Studies in Literature and Environment* 13, no. 2 (2006): 73–92, here 81.

44 Chute, *Graphic Women*, 4.

45 Pirmin Beeler, *Hat man erst angefangen zu reden, kann alles Mögliche dabei herauskommen* (Zurich: Edition Moderne, 2018), 57. Translations are mine.

overlayed with the textual voice of the adult narrator: "Ich halte eine Wunderkerze in der Hand. Und dann höre ich, wie sich meine Eltern fürchterlich streiten. Meine Mutter läuft davon und ich weine. Aber Erinnerungen sind unzuverlässig" (I am holding a sparkler in my hand. And then I hear how my parents are fighting terribly. My mum runs away, and I cry. But memories are unreliable).[46] While visually the scene is narrated from the perspective of the child, the voice of the adult narrator verbally frames the narrative in a different light. Chute finds that most women's autobiographical comics are narrated, at least partially, from the perspective of a child, highlighting an ongoing open-ended project of self-representation and self-narration with multiple graphic selves that change over time.[47] Beeler's multi-layered narration in different temporalities similarly creates a hybrid subjectivity that allows the narrator to express traumatic childhood memories while distancing his adult self from them. By questioning the authenticity of the childhood memory, the adult narrator "manifests an awareness of the lines of fiction and nonfiction as discursive and their blurring as productive" and self-reflexively calls attention to the construction of the comic at different temporal layers of experience without reifying experience itself.[48]

The metaphorical image of the emotional waves is taken up in the father's fragmentary flashback narrative of his life as a sailor and his wife's psychiatric hospitalization in Switzerland, where she stayed for the duration of one year after the narrator's birth. In a conversation between Anne's treating physician and her former husband, the physician uses the image of a sailboat and storm to explain her condition to her husband: "Einen Patienten kann man mit einem Segelboot vergleichen. ... Er muss lernen, das Boot zu navigieren. Wenn er das nicht kann, kommt das Boot vom Kurs ab und fährt in einen Sturm hinein!" (A patient can be compared to a sailboat. ... He has to learn how to navigate the boat. If he is unable to do so, the boat will steer off course and into a storm).[49] In reaction to the storm metaphor, the narrative shifts to the father's narrative of his life as a sailor. He remembers a traumatic episode on a container ship when he and his colleagues experienced a dangerous storm. Images of high waves and the struggling team represent both the actual storm and the affective intensity of their existential fear. Contrasting with the visual expressivity, the father admits their inability to speak: "Wir hatten Angst. Darüber wurde nicht geredet, aber ich konnte es den anderen ansehen" (We were scared.

---

46   Beeler, *Hat man erst angefangen*, 102.
47   Chute, *Graphic Women*, 5.
48   Chute, *Graphic Women*, 6.
49   Beeler, *Hat man erst angefangen*, 83.

Nobody talked about it, but I could see it on the others' faces).[50] Beeler's concrete and metaphorical oceanic images connect inner life and outer worlds and the traumatic memories of the distant and silent couple. However, both the physician's and the father's storm narratives also point towards gendered injustices within the life of the couple and beyond. During the conversation between physician and husband, Anne is (imagined as) absent, and over the course of the husband's narrative, he proudly reports forced prostitution with a local woman of color (in exchange for alcohol) in foreign locations. Even though the memories are narrated from the male perspective, they reveal silenced experiencess of female abuse and neglect at the edges of male-dominated cultures of medicine and marine life in the post-war period and trace subtle links between gendered injustices across cultures, race, and class.

The ocean and landscape images thus connect traumatic memories of ethnic conflict and death, mental illness, marriage struggle, gendered violence, and life-threatening work at sea. Through the transnational landscape imagery, the comic further relates different affective memories with distant spaces of the Kurdish mountains, the Swiss Alps, the Pacific Ocean, and a psychiatric hospital, and with different narrative perspectives and genres. The son's travel narrative, Ali's mythological histories, the physician's medical drama, and the father's nautical fiction fluidly melt into each other and connect different affective registers of loss, mourning, anxiety, uncertainty, and hope. Chute has recognized the power of the radically inadequate in representations of trauma in comics: comics rely on "the power of the visual to represent an important emotional landscape, which is paradoxically moving because of its distance from and proximity to the realities it references."[51] Beeler's large and affective landscapes open an affective closeness to the different traumatic memories that resist written and verbal forms of representation. In addition, rather than conceiving of trauma as individualized events, the landscape imagery allows a fluid merging of different voices, affective genres, and spaces. This, in turn, leads to a relational, transnational, and affective representation of traumatic memories that opens questions about voice and authenticity.

In addition to landscape imagery, Beeler's comic is populated with animals that serve to fill in and connect affective memories of the past with the present. The narrative features several cats and goats that appear repeatedly in scenes around the house in Turkey and that Anne, Ali, or the son cuddle and feed as practices of reciprocal care. In addition, like in *Madgermanes*, birds appear in the comic, starting with the flashback narrative of Anne's hospitalization. While the narrator indicates that he has

---

50   Beeler, *Hat man erst angefangen*, 95.
51   Chute, *Graphic Women*, 152.

no memories of her hospitalization and Anne prefers to let the past rest, he fills this gap through imagination: "Ich stelle mir vor, wie Anne die Meisen in den Bäumen beobachtet hat" (I image how Anne has observed the tits in the trees).[52] The visual track replicates this imagined bird watching: In large entirely green panels, a single small bird is first shown sitting on a naked branch at the edge of the panel, then flying away, only to appear again in magnification a few panels later. By imagining how his mother carefully watched birds, Beeler hints at a practice of mindful birding that combines mindfulness with nature observation, a practice of self-care and wellbeing that attempts to form deeper relationships with the birds surrounding us.[53] Based on his experience as a psychiatric nurse, who later worked at the same hospital where his mother was hospitalized, the narrator explains how mindfulness training was a common treatment option in his ward. The panels connect his animal-loving mother with bird-watching and fill in the son's missing family memories. In addition, the images' large size, pastel colors, and focus on individual birds create a meditative and caring atmosphere that also draws in the reader to engage in mindful watching of the bird and the comic and to relate to Anne's unspoken experience of illness.

The image of the birds returns in an anecdote about another psychiatric patient and in the epilogue. Like the previous scene, the narrative of another patient's hospitalization reshapes the narrator's missing or traumatic memories of Anne's hospitalization in a relational way. During a car ride, an older colleague in psychiatric nursing tells the narrator the story of Erich, who was one of his patients in a psychiatric hospital twenty years ago. While Erich is drawn and described as small, bent, self-absorbed, and aggressive towards other patients, he takes care of a canary, whispering to it ("Hast du Angst"; Are you scared?[54]), cleaning his cage, and feeding it with peeled apples. The hospital bird connects Anne's and Erich's hospitalizations which might have occurred at the same time. Like Anne's care for her cats and goats and her (imagined) observation of birds, Erich's narrative highlights how relations to the more-than-human can have healing effects and have a long history in psychiatric care.[55] Moreover, the

---

52 Beeler, *Hat man erst angefangen*, 63.

53 See: Mindful Birding Network, "Mindful birding," https://www.themindfulbirdingnetwork.com/mindful-birding, accessed December 3, 2024.

54 Beeler, *Hat man erst angefangen*, 73.

55 While animals have been incorporated into mental health institutions since the late eighteenth century, primarily to increase socialization among patients, more recent research in psychiatric care has shown the therapeutic benefit of animals, for instance, for the quality of life of patients with chronic psychiatric illness that are living in residential care homes. See Mohammad Sahebalzamani, Omid Reyaei, and Ladan Fattah Moghadem, "Animal-Assisted Therapy on Happiness and Life Quality of Chronic Psychiatric Patients Living in Psychiatric Residential

bird in the cage metaphorically points to the traumatizing conditions of forced and long-term psychiatric care, reinforced by the shift to shades of grey in the flashback narrative. The epilogue further links Anne's and Erich's narratives and connects the image of the bird with a complex notion of freedom. In the scene, Anne tells her son, who is about to fly back to Switzerland, how a "komischer Vogel" (strange bird) flew into their home, turned in circles, but finally found its way out.[56] This symbolic scene allows the reader to envision both Anne's and Eric's life narratives from their struggles with (traumatizing) psychiatric hospitals to their negotiation of lives in freedom and peace: While Erich suddenly escaped the closed ward one day and was never found again, Anne migrated to Turkey with her new partner. Like in *Madgermanes*, the bird signifies complex feelings of isolation, confinement, migration, freedom, love, or care. By connecting different affects, temporalities, spaces, and voices, the bird imagery represents traumatic memories as affective, relational, transnational, and in between reality and fiction. Thus, it invites the reader to witness complex and marginalized (traumatic) histories of illness and migration.

The comic's cover exemplifies its relational and transnational landscape aesthetics. It features a large aquarelle landscape image in pastel colors, with the narrator seen from behind on a little rocky hill overlooking the Kurdish landscape of small towns, green-grey valleys, and small mountains against the immense white-bluish sky. The isolated male figure shown from behind and positioned in a landscape is reminiscent of Caspar David Friedrich's famous painting *Der Wanderer über dem Nebelmeer* (Wanderer above the Sea of Fog, ca. 1817), which has been framed as a symbol of German Romanticism and shows a view of the mountains of Saxon Switzerland, where Friedrich had been hiking. In contrast to the older painting, Beeler's painting expands the framework of the German cultural landscape to a transnational one, and the title of the comic moves beyond a description of the scene. Rather, *Hat man erst angefangen zu reden, kann alles Mögliche dabei herauskommen* is indicative of Beeler's play with associations. The title indicates the family's wariness or uneasiness about speech and language, but it also suggests that the work opens narratives in multiple unexpected ways and invites the reader's imagination to fill the gaps in between. In an interview, Beeler revealed that the title is a quote from Marilynne Robinson's novel *Lila* (2014), which centers on the protagonist Lila, a foundling with a childhood of violent neglect and poverty, who becomes a migrant wanderer. The two works bear stylistic and thematic similarities. Like Anne and the

---

Care Homes: a Randomized Controlled Study," *BMC Psychiatry* 20, no. 575 (2020): 1–9, here 5–6.

56 Beeler, *Hat man erst angefangen*, 109.

other protagonists, Lila has few words to express herself, yet her questions and comments are deep and authentic, and she also finds new love in her life.[57] Like the comic, the novel interweaves memories, wishes, dreams, conversations, and encounters in the past and present, in an attempt to deal with traumatic memories and ongoing struggles. In contrast to Robinson and Friedrich, Beeler juxtaposes image and text in the medium of the comic. It opens "gutters" that invite the viewer to imagine narratives in between the visual and textual, human and nature, Switzerland and Turkey, thus highlighting the relational and transnational practice of remembering and witnessing.

Conclusion

Nuancing trauma theory's tenet of non-representability, Beeler's and Weyhe's affective landscapes and animal imagery open an affective closeness to traumatic events that resist written and verbal forms of representation or that do not get much public recognition and witnessing. The repetition and interrelation of landscapes, vegetation, animals, and birds (among other more-than-humans) in these comics indicate how painful memories of migration, racism, and illness are not single events but ongoing and relational experiences in which the (Western) reader is continuously implicated. In both narratives, trauma is recognized as a series of transnational, relational, and long-term experiences that are situated within specific cultural and political histories and spaces of migration, postcolonialism, and mental health care. The comics' use of landscapes, animals, and vegetation in the Global South and East mirror and relate individual affective experiences to transnational histories and spaces of violence, mourning, and belonging. The comics invite the reader to serve as witness to multi-voiced narratives of racism, sexism, and migration and to contemplate their own relationality to these larger cultural and political landscapes of oppression. Going beyond traditional first-person illness narratives, these comics expand the field of German life writing and comics beyond the borders of the individual and the national and open the possibility for social justice and ethical engagement with narratives of colonial legacies and trauma.

---

57 See: Marilynne Robinson, *Lila* (New York: Farrar, Straus & Giroux, 2014).

2: Going Home: East German Trauma in Olivia Vieweg's Graphic Novels

Evelyn Preuss

> *"literature as such ... represents the ultimate coding of our crises, of our most intimate and serious apocalypses."*
>
> —Julia Kristeva, *Powers of Horror*[1]

IN HER GRAPHIC novels *Huck Finn* (2013), *Antoinette kehrt zurück* (Antoinette Returns, 2014), and *Endzeit* (*Ever After*, 2018), Olivia Vieweg addresses the traumatic effects of global neoliberalism. By far outpacing similar developments in the West, neo-liberalization in post-1990 East Germany, where Vieweg grew up and continues to live and work, had particularly harsh consequences. In contradistinction to other artists, Vieweg openly identifies as an "Ossi," and even tries to create an understanding of what East Germans experienced post-1990—and what they lost—in highly visible interventions, such as contributions to public television: socialized with firm expectations of social stability, egality, and the relevance of each individual, as well as the materialization of a more equitable society within their lifetime, East Germans had been affected all the more by deindustrialization, ghettoization, and the exclusion from the Western-dominated public sphere and politics. Post-1990 protests outnumbered those of 1989 but went unreported in the global press. As a result, psychological disorders spread like an epidemic. Vieweg works through the trauma caused by the Western takeover in what can be understood as her East German trilogy, *Huck Finn*, *Antoinette kehrt zurück*, and *Endzeit*, whose two versions bracket the other two texts. The trilogy transposes Western narratives either onto a concretely East German landscape (*Huck Finn* and *Endzeit*) or onto a landscape that is deliberately not identified as East or West: the Harz Mountains (*Antoinette*), the only geographical location that the German-German border divided in equal parts. This ambiguity as well as the superimposition of Western narratives

---

1 Julia Kristeva, *Powers of Horror: An Essay on Abjection*, trans. Leon Roudiez (New York: Columbia University Press, 1982), 208.

draw attention to the global continuities of the East German situation, while making East Germans visible in Western media.

The trilogy explores the loss of *Heimat* (home; homeland) and reflects on the human costs of East Germany's post-1990 neo-liberalization.[2] Vieweg's protagonists experience socio-political trauma as personal history and personal trauma as socio-political history.[3] Bullying, abuse, and betrayal derail their lives and turn them into wanderers between the worlds: migrants navigating hostility and lawlessness in the Wild East. The novels' highly ambivalent endings do not resolve the dystopia, but give the protagonists an alternate space that, although geographically defined, remains literally a utopia—an empty non-space—in which her characters can reinvent themselves and their social relationships.

Hinting at ways out of their crisis, Vieweg's novels not only respond to the social alienation and economic and political disenfranchisement in the wake of neo-liberalization, but also take up fundamental problems in trauma theory. First of all, her endings controvert the assumption that victims cannot recover from trauma, because trauma remains unspeakable and thus reinscribes itself. Finding solidarity and friendship that help them recuperate their sense of self, Vieweg's protagonists work through their traumatization. In connection with this, the trilogy also presents different scenarios of perpetrator trauma,[4] an underexplored area in trauma theory. Finally, Vieweg's trilogy also speaks to the spatial dimensions of trauma, that is, to what extent landscapes bear witness to trauma, hold it as sites of memory, reinscribe it, or offer a space for redemption and recuperation. Employing aesthetics, which layer and imbricate meaning while refusing definition at decisive points, her novels empower readers to bring their own experiences and visions to bear.

---

2   Philip Ther, *Europe since 1989: A History*, trans. Charlotte Hughes-Kreutzmüller (Princeton, NJ: Princeton University Press, 2016), 40.
3   Olivia Vieweg, *Endzeit* (Hamburg: Carlsen, 2018), in the following, *EZ*; simultaneously published in English translation as Olivia Vieweg, *Ever After* (Minneapolis, MI: Graphic Universe, 2018); Olivia Vieweg, *Antoinette kehrt zurück* (Cologne: Egmont, 2014) in the following, *A*; Olivia Vieweg, *Huck Finn: Die Graphic Novel* (Berlin: Suhrkamp, 2013), in the following, *HF*.
4   Perpetrator trauma refers to those who become victims of the trauma they inflict as well as victims of trauma who in turn become perpetrators.

No Place Like Home: East German Trauma in *Endzeit*

Described by Zygmunt Bauman as liquifying all and even the most intimate social relationships,[5] neo-liberalization results, for many, if not most, in a migrant experience whose most salient manifestations include itinerant working conditions and holding camps. But the migrant experience also exists in many other shapes and meanings that deprive huge populations of a sense of home. Their status as human surplus sustains the race-to-the-bottom logic of neoliberalism. According to Jana Hensel, the migrant experience has come to define East German identity.[6] "Der migrantische Kern ostdeutscher Identität" (the migrant core of East German identity) is, in Jana Hensel's words, "am besten mit Heimatlosigkeit zu beschreiben, mit einem Unbehaustsein, das viele Facetten kennt" (best described as a homelessness, as having no abode in so many different respects).[7] Corresponding with the global trends described by Bauman, Hélène B. Ducros, Quinn Slobodian, and others, the East German experience is marked by living in a traumatic social space, by being excluded from representation in the double sense of the word. Gerhard Gundermann's song "Ossi-Reservation" about the post-1990 changes in East Germany is a telling example: it exists only in a bootlegged concert recording on the internet, despite the East German singer-songwriter's fame and the posthumous appropriation of his biography.[8] Much in line with the scholarship cited above, the song defines East Germany as an extra-legal space—a reservation—from which the people,

---

5   E.g., Zygmunt Bauman, *Liquid Modernity* (Cambridge: Polity, 2000); Zygmunt Bauman, *Liquid Love: On the Frailty of Human Bonds* (Cambridge: Polity, 2003); and Zygmunt Bauman, *Liquid Times: Living in an Age of Uncertainty* (Cambridge: Polity, 2006).

6   See Daniel Schulz, "Professorin über 'Ostdeutsche sind auch Migranten,'" *Die Tageszeitung*, March 13, 2018, https://taz.de/Professorin-ueber-Identitaeten/!5501987/. See also Naika Foroutan, Frank Kalter, Coskun Canan, and Mara Simon, *Ost-Migrantische Analogien I: Konkurrenz um Anerkennung* (Berlin: DeZIM-Institut, 2019); Naika Foroutan and Coskun Canan, "Ost-migrantische Analogien der Konkurrenz um Anerkennung und Teilhabe? Schlaglichter aus einem repräsentativen Survey," *Forschungsjournal Soziale Bewegungen* 32, no. 3 (2019): 424–29.

7   Wolfgang Engler and Jana Hensel, *Wer wir sind: Die Erfahrung, ostdeutsch zu sein* (Berlin: Aufbau, 2018), 143.

8   See Evelyn Preuss, "Goodbye, Sonnenallee, Or How Gundermann Got Lost in the Cinema of Others," in *Edinburgh German Yearbook* 14: *Politics and Culture in Germany and Austria Today*, ed. Frauke Matthes, Dora Osborne, Katya Krylova, and Myrto Aspioti (Rochester, NY: Camden House, 2021), 183–206.

whose culture, livelihoods, and futures have broken away, emerge with a vengeance as "ein Volk der kalten Barbaren" (a people of cold savages).[9]

In *Endzeit*, the "kalten Barbaren" quite literally emerge from the landscape in the form of zombies. Having already overtaken the rest of the globe, they invade the East German provinces, where only two towns, Weimar and Jena, have so far withstood the zombies' onslaught. A relentless predatory instinct drives them to inflict their own wound onto others. Apparently without agency, the zombies are caught in a seemingly unstoppable cycle of violence, since killing them, in turn, traumatizes their killers. Thus, Vieweg's graphic novel illustrates how "trauma affects not only those who are directly exposed to it, but also those around them,"[10] as it triggers relay mechanisms that lead victims to spread their trauma through their social relationships, rendering trauma as infectious as a viral disease. Thus, Vieweg uses the narrative tropes of the zombie genre to draw out the social and collective dimensions of trauma.

In the same vein, the zombies' ambivalent undead mode of existence and their locked-out status echo Butler's reading of Giorgio Agamben's *Homo Sacer: Sovereign Power and Bare Life*, which suggests that the lives of those who are systematically disenfranchised are not "genocidally destroyed, but neither are they being entered into the life of the legitimate community in which standards of recognition permit for an attainment of humanness."[11] Just as trauma denotes an experience that cannot be grasped with the frameworks of our language and expectations, so these populations exist outside of the legal syntax and semantics that define personhood. Since migrants lose all legal protection because of their *de facto* statelessness, including basic human rights, as Bauman and others note, their existence is in itself traumatic. Philip Ther characterizes post-unification East Germans as stateless and surmises that their post-1990 protests went unnoticed and unheeded because they had no state to represent them. The same is true for populations in the extra-legal zones, which states increasingly use as a political and economic tool, as Slobodian points out.[12] As the territory of the former GDR was excluded

---

9   Gerhard Gundermann, "Ossi-Reservation," *Alphazalpha*, http://www.alphazalpha.de/musik/gundermann/texte/ossi.html, accessed December 3, 2022.

10 Bessel van der Kolk, *The Body Keeps the Score: Brain, Mind, and Body in the Healing of Trauma* (New York: Viking, 2014), 1. See also Cathy Caruth, *Unclaimed Experience: Trauma, Narrative and History* (Baltimore, MD: Johns Hopkins University Press, 1996). Vieweg does not conceive the zombie invasion as a resurrection of the dead. As Eva tells Vivi, "immerhin sind nicht die Toten aus den Gräbern gestiegen" (*EZ*, 98; At least the dead didn't rise from their graves).

11 Judith Butler, *Antigone's Claim: Kinship Between Life and Death* (New York: Columbia University Press, 2000), 81.

12 E.g., Ther, *Europe since 1989*, 88; Zygmunt Bauman, *Wasted Lives: Modernity and its Outcasts* (Cambridge: Polity, 2003), 76; Quinn Slobodian, *Crack-Up*

from basic stipulations of the FRG's constitution, such as the equality before the law, it again serves as an example for neoliberalism's unhinging of civil society. In this context, Vieweg's zombies call to mind "populations without full citizenship [that] exist within states,"[13] and thus reflect on the way in which statelessness and extra-legal status affect populations. Vieweg's zombies, dialectically perpetrators and victims at the same time, thus mirror the values and workings of post-1990 society, not only in East Germany, but globally, and show its traumatizing effects.

In keeping with this logic of defining who is deemed worth existing and who is not, Weimar and Jena conceive of themselves as the last remnants of civilization, which they defend with flimsy, dilapidated fences and a brutal border regime. Superimposing references to pre-1990 German history with allusions to the global post-1990 political and economic restructuring, Vieweg puts the present strategy of walling-in and walling-out into historical perspective and before audiences who might be unaware that 15,551 people perished trying to scale the still existing walls of Fortress Europe in the thirty-three years between 1988 and April 2011, while the 125 people who died trying to cross the Berlin Wall during its entire twenty-eight-year history still make headlines even thirty-five years after the dismantling of that wall.[14] "New barricades replaced old ones as the Cold War ended," her narrative reminds readers. "Walls were built the world over."[15]

Continuities in Time and Space, or Breaking Down the Binary

Since "walls ... in concrete and in barbed wires (Ceuta and Mellila) ... were not sufficient and were too visible,"[16] physical barriers were extended and fortified by mental and emotional ones congealing into an ideology of Othering that legitimizes the various kinds of extra-legal zones. Casting Weimar's response to the zombies as a trope for histories

---

Capitalism: Market Radicals and the Dream of A World Without Democracy (New York: Metropolitan Books, 2023), 236.

13   Butler, *Antigone's Claim*, 81, again summarizing Agamben's *Homo Sacer*.

14   Matthew Carr, *Fortress Europe: Dispatches from a Gated Continent* (New York: The New Press, 2012), 4. E.g., Christopher Schuetze, "50 Years After Killing, a Berlin Court Convicts Stasi Officer of Murder," *New York Times*, October 14, 2024, https://www.nytimes.com/2024/10/14/world/europe/stasi-murder-convicted-1974.html.

15   Slobodian, *Crack-Up Capitalism*, 6.

16   Paul Vieille, "Globalization and the Walls," in *Language and Power: The Implications of Language for Peace and Development*, ed. Birgit Brock-Utne and Gunnar Garbo (Dar es Salaam: Mkuki na Nyota, 2009), 79–83, here 82.

both past and present, Vieweg asks about continuities in the ongoing traumatization of entire populations and puts the Othering that has been central to the FRG's state-mandated memory into a historical and global perspective. At the same time, *Endzeit* also proposes an alternative to these politics by setting up binaries of "inside" and "outside," "Self" and "Other," or human and zombie, only to analyze, question, and transcend them.

Vieweg first establishes the binary by presenting Weimar's ideology as blambing the zombies' presence for the transformation of the landscape inside and outside the fence. The zombies seem to change the landscape's meaning, rendering it fraught with danger, inhospitable, and, seemingly, uninhabitable. They seem to turn home into a place that denies the future: in- and outside the fence, the wrecks of a lost civilization litter what otherwise could be an idyllic scenery; enclosures fragment the space and the self; and the repurposing of landmarks erases previous cultural meanings.

However, as the story unfolds, the response of Weimar citizens to the zombies reveals that their alleged civilization is a thin veneer. As the Weimar government uses the zombie threat to legitimize a regime that recalls Nazism as well as problematic aspects of pre- and post-1990 East Germany, the Othering of the zombies imposes a rigid form of belonging on Weimar citizens that, as a measure of hygiene, punishes any sort of exposure to the zombies with death. Alluding to the current politics of Fortress Europe as well as xenophobia and economic protectionism elsewhere, Weimar citizens invest their precarious resources into maintaining a crumbling fence that protects the privilege of few while sacrificing those in the first line of defense—and the vast number of disenfranchised in no man's land.

But the fence not only reinforces a binary between inside and out, human and zombie, Self and Other. The stratagems of inclusion and exclusion continue internally, dividing the Weimar citizenry according to prerogatives and tasks, unequally distributing resources and risks. The state of emergency serves as a justification for command structures, control, and stratification. Vieweg highlights the traumatic structure of these politics through the city government's prohibition to leave the city: the place literally possesses its subjects. "Die kalten Barbaren," whether as an actual threat or as a legitimation for barbarous power structures, turn home itself into a barbaric place. Vieweg blends past and present into a future that could be tomorrow or that has perhaps already begun.

Poignantly, *Endzeit*'s opening panel introduces the theme of inclusion and exclusion with a provocation evocative of the opening lines of Christa Wolf's 1976 novel *Kindheitsmuster* (Patterns of Childhood), whose title signals a continuity between pre- and post-1945 regimes in the face of alleged caesuras on both sides of the Wall. Wolf prefaces her novel with a quote by William Faulkner that rejects the Othering of history: "Das Vergangene ist nicht tot; es ist nicht einmal vergangen. Wir trennen es ab und stellen uns fremd" (The past is not dead; it is not even past. We split it off and regard it as foreign).[17] Likewise, Vieweg's panel, taking up the entire page, resonates Nazi and GDR pasts. While showing Weimar as an idyllic cityscape, in the near distance overlooking the town, almost at the vanishing point, stands the Bell Tower that the GDR had erected in commemoration of the victims of the Nazi concentration camp Buchenwald just beyond that hill. To this day the largest monument to camp victims worldwide, the Buchenwald Monument reminds citizens of the crimes perpetrated barely out of their sight, for such inhumanity never to be repeated.[18] The Bell Tower overlooks not only a series of mass graves in which inmates of over thirty nations and all social strata are buried together in large pits,[19] but also the city of Weimar. Thus, it sets Weimar and the camp in relation to one another in both contrast and continuity.

While the small sketchy Bell Tower on the horizon opens up these meanings only for readers who are acquainted with Weimar's landmarks and history, Vieweg invokes the relationship between town and countryside more directly, when she lets one of *Endzeit*'s protagonists, Eva, muse about the luck of Weimar citizens:

> Weißt du, dass wir eigentlich noch Glück haben mit unserer Apokalypse? ... Immerhin sind nicht die Toten aus den Gräbern gestiegen. Das wäre für Weimar nicht gut ausgegangen ... Oben in den Bergen um Buchenwald, da liegen die armen Seelen. (*EZ* 98)
>
> [You know that we were actually lucky with our apocalypse? ... At least, the dead didn't rise from their graves. That wouldn't have ended well for Weimar. ... Up in the mountains around Buchenwald, that's where the poor souls lie.]

Eva's comments speak to the historical debt of Weimar's "civilization," which would overwhelm the town if it was called in. As in the visual reference to the Bell Tower, Vieweg again relies on the reader to understand

---

17 Christa Wolf, *Kindheitsmuster* (Berlin: Aufbau, 1976), 9.

18 "Buchenwald Memorial/National Memorial of the GDR," *Buchenwald Memorial*, https://www.buchenwald.de/en/geschichte/historischer-ort/gedenkstaette/mahnmal; "Design of the Mass Graves as a National Memorial of the GDR," *Buchenwald Memorial*, https://www.buchenwald.de/en/geschichte/chronologie/gedenkstaette/gestaltung-massengraeber, both accessed December 3, 2022.

19 The GDR-era introductory film at the Buchenwald Memorial Site showed how the inmates' corpses were bulldozed into the pits in a most radical erasure of national and social boundaries.

what the reference to Buchenwald means and thus reserves her commentary on present politics for those who conscientiously share in this history.

Another such potent, complex reference is the bitten-into strawberry on the page opposite the opening panel, in the space where publishers usually print copyright information. Linking *Endzeit* to more global and likewise historically informed discourses, it combines references to Genesis, the Hollywood film *The Strawberry Statement*, and the stratification of Weimar society in *Endzeit* itself.[20] Under the title *Blutige Erdbeeren* (literally, Bloody Strawberries), *The Strawberry Statement* was a popular film in East Germany. Its final sequence is quoted in the last scene of Leander Haußmann's 1999 film *Sonnenallee*, which Vieweg considers a seminal film that gave East Germans a platform to resist the obliteration of their memory.[21] Based on a student's first-hand account of the uprising at Columbia University in May 1968, *The Strawberry Statement* takes its title from the remark of a university dean that students' political opinions and their demands for inclusion in decision-making mattered as much to him as if they told him that they like strawberries;[22] in other words, it speaks to the lack of political representation that presents a continuity between Western democracy and the GDR.

The film's invocation of the American dream, not as the individualistic, consumerist gratification to which it has been reduced, but as a social, collective vision for a better society, also echoes in Eva's remark, "Hauptsache, man hat Träume!" (*EZ*, 132; The main thing is that one has dreams). Dreams present a utopia, which is necessary to drive social change, as the main character of *The Strawberry Statement* puts it: "This country used to have a dream about things being different … and now everybody is just sitting back and leaves things the way they are … Maybe they should dream again." The film's popularity in East Germany points to a continuum between Western and Eastern Bloc societies, both in their utopian aspirations and in their failure to accomplish their social goals and live up to their ideology. Thus, *Endzeit*'s reference calls to mind the revolutionary momentum that had informed societies in East and West and by the same token also challenges the Othering that perpetuates Cold War thinking post-1990. Reading Vieweg's novel against the filmic references—for example, the recurring theme of people behind

---

20 Stuart Hagman, dir., *The Strawberry Statement* (Metro-Goldwyn-Mayer, 1970).

21 Frank Blum, *Angelica mit C: Die Schauspielerin Angelica Domröse* (Frankfurt am Main: Lang, 1992), 158; Olivia Vieweg, dir., *Land vor unserer Zeit* (ZDF, 2020) https://www.zdf.de/filme/das-kleine-fernsehspiel/meine-wende-kurzfilm-land-vor-unserer-zeit-100.html; Leander Haußmann, dir., *Sonnenallee* (Boje Buck Produktion, 1999).

22 James Simon Kunen, *The Strawberry Statement: Notes of a College Revolutionary* (New York: Random House, 1969).

fences—suggests a floating meaning of zombiedom and draws attention to the politics of inclusion and exclusion.

Like the reference to the Hollywood film, the biblical allusion, in the form of the bitten-into strawberry, also thematizes expulsion and demarcation. In Genesis, Adam and Eve are driven from paradise after tasting the fruit from the Tree of Knowledge, typically presented as an apple. Further developing this reference, Vieweg names the initially more knowledgeable of the two protagonists in the German version "Eva." Like Eve, who must leave the walled-in enclave of paradise because her knowledge renders her tainted, Eva must leave Weimar because she has been infected with the zombie virus. Being infected thus also means coming to understand the Other's perspectives and experiences, which makes living within "civilization" impossible. The biblical reference points to a false sense of security in the "paradise" that Weimar's society represents: ignorance allows its inhabitants to discount the human cost of their lifestyle.

In the graphic novel itself, Vieweg uses strawberries as a symbol of both privilege and the transgression of social demarcations. Although strawberries are officially deemed "unnütze Lebensmittel" (useless, non-essential foodstuff), Vivi locates a tray in a pantry for the ward's officials. She steals them for an old man on death row whom the regime considers "human waste," even deeming a lamp for him a squandered resource.[23] With the strawberries, she wants to remind him of his past, his identity, and thus restore his humanity to him. When Vivi's theft is discovered, she escapes the awkward situation by volunteering for fence duty and ends up giving the strawberries to a less privileged girl. In a cruel twist, Eva kills the same girl shortly thereafter: she is under orders to shoot her after having tried to save her life because she was injured in a zombie attack. The narrative twist highlights Weimar society's zombie-like inhumanity.

Finally, red fruits like strawberries invite Vivi to sit down for *Kaffeetrinken* (a German afternoon meal of sweet baked goods and coffee) on the way from Weimar to Jena. In Thuringia, Vieweg's home region, the image of a table set for *Kaffeetrinken* invokes traditional sociability with friends and family and conveys a sense of home and safety. This sense, however, is soon betrayed. The table stands in the garden of a woman, who, half human, half zombie, has been involved in the creation of the zombie virus. The lush growth of fruit and vegetables in her garden results from composting zombies. Again, the strawberries signify that civilization comes at a human cost. Again, Vieweg presents civilization as a contradiction in terms, since it implies a body politics premised on the

---

23   Here, Vieweg also thematizes the valorization of human life according to a given society's productivity standards, which Bauman repeatedly remarks upon in his work and which, of course, was also a basic characteristic of the Nazi camp system; see, for instance, Zygmunt Bauman, *Liquid Modernity*.

violation of some bodies and the preservation of others.[24] The strawberries figure as the forbidden fruit of knowledge, which Vivi and Eva tasted with traumatizing effect.

Like the forbidden fruit, the metaphor of the dilapidated fences visualizes these body politics in a way that speaks to their traumatic character. Erikson defines trauma as a violation of physical, mental, and emotional boundaries and describes it as "something alien [that] breaks into you, smashing whatever barrier your mind has set up as a line of defense."[25] *Endzeit*'s fences bear witness to a continued assault and, as much as they separate those inside and outside, they also connect both, structuring Weimar society, and, as Vivi at the end of the novel surmises, also Jena's. Even though meant to protect, the fences inflict violence on those on the inside and outside. Hence, the demarcation of Otherness fails, because Othering is ultimately a dialectical process that also alienates the Self.

Like the fences, the zombies and the zombie virus figure as trauma, which Erikson defines as something that "invades you, takes you over, becomes a dominating feature of your interior landscape—'possesses' you."[26] Just as the breached fences point to a continuity in trauma between zombies and the still-human, so humans and zombies also share trauma symptoms. Like the zombies—and indeed all protagonists of Vieweg's East German trilogy—Vivi and Eva migrate. Their "feelings of restlessness" present one of "[t]he classic symptoms of trauma."[27] Moreover, zombies and still-humans share the "numbness and bleakness" that Erikson considers a classic trauma symptom and that Vieweg thematizes throughout her novel. Finally, the metaphor of the virus and the changing physique that marks the transition from human to zombie corresponds with Bessel van der Kolk's observations that trauma changes the body, impacting social abilities and the immune system, which further underscores the continuity between the still- and the no-longer-humans.[28]

In *Endzeit*, the definition of 'in' and 'out', although seemingly clear at first, gets murky once the narrative reveals more of the underlying motives and structures. This dissolve calls to mind Kristeva's localizing

---

24 See Kristen Ghodsee and Mitchell A. Orenstein, *Taking Stock of Shock: Social Consequences of the 1989 Revolutions* (Oxford: Oxford University Press, 2021).

25 Erikson, "Notes on Trauma and Community," 183.

26 In Vieweg's original version, the virus was cultivated in the Max-Planck-Institute, see Christian Werner, "Im Sog der Zombies," *UniSpiegel* 3 (2011), 40–43, here 40. http://magazin.spiegel.de/EpubDelivery/spiegel/pdf/78490674.

27 Kai Erikson, "Notes on Trauma and Community," in *Trauma: Explorations in Memory*, ed. Cathy Caruth (Baltimore, MD: Johns Hopkins University Press, 1995), 183–99, here 183.

28 Van der Kolk, *The Body Keeps the Score*, 102, 126–27.

of abjection, horror, and Othering not just in a narrowly defined genre but in "all literature" as "a version of the apocalypse that seems ... rooted ... on the fragile border ... where identities (subject/object, etc.) do not exist or only barely so—double, fuzzy, heterogenous, animal, metamorphosed, altered, abject."[29] As the binary between human and zombie, inside and out, Self and Other gradually breaks down, the graphic novel reveals various structures of inclusion and exclusion that show humanity as compromised and zombie-like. Vivi learns of the cruel conditions in the psychiatric clinic, where patients/inmates are routinely left to die unseen, unheard-of deaths, while she receives special favors. Likewise, Eva is weary of the border killings and violates government regulations to save lives, but in defending the city, becomes infected herself. In their conversations, she recounts her friends' betrayal. Conversely, Vivi, talking with Eva, admits her guilt in her younger sister falling prey to the zombies. Vivi's and Eva's stories present mirror images of a perpetrator and victim involved in the same offense: Eva's friends leave her to die; Vivi leaves her sister to die. The motive of Eva's friends is fear for their own lives, Vivi's is envy and ignorance.

However, it is not the exposure to zombies that is most traumatic for the protagonists but the failure of quotidian relationships, of sisterhood, and of friendship. The zombies merely bring out the zombieness of humans. They externalize the trauma that humans suffer by functioning in predatory structures. The outside threat is complemented by the enemy within: "die kalten Barbaren" inside the fence, the human, the Self. The humanity that the protagonists had taken for granted breaks down, and they can recover from the trauma only by finding, once again, sisterhood, friendship, and understanding—in each other.

To underscore that the zombies are not an Other but frail humanity, Vieweg endows them with individual markers that connect them to their former lives. Thus, she shows them not merely as automaton perpetrators but also as victims. In a haunting scene, a zombie pursuing Vivi and Eva still wears her bridal gown and a white veil. Her predatory demeanor stands in stark contrast to the innocence that her dress signifies. Displaced in the fields between Weimar and Jena, she is cut off from her wedding party, her life plans interrupted, her body and mind disfigured, a lost soul. The protagonists' conversations and the zombies' behavior likewise suggest a continuity between humanity and zombiedom. Eva, for instance, tells Vivi: "Meine Family rennt da draußen auch noch rum ... und schlägt sich die Köpfe ein. Also kein großer Unterschied zu früher" (*EZ*, 131; My family also still runs around out there somewhere ... and bangs in each other's heads. So, no big difference to before). To Eva, the behavior of her family-turned-zombies is a mere extension of their behavior as humans.

---

29 Kristeva, *Powers of Horror*, 207.

At the same time, zombies not only embody negative human traits but can show more care and compassion than humans. While Vivi did not care for her little sister, a zombie man takes her by the hand (*EZ*, 134). Even though this scene may only play in Vivi's imagination, it shows that she does not imagine the zombies as Other, but as continuous with humanity—and with values to which she herself did not live up. This connection between human and zombie unfolds also in a tender scene in which Vivi finds the bodily remains of her little sister-turned-zombie. Like Antigone, she tries to give her sibling a dignified burial (*EZ*, 88 and 268).

Finally, Eva herself represents the continuity between zombie and human. As she succumbs to the virus, which she contracted at her job defending Weimar's border, she gradually turns into a zombie. Her metamorphosis does not alter Vivi's feelings for her. Instead of fleeing from Eva as a source of danger, Vivi saves her repeatedly. Vivi's solidarity and care seem to prevent Eva's zombie self from becoming a predator, which Vieweg marks by gracing her features with flowering vines instead of the harsh cracks and fissures with which she characterizes others. In turn, Eva consoles Vivi in her despair over her survivor's guilt. To Vivi's comment, "Nur die Arschlöcher haben überlebt" (Only the assholes survived), Eva replies: "Du hast mein Leben gerettet. Du bist der beste Mensch, der mir je begegnet ist" (*EZ*, 223; You saved my life. You are the best person whom I ever met). When they reach their destination at the end of the novel—the fence of the city of Jena—Vivi decides to turn around to protect Eva. While they had hoped to find a cure for the zombie virus there, Vivi realizes that Eva will not be healed but only encounter discrimination—or worse. She holds Eva back: "Geh nicht. Sie werden dich dort nicht mögen" (*EZ*, 280; Don't go. They are not going to like you there). The inside is no more desirable—or welcoming—than the outside.

This distinction has become irrelevant for the protagonists. Their relationship with one another is more important than being accepted by a society that would destroy it, because it transcends the exclusionary distinction between human and zombie, Self and Other. As Vieweg's protagonists move beyond binary distinctions, the self-proclaimed civilization provides no home or future for them. They come to understand that the social and political institutions that are supposed to protect them from the zombie epidemic reproduce it.

Vieweg's protagonists refuse to be victimized. Instead, they use these traumatic spaces of transience and homelessness to test modes of survival. Their trauma prompts them to reinvent themselves and their relationships. As they come to rely on peers and fellow travelers in making their way through the no man's land of their lost home, they learn coping strategies. Thus, this post-1990 generation's reinvention of self and social relations resonates with the pre-1990 cultural memory of the East German space, as it validates equality, social connectivity, and collective *Eigensinn*. Asserting there is a freedom that does not come at the cost of others, *Endzeit*—like the other two novels of Vieweg's trilogy—value each individual and present, if somewhat precarious, models of inclusivity and equity.[30]

Unlike the cityscapes, the open landscape allows Vivi and Eva to experience mutual respect, solidarity, and friendship. At the beginning of their journey, Vivi associated the town of Weimar with home, asking Eva, "Bringst du mich bitte nach Hause?" (*EZ*, 11; Could you please bring me home?) and even screaming, "Ich will nach Hause" (*EZ*, 88; I want to go home). Now she locates home in her relationship with Eva. In this sense, Eva has indeed brought her home.

Paradoxically, even though—or precisely because—they turn away from Jena, Vivi and Eva also reach it in a more metaphorical sense and, possibly, find healing in a utopian understanding of Jena rooted in the late eighteenth century, when the university town became synonymous with a spiritual upheaval that restructured the universe.[31] This intellectual revolution empowered the Self with agency and thus stands in stark opposition to trauma, which results from experiences that deny individuals or groups their subject position and objectify them.[32] It is these powers that Vivi and Eva claim for themselves when they decide not to enter the town but remain in no man's land.

Home without Home: No Happy, But an Open Ending

Endzeit shows the sky superimposed with lyrics of a song, to which Vivi's sister had listened. The text continues from the previous page: "Ich bin ein Felsen" (I am a rock), as in the refrain of the well-known 1966 song "I Am a Rock" by Paul Simon and Art Garfunkel, which Vieweg seems to quote, especially since *The Strawberry Statement* referenced in the graphic novel features similar songs of the same era:

> I am a rock
> I am an island

---

30 Elizabeth Emery, Matthew Hines, and Evelyn Preuss, "Introduction: The GDR Tomorrow," in *The GDR Tomorrow: Rethinking the East German Legacy*, ed. Elizabeth Emery, Matthew Hines, and Evelyn Preuss (Oxford: Lang, 2023), 1–23, here 4–14.

31 Andrea Wulf, *Magnificent Rebels: The First Romantics and the Invention of the Self* (New York: Knopf, 2022), 43.

32 Wulf, *Magnificent Rebels*, 43; Peter Neumann, *Jena 1800: The Republic of Free Spirits*, trans. Shelley Frisch (New York: Farrar, Straus, and Giroux, 2022), 32.

> I've built walls
> A fortress deep and mighty
> That no one may penetrate
> I have no need of friendship
> Friendship causes pain
> It's laughter and it's loving I disdain
> I am a rock I am an island.[33]

This quote sets up an audience expectation that corresponds to the protagonists' decision to eschew society and strike out on their own. The visual corroborates this interpretation, as it shows Vivi and Eva walking through a seemingly deserted landscape. Despite being in the foreground, Vivi seems remote. She wears earbuds and holds her player, which, the reader is led to surmise, plays the song whose text is written in the sky.

Only the white dog who joined Vivi on the outskirts of Jena looks at the reader and the way ahead, engaging them with the question of where Vivi and Eva will go. While this question expresses the precarity of Vivi's and Eva's future, it also speaks to their emancipation from the confinement of compartmentalizing, hierarchizing, and Othering civilization. Thus, it opens the horizon toward the possibility of overcoming trauma. The undetermined space of the open landscape allows Vieweg's protagonists to regain their agency.

Their new-found agency also entails a different relationship to life, its interconnectedness with the world, and a sense of responsibility. As readers turn the page, they find that the song does not continue with Simon and Garfunkel's lyrics of social isolation, frustration, and alienation quoted above. Instead, it speaks to a sense of determination, preparedness, and guardianship: "ich habe Leben und Tod gesehen … Ihr bösen Geister sollt wissen … ich schlafe nicht" (*EZ*, 15–16; I have seen life and death … you evil spirits should know … I don't sleep).[34] The text is a version of a Hopi prayer that has gained popularity on the German-speaking web as an alternative to Western society's extractive and exploitative relationship to the world.[35] Already earlier in the graphic novel, Vieweg lets

---

33 Paul Simon, "I Am a Rock," *Paul Simon: The Official Site*, https://www.paulsimon.com/track/i-am-a-rock-2/, accessed December 3, 2022.

34 Vivi recited the same text at the beginning of the graphic novel during a sleepless night in the psychiatric ward, when the memory of her sister's death kept her awake, and later when she saw her little sister during the night on the train (*EZ*, 15–16 and 104–5), but the prayer did not provide her with comfort or help then (*EZ*, 107).

35 The prayer enjoys many German-language iterations on the internet; to cite but three examples: Ortlieb Schrade, "Ortlieb-Schrade_mehrlebensfreu.de_Ich_bin_ein_Felsen_von_Cesspooch.pdf," *Lebensweisheiten: Eine Textauswahl als Downloads* https://www.shamans-of-the-new-world.de/informationen/downloads-links/

Eva echo Native American worldviews when she tells Vivi: "Die Erde ist ne kluge alte Frau … und die Menschen haben ihr zu lange keine Miete gezahlt. Und das da draußen … das ist jetzt die Räumungsklage" (*EZ*, 135; Earth is a wise old woman … and humans didn't pay her any rent for too long. And this out there … that is now the eviction proceeding).[36] Likewise, the white dog refers to Native American mythology. Called Ofi' Tohbi' in the legends of the Chickasaw, it is "a symbol of strength and courage [that] continues to inspire loyalty and friendship"; it scouts the way on the tribe's travel in search for new homelands.[37] Expressing the Native belief in the animatedness of and the human interconnectedness with the natural world as well as the reciprocity of communication and solidarity, the prayer counters the isolation and disdain for human connection that Simon and Garfunkel's song expresses.

By quoting a commercial pop song and then contradicting that expectation with an alternative text, which also originates from the United States, but has been suppressed there, Vieweg calls attention to alternative modes of social relations and of relating to our environment, which are already part of our political and cultural heritage but have been sidelined by Western society. Defining itself as "civilization," the West Orientalizes and Others modes of living that defy its logic. Like Gundermann in his song "Ossi-Reservation," Vieweg overlays the colonization of the American continent onto the East German landscape and thus invites us to reflect on the legacy of the GDR, which, like Gundermann's song, is not easily accessible but survives only in marginal spaces.

Although the prayer does not elaborate on its reference to "evil spirits," its text is associated earlier in the graphic novel with Vivi's younger sister, whose fears, Vivi surmises, anticipated the apocalyptic advent of the zombies. Thus, the "evil spirits" could refer to the "cold barbarism"

---

lebensweisheiten.html; https://www.pinterest.de/pin/642255596832727778/; https://ateliertraumwelle.net/2017/05/27/der-stein-spricht-gebet-der-hopi-indianer/; https://welt-der-indianer.de/verschiedenes/indianer-weisheiten-zitate/, all accessed December 3, 2022.

36 "We are the landlords of the country, it is the end of the month, the rent is due, and A.I.M. is going to collect," Clyde Bellecourt stated during the 1973 standoff at Wounded Knee. Quoted in Sam Roberts, "Clyde Bellecourt, a Founder of the American Indian Movement, Dies at 85," *New York Times*, January 13, 2022, https://www.nytimes.com/2022/01/13/us/clyde-bellecourt-dead.html?searchResultPosition=1. Vieweg fuses that quote with Russell Means's comment on Mother Earth's limited tolerance for abuse: Russell Means, "'I Am Not a Leader': Russell Means' 1980 Mother Jones Cover Story," *Mother Jones*, October 22, 2012, https://www.motherjones.com/politics/2012/10/russell-means-mother-jones-interview-1980/.

37 N.a., "Great White Dog Ofi' Tohbi'," *National Park Service*, https://www.nps.gov/articles/great-white-dog.htm, accessed December 3, 2022.

to which humans have fallen victim, including the competitiveness and envy that prevented Vivi from helping her sister. Through the solidarity she experienced with Eva, Vivi has learned to guard against these spirits instead of being possessed by them; and in turn, she decides to care for Eva-turned-zombie rather than enter a civilization where she might once again become complicit in abusive behavior. In an understated and tentative gesture, Vieweg suggests here that change is possible. She thus stakes out a utopia in a dystopian landscape marked by climate change, the vestiges of consumer culture, and disregard for Others.

This change, however, does not imply a final resolution of conflict, a happy ending, or a suturing return to the safe zone of home, which the *Heimat* genre conventionally narrates. On the contrary, it implies the persistence of conflict, a story without a certain end, and it puts the protagonists into the very space that has been, from the beginning, identified with danger. Vieweg's ending resonates with Bauman's account of the indeterminate future that migrants face: "they are on a journey never to be completed ... They are never free from the gnawing sense of transience, indefiniteness and provisional nature of any settlement."[38] Yet, because of Vivi's development, this space has lost its confining character. Its trauma has been transformed into "the ethical imperative of an awakening," to use Cathy Caruth's words.[39] But unlike in Caruth's theory of trauma, the awakening is not indefinitely deferred. Instead, Vivi is "awake" enough to prevent Eva from going to Jena and to stay with her.

As Vivi's name, abbreviated from the Latin "Vivian," derives from the adjective "vivus" and literally means "alive," Vieweg may have meant Vivi to stand for what it means to be "alive" in an ethical sense. In the same purplish color as that of the open sky, the last image of the graphic novel shows, above a phantastic meadow, again the starry sky, which Eva had called "was Gutes an unserer Apokalypse" (something good in our apocalypse) and which connoted openness, self-determination, and a new beginning in the previous image (*EZ*, 56). "Nein, ich schlafe nicht" (No, I am not asleep) is written into the stylized vegetation in the lower third of the page. It refers to Vivi's inability to sleep after she leaves her sister's calls unanswered (*EZ*, 133) and to the way in which her and Eva's minds constantly return to those in whose death or zombiedom they feel implicated (*EZ*, 222).[40] At the same time, it also refers to the sense of aware-

---

38 Bauman, *Wasted Lives*, 76.
39 Caruth, *Unclaimed Experience*, 112.
40 Vieweg's depiction of the way in which Vivi's younger sister reappears wherever Vivi goes and thus accompanies her on her journey recalls a passage from Freud's *Interpretation of Dreams* (and Jacques Lacan's reiteration of Freud in his seminars): a father dreams of his child awakening him from a dream of a fire in which the child perished. "To awaken is thus precisely to awaken only to one's

ness and wakefulness that Vivi gained in coming to terms with her (in)
action. It contrasts with her account during her first night with Eva in the
open landscape, "Dabei habe ich früher nur geschlafen. Auch wenn ich
wach war" (*EZ*, 133; Before I only ever slept. Even when I was awake).
As if to underscore Vivi's new awareness of her world, her own thoughts,
and feelings, Ofi' Tohbi', the guide dog, stands in the distance on the
horizon. It could be showing the way ahead, or the way they have already
gone, or the place where they stay for the night. Here, *Endzeit* lets its
readers, like its protagonists, determine the space.

After *Endzeit*: The Trauma of 1990s East Germany

Vieweg's new-found sense of home relates directly to her generation's
trauma of growing up in East Germany in the years following the country's incorporation into the Federal Republic of Germany. The FRG's
memory politics sought to recast the GDR as an Orientalist caricature
in order to drown out East German voices and legitimize the Western
takeover,[41] and many of Vieweg's generation, lacking a sense of future,
developed a cynical culture that imitated neoliberal social stratification
and cut-throat exploitation, fulfilling Gundermann's prediction that such
disenfranchisement will produce "ein Volk der kalten Barbaren."[42] In
contrast, Vieweg cherished the egalitarian conviviality in her childhood
home of Jena-Neulobeda, a vestige of the GDR's socialist vision turned
concrete in prefab developments. She talks about the defamation and
suppression of the East German legacy in the graphic novel *Antigone*,
which she published immediately after her East German trilogy, and in
her subsequent autobiographical short film *Land vor unserer Zeit* (Land
before our Time, 2020).[43] In the same way in which East German artists

---

repetition of a previous failure to see in time," which leads Caruth to conclude that
"awakening ... is itself the site of trauma," Caruth, *Unclaimed Experience*, 100.

41 See for instance, Dirk Oschmann, "Deutsch-Deutsche Verhältnisse: Wie
sich der Westen den Osten erfindet," *Frankfurter Allgemeine Zeitung*, April 4,
2022, https://www.faz.net/aktuell/feuilleton/deutschland-wie-sich-der-westen-
den-osten-erfindet-17776987.html.

42 Clemens Meyer and Anna Rabe vividly portray this youth culture in their
recent novels: Clemens Meyer, *Als wir träumten* (Frankfurt am Main: Fischer,
2006); Andreas Dresen, dir., *Als wir träumten* (Rommel Film, 2015); Anna Rabe,
Die Möglichkeit von Glück (Stuttgart: Klett-Cotta, 2023).

43 *Antigone* was published a year before *Land vor unserer Zeit* aired on German public television as part of a series that showcased responses to the Federal
Republic's absorption of the former GDR; Olivia Vieweg and Sophocles, *Antigone* (Hamburg: Carlsen, 2019); Vieweg, *Land vor unserer Zeit*.

employed classical models before 1989 to criticize the GDR regime,[44] Vieweg uses Sophocles' eponymous drama to parabolize the German post-1990 public sphere that, dominated by Western media and money, suppressed East Germans' ability to work through their past and thus deepened the trauma of a revolution—and a home—lost.[45] By drawing a connection between the censorship of the past and the glaring democratic deficit, Vieweg points to the more fundamental issues underlying East Germans' grievances, again extending her critique beyond the German context to the rampant democratic backsliding globally that has been corollary to the neoliberalist restructuring of societies on all continents:

> Alles wie ehedem. Willkür, Tyrannei und Menschenmissachtung: Gibt's alles noch … Als Sophokles sich vor gut 2500 Jahren hinsetzte und sein Stück schrieb, war die Demokratie seiner Zeit so schwer krisenbefallen wie es die unsrige ist.
>
> [All is like before. Arbitrariness, tyranny, and disrespect for people: it is still there. When Sophocles sat down and wrote his drama more than 2,500 years ago, the democracy of his age was as crisis-ridden as ours.][46]

Vieweg's *Antigone* draws the political consequences from the trauma that the protagonists of her three previous novels, *Huck Finn*, *Antoinette*, and *Endzeit*, suffer. While the protagonists of her trilogy navigate loss, disenfranchisement, and feelings of powerlessness by migrating in search of home and belonging, Antigone confronts the powers that be with outright disobedience.[47] But while her trilogy held out hope and carved out an albeit precarious utopia for her protagonists, *Antigone* does not.

---

44 Works engaging the classical heritage or mythology often had a decidedly political meaning; examples include Bertolt Brecht's adaptation of *Antigone* (1948), Heiner Müller's *Sophokles: Oedipus Tyrann* (Sophocles: Oedipus the King, 1966/67), *Philoktet* (1958/64), and *Der Horatier* (Berlin: Henschel, 1969), and Christa Wolf's *Kassandra* (1983).

45 For information on the suppression of East German media, see Christoph Links, *Das Schicksal der DDR-Verlage: Die Privatisierung und ihre Konsequenzen* (Berlin: Edition Berolina, 2016); Philip Ther notes: "These protesters [of Berlin's Alexander Square in the fall of 1989] had presumed that the accomplishments of socialism, in which the large majority believed, would be retained when a democratic order was established." Ther, *Europe since 1989*, 75.

46 Dirk Pilz, "Schlimm ist es, sehr schlimm," *Berliner Zeitung*, March 23, 2014, https://www.berliner-zeitung.de/archiv/antigone-im-dresdner-theater-schlimm-ist-es-sehr-schlimm-li.1156734.

47 E.g. Egon Krenz, *Herbst '89* (Berlin: Neues Leben, 1999), n.p. There are relatively few accounts revealing social conditions in the East German states. Notable exceptions are Clemens Meyer's *Als wir träumten* (As We Were Dreaming),

In contrast to the protagonists of her East German trilogy, Vieweg's Antigone is alone, buried alive, left to die. While Vieweg again shows trauma as interfacing individual and social spheres, this time it is with deadly consequences. Extending from Antigone's cell, countless more are visible in the graphic novel's final image, beneath a sky filled with crows carrying off the carcass in bits and pieces. The page is overlaid with downward splashes of red, evoking blood splashed on a camera lens. While the empty last pages of the trilogy's graphic novels invite the audience's own ideas about a livable society, *Antigone*'s audience seems separated by a lens and a curtain of blood. Showing here in a stark image how post-1990 developments betrayed expectations, hopes, and projections of the future, Vieweg does not merely lament the loss, but implicates all who watched—and unlike Antigone—did not act, letting her readers connect the dots between traumatization and perpetration.

Andreas Dresen's eponymous film adaptation of Meyer's novel, and, more recently, Anna Rabe's *Die Möglichkeit von Glück* (The Possibility of Happiness).

3: Olivia Vieweg's *Endzeit*: The Trauma of Climate Change, Disease, and Plants Run Amok

Heather I. Sullivan

WITH AN ECOCRITICAL and plant-focused perspective, this essay considers how Oliva Vieweg's 2018 graphic novel *Endzeit* (meaning "End Time" but published with the English title of *Ever After*) documents the trauma and impact of climate change on both human and nonhuman-vegetal beings. Additionally, it is a traumatic zombie story of humans transformed into the wandering dead via a species-crossing plant infection.[1] The tale traces two girls, Eva and Vivian, on a journey through a heat-hazed, post-apocalyptic German landscape emptied of people. The girls escape from brutal situations in Weimar with fairy-tale hopes of a better life in Jena while facing the constant horror of needing to flee from zombies whose orifices sprout roots, leaves, and eventually even flowers. The plants that we see in the comic are flourishing but have themselves become agents of infection. While we know that much vegetation has been negatively impacted by human activities and their consequences, such as climate change, industrial toxins, deforestation, and expanding urban zones, some invasive, pesticide-resistant, or hardy weed plants are actually thriving in our ever hotter and radiated world.[2] Plants have not (yet) become such a disease vector, though their partners in root collaboration, the fungi, certainly have infected other species, such as the spore-sprouting ants of the rain forest whose brains are controlled by a fungal infection. Indeed, fungi are often featured in science fiction texts as zombie-inducing agents of infection (including a vast array of novels and the

---

1   I have written at greater length on the species-crossing, kingdom-crossing disease aspect. See Heather I. Sullivan, "Cross-Infections of Vegetal-Human Bodies in Science Fiction," *Science Fiction Studies* 49, no. 2 (2022): 342–58.

2   For discussions of plant death and plant expansion in the Anthropocene in the US and Germany, see Emily Grebenstein, "Escape of the Invasives: Top Six Invasive Plants Species in the United States," *Smithsonian Insider*, April 19, 2013; and Josef H. Reichholf, *Der Tanz um das goldene Kalb: Der Ökokolonialismus Europas* (Berlin: Wagenbach, 2006).

recent television series based on a video game, *The Last of Us*).[3] Vieweg's *Endzeit* transforms the fungal-infection trope into a plant-infection zombie trope, but with no explanation. Originally published in a much shorter form and without the plant-infusion as her 2012 *Diplomarbeit*, Vieweg revised it into the longer 2018 version in which plants are retaking the world with human bodies as convenient carriers. Plants have always (quietly) dominated most earthly ecosystems, at least in terms of the multicellular species, in that they transform the sun's energy into plant sugars through photosynthesis and so feed us all, but also in the oceans in the form of single-celled photosynthetic algae and cyanobacteria. In *Endzeit*, the vegetal beings reassert themselves by conquering human bodies and brains in a new zombie embodiment, and their vegetal selves flourish in the climate-change induced heat.

Endzeit begins with a full splash-page view from above Weimar where the sky is vivid red and orange suggesting intense heat; no human beings appear for several pages. We see instead the city surrounded by vegetation and filled with trees and potted plants, crows, a barbed-wire fence, and bloody gardening tools. Something is very wrong. The first image of a human being occurs only several pages later, and it includes her complaints about the heat: "Das ist eine gottverdammte Hitze heute" (It's a goddamned heat[wave] today).[4] The comic's imagery features plants with three specific emphases: first, Germany's now very hot climate is revealed with vibrant reddish-orange tones that are matched in color by what looks like a savannah of lush grasslands flourishing in the absence of most people and occupied instead by (zoo-escaped?) giraffes who look quite well adapted to this vegetal world; second, the text repeatedly presents vibrant

---

3   For the science of fungi broadly, and a discussion including images of the ants whose brains are controlled by the fungus as they sprout spores from their heads to infect their fellow ants, see Merlin Sheldrake, *Entangled Lives: How Fungi Make our Worlds, Change our Minds* (New York: Random House, 2020). In terms of cultural texts, fungal zombie texts compose an entire genre. Beyond the 2023 HBO series, *The Last of Us*, written by Timothy A. Good, Mark Hartzell, Emily Mendez, and Cindy Mollo, I mention just a few recent examples: Mike Carey's *The Girl with All the Gifts* (New York: Orbit Books, 2014) and *The Boy on the Bridge* (New York: Orbit Books, 2017); T. Kingfisher's *What Moves the Dead* (New York: Tor Nightfire, 2022); David Koepp, *Cold Storage* (New York, HarperCollins, 2019); Benjamin Percy's trilogy of alien fungi that begins with *The Ninth Metal (The Comet Cycle, 1)* (New York: William Morrow Paperbacks, 2021); Scott Siegler's trilogy that begins with *Infected* (New York: Three Rivers Press, 2008); Jeff Vandermeer, *City of Saints and Madmen: The Ambergris Series, Book 1* (New York: Picador, 2002); David Walton, *The Genius Plague* (Amherst: Pyr, 2017); and many others.

4   Olivia Vieweg, *Endzeit* (Hamburg: Carlsen Comics, 2018), 8; all translations from the German are mine.

images of potted plants, gardens, trees, grasses, vegetables, and fruits; and, third, the zombies themselves clearly suffer from a botanical infection transforming human beings into root- and branch-sprouting bodies. Interestingly, none of the dialogue ever addresses directly either climate change or the vegetal dominance and take-over. Instead, Vivian and Eva journey through the overgrown landscape seeing birds, bugs, giraffes, and zombies yet their conversations pertain only to their past lives, families, anxieties, losses, hopes, and dreams. Vivian used to repair and sell stolen cameras on eBay, whereas Eva had just received a scholarship to study in the US and had her ticket ready to fly; all such plans were disrupted by the zombie attack. Their ensuing conversations fail to address either the plant-zombies or their real traumas such as Vivian's PTSD-induced hallucinations about her dead younger sister and Eva's spreading vegetal-zombie infection slowly taking over her mind. The text presents graphic details of both problems while the characters avoid speaking directly of them. The dual nature of graphic novels that can include dialogue and images that complement or contrast each other allows Vieweg to feature, on the one hand, spoken language focusing on daily human issues, such as relationships and food, and, on the other hand, images of unspeakable trauma juxtaposed with a bright vegetal world of plant-human bodies spreading, growing, and flourishing. The contrast powerfully drives the narrative: even in the visually blatant vegetal-zombie apocalypse, people obsessively converse about their small-scale issues while failing to mention the major crises, the climate, or the rampant zombies.

Vieweg's *Endzeit* does significant work towards visualizing plant power while leaving the readers the task of understanding the implications of the images without verbal explanations. The ability of graphic novels and comics to allow doubled insights in this particular combination and/or juxtaposition of text/imagery is significant here. Tammy Horn explains that "comics enact 'transmediation,' or the translation of content from one sign system to another."[5] "Transmediation" refers to how comics actively engage two or more kinds of codes simultaneously, in this case, images and words. Such a layering of codes allows manifold meanings to emerge from the more-than human plant lives in Vieweg's work. Hillary Chute's *Why Comics* similarly notes that "comics is not an illustrative form, in which the words and images match, but rather … 'narrative drawing' … and 'picture writing,' in which the words and the images each move the narrative forward in different ways the reader creates out of the relationship between

---

5   Tammy Horn, "The Graphic Novel as a Choice of Weapons," in *Teaching the Graphic Novel*, ed. Stephen E. Tabachnick (New York: The Modern Language Association of America, 2009), 91–98, here 79.

the two."[6] And Scott McCloud's famous *Understanding Comics* describes seven different types of word-image relationships characterized, respectively, by harmony, tension, contrast, and enhancement.[7] In other words, the medium of the graphic novel provides rich possibilities for portraying simultaneously the plant and human expressive existences in juxtaposition to one another. Vieweg's graphic novel presents a compelling version of this doubled perspective of the plant-based, non-human communication and action in imagery that contrasts with the language-based human experiences of the two aptly named protagonists Vivian (like "vie," "vivus," or life) and Eva (like the biblical Eve). Indeed, our two females suggesting life and the "first" female will transform by the end of the text into new, hybrid beings just as the dialogue is abandoned and replaced, much like in Goethe's infamous 1828 *Novelle*, which also ends with a song of harmony (but does not offer an explanation).

I address here the question of plant power and the implications of the vegetally infected zombies in the climate-changed landscapes of Germany; the multispecies aspect of virtually all life forms that are always already in a state of shared bodies (consider all the bacteria, viruses, etc. that exist on and in your body), which Vieweg makes visually overt with the plant-infected zombies; and how Vieweg's comic form more dramatically presents this hybridity in images but not words. First, then, is the visual portrayal of plant horror in this apocalyptic story that provides conversations only about human feelings and experiences while presenting the radically changed environment in imagery. For one thing, the images-versus-text contrast reveals a world dominated by plants that certainly do not have human voices nor do they communicate with human words. Instead, vegetal beings are wildly different life forms upon which we are fully dependent for our food, oxygen, local environmental conditions, and caffeine—and yet they are as alien as we can imagine with their dual lives above and below ground, their rooted entwining and communication with fungi, their distributed intelligence that has no central nervous system and requires no brain, their vast physical scale, potential to live for tens of thousands of years, and slower physical movements. As Dawn Keetley notes in the introduction to *Plant Horror: Approaches to the Monstrous Vegetal in Fiction and Film*, "plants embody an absolute alterity," beyond "the outer limits of what we know."[8] Additionally, she notes

---

6 Hillary Chute, *Why Comics? From Underground to Everywhere* (New York: HarperCollins, 2017), 21.

7 See Scott McCloud, *Understanding Comics: The Invisible Art* (New York: HarperCollins, 1994), 138–61 (Chapter 6: "Show and Tell").

8 Dawn Keetley, "Introduction: Six Theses on Plant Horror; or, Why are Plants Horrifying?," in *Plant Horror: Approaches to the Monstrous Vegetal in Fiction and Film*, ed. Dawn Keetley and Angela Tenga (London: Palgrave Macmillan, 2016), 1–30, here 6.

that we tend to be "blind" to their lush growth that seems not to threaten us; and yet when plants do become a menace, when their "wild, purposeless growth" extends beyond the spaces we allot to them or expect them to be and spreads faster and more intimately onto and into our bodies, then real horror ensues.[9] In that we tend not to see plants as active, the horror becomes all the more overt when they manifest themselves in a manner that brings to our attention their power and our full dependency on them. Jessica George's essay for the volume *Plants in Science Fiction* notes that "the tension between our awareness of a 'non-human world'—what [Eugene] Thacker calls the 'world-in-itself'—our embeddedness in it, and our inability to access it, manifests itself in horror."[10] Similarly, Christina Becher's discussion of "Pflanzliches Aufbegehren in Frauke Bergers *Grün*" (Vegetable Rebellion in Frauka Berger's *Grün*) also discusses the horror of plants on an alien planet altered by human activity that transform into green predatory invaders and a "vegetabile[] Seuche" (vegetal plague).[11] Like Vieweg's comic, Berger's presents human-plant hybrids emerging from human destruction of their environment.

In this essay, I consider how Vieweg's text is able to represent both the potential power and vitality, even agency, of plants through images while simultaneously having words—human words—present the human perspective that remains so typically self-focused (even rather narcissistic, one might say) and thereby relegates the surrounding environment, particularly the green beings, to the background. The plant-zombies reassert themselves in the foreground, albeit visually. *Endzeit* provides a rich textual landscape for critical plant studies, and its zombie narrative transforms the horror of shared bodies with what looks like a final embrace of what Donna Haraway would call multispecies kinships in *Staying with the Trouble: Making Kin with the Chthulucene*.[12] Ecocriticism broadly, and the fields of plant and animal studies specifically, reconsider our human relationships with the non-human in terms of entanglements and ecological systems, positioning human beings fully within the world of living things rather than outside of it as exceptional, almost non-material beings who rule with seemingly "rational" minds. After all, we humans, like all large, living animals, exist *because* of plant sugars, and horror tales of plants changing the game to reclaim their energy provide relevant insights into our actual dependency on their green lives, bodies, and activities.

9   Keetley, "Introduction: Six Theses on Plant Horror," 10 and 13.
10   Jessica George, "Weird Flora: Plant Life in the Classic Weird Tale," in *Plants in Science Fiction: Speculative Vision*, ed. Katherine E. Bishop, David Higgins, and Jerry Määttä (Cardiff: University of Wales Press, 2020), 11–31, here 17.
11   Christina Becher, "Nach dem Kollaps: Pflanzliches Aufbegehren in Frauke Bergers Grün," *Closure: Kieler e-Journal für Comicforschung* 7 (2020): 66–89.
12   See Donna Haraway, *Staying with the Trouble: Making Kin in the Chthulucene* (Durham, NC: Duke University Press, 2016).

In the humanities and social sciences, critical plant studies explores portrayals and understandings of plants in both scientific and cultural forms.[13] The history of plant studies more broadly is quite mixed: most ancient cultures grasped the relevance and lively nature of the most readily available food and green beings surrounding them, though already the ancient Greeks claimed that plants were barely alive and certainly at the very bottom of the hierarchy (with humans at the top). Much of Western philosophy has had a messy response to vegetal lives with diminished attention to the green—literally—energy that fuels our existence and with the refusal to attribute an animated state to plants. Bruno Latour critiques the tendency of Western cultures to treat the world as mere passive matter, noting that: "One of the main puzzles of Western history is not that 'there are still people who believe in animism,' but the rather naïve belief that many still have in a de-animated world of mere stuff."[14] This essay adopts, in fact, a perspective of animism, asserting that the wild activity of plants is quite "animated" even though we tend not to see it due to their different time scales and forms of movement. One of the most brilliant portrayals of ancient indigenous knowledge together with contemporary "Western" science is Robin Wall Kimmerer's essential book, *Braiding Sweetgrass*; Kimmerer is a member of the Potawatomi tribe and has a PhD in plant science. She describes how Native American indigenous thinkers see plants as older cousins:

> In the Western tradition there is a recognized hierarchy of beings, with, of course, the human being on top—the pinnacle of evolution, the darling of Creation—and the plants at the bottom. But in Native ways of knowing, human people are often referred to as "the younger brothers of Creation." We say that humans have the least experience with how to live and thus the most to learn—we must look to our teachers among the other species for guidance. Their wisdom is apparent in the way that they live. They teach us by example.[15]

Let Kimmerer here serve as a counter-voice to "Western" thinking, a guide through an animist reading of Vieweg, a voice that knows and

---

13 For a marvelous summary of recent work in critical plant studies, especially on trees, see Solvejg Nitzke and Helga G. Braumbeck, "Arboreal Imaginations: An Introduction to the Shared Cultures of Trees and Humans," *Green Letters* 25, no. 4 (2021): 34–55.

14 Bruno Latour, "Agency at the Time of the Anthropocene," *New Literary History* 45 (2014): 1–18, here 8.

15 Robin Wall Kimmerer, *Braiding Sweetgrass: Indigenous Wisdom, Scientific Knowledge, and the Teaching of Plants* (Minneapolis, MN: Milkweed Editions, 2013), 9.

utilizes but also enhances more traditional science with a broader understanding of plant life.

Indeed, plants tend to receive the brunt of philosophical and economic brutality in terms of denials of their active lives, their sexuality (despite the wildly sexual floral displays and fruits), intelligence, communication, and even their status as living things.[16] In the 2022 volume, *Literaturen und Kulturen des Vegetabilen: Plant Studies—Kulturwissenschaftliche Pflanzenforschung* (Literatures and Cultures of the Vegetable: Critical Plant Studies), the editors Urte Stobbe, Anke Kramer, and Berbeli Wanning present studies that "begegnen Pflanzen nicht länger mit der auf Aristoteles zurückgehenden Haltung, dass sie in der Hierarchie unter den Menschen und den Tieren stehen und zum Nutzen des Menschen frei verfügbar sind" (no longer encounter plants with the attitude that goes back to Aristotle, indicating that they [plants] stand in the hierarchy under human beings and animals, and are readily available for the use of humans).[17] Similarly, the preeminent plant philosopher, Michael Marder, dedicates his book *Plant Thinking: A Philosophy of Vegetal Life* to surveying "Western" philosophy from the ancient Greeks through Heidegger in terms of their faulty vegetal thinking. He explains that "non-Western and feminist philosophies contain a wealth of venerable traditions much more attuned to the floral world than any author or mainstream current in the history of Western thought."[18] In his discussions, Marder both critiques and attempts to redeem "Western" philosophy, claiming that "although in denying to vegetal life the core values of autonomy, individualization, self-identity, originality, and essentiality, traditional philosophy marginalizes plants, it also inadvertently confers on them a crucial role in the ongoing transvaluation of metaphysical value systems."[19] His most rele-

---

16   On current debates regarding plant intelligence, see Monica Gagliano's works, for example: Monica Gagliano, John C. Ryan, and Patricia Vieira, eds., *The Language of Plants: Science, Philosophy, Literature* (Minneapolis: University of Minnesota Press, 2017). Regarding the "soul" of plants, see the confirmative study by Gustav Theodor Fechner, *Nanna: oder über das Seelenleben der Pflanzen* (orig. 1848), on Projekt Gutenberg, https://www.projekt-gutenberg.org/fechner/nanna/nanna.html. On plant sexuality, see Lincoln Taiz and Lee Taiz, *Flora Unveiled: The Discovery & Denial of Sex in Plants* (New York: Oxford University Press, 2017).

17   Urte Stobbe, Anke Kramer, and Berbeli Wanning, "Einleitung: Plant Studies—Kulturwissenschaftliche Pflanzenforschung," in *Literaturen und Kulturen des Vegetabilen: Plant Studies—Kulturwissenschaftliche Pflanzenforschung*, ed. Urte Stobbe, Anke Kramer, and Berbeli Wanning (Berlin: Peter Lang, 2022), 11–31, here 19–20.

18   Michael Marder, *Plant-Thinking: A Philosophy of Vegetal Life* (New York: Columbia University Press, 2013), 6.

19   Marder, *Plant Thinking*, 55.

vant comment for this study of Vieweg's *Endzeit*, though, is his admission that, in the overall picture, non-Western and feminist philosophies offer the most insights into more accurate knowledge of plants. Consider this our frame: eco-feminist thinking shaped by critical plant studies with animism and the vitality of material ecocriticism. In terms of agency, plants are definitely responding actively to the terrible impacts of industrialization by languishing or even going extinct, and yet some species are, in contrast, becoming resistant to the petrochemical poisons we dump daily into the fields of our food plants and into the air, soil, and water as we deforest the world. Vieweg's contemporary zombie text reminds us of the resistant and invasive plants that, aided by humans, traverse the world or "learn" to defy human power; she overtly vegetalizes the world with vivid imagery of lush plant-scapes in which humans roam, now driven only by their plant infections. This vision is both much more contemporary and, simultaneously, much more ancient.

Indeed, after the opening pages of heat and plants, Vieweg's graphic novel has another two pages devoid of people that show trees, cars as places on which to place plants, watering cans, the iconic statue of Goethe and Schiller with more water cans, and a sign asking people not to hoard water. While the proliferation of plants everywhere in the city looks lovely, a crisis situation is indicated by a fence topped with barbed wire surrounding the human space. The first person shown is a typical fairy-tale-like evil mother figure in the form of a psychologist up on a roof hanging laundry to dry and complaining about the extreme heat. She is treating Vivian for her trauma, which appears in terrifyingly repetitive nightmares and daytime hallucinations of the appearance of the zombies who took her sister. The doctor, herself traumatized by the loss of her own daughter, has the teenage Vivian inappropriately sit on her lap during therapy, feeding the girl strawberries before sending her back to her room in the psychiatric ward. Because Vivian later helps another inmate to get strawberries, she is punished by the doctor by being sent to work the fence the next day, that is, she must reinforce the barriers and fight any zombies trying to break through. The doctor's own trauma makes her try to control Vivian in highly problematic ways and to reshape her into a replica of her daughter, to slap her like a child when she disobeys, and to fulfill the stepmother role of fairy tales whose behavior sends the young heroine fleeing out into the world. This time, however, it is not the forests of the Brothers Grimm but rather the overheated grasslands of the transformed German lands filled not with wolves, ogres, or magical creatures, but rather zombies and plants with an agenda. Of course, there is a witch of sorts, or a scientist, whom Vivian later encounters: the Gardener, whom I discuss below.

Vivian goes to work on the fence in this fairy-tale situation of navigating terribly behaving older adults, only to face the horror of an attack before she learns any active resistance strategies against the zombies. Her new friend Isabelle is bitten and then shot and killed immediately for fear of infection by the tough girl, Eva, who always works on the fence, unhappily and unhelpfully. Vivian is so upset that she tries to kill herself that night; the next day she and Eva escape from Weimar separately, but end up together on an unmanned, empty train to Jena that carries supplies from city to city. The two girls thus begin to traverse the wilds outside of the city, despite not liking each other at all, at least at first. In the typical manner of road-trip narratives, they despise each other initially but gradually develop a friendship; this road trip is, however, a truncated train journey that turns into a hike through the plant-dominated landscape where cars, freeways, and most remaining human structures are hidden under luxuriant vegetation. The power of plants reveals itself in the comic in a variety of vivid images.

Indeed, as the girls hike through the lush landscape after Vivian's hallucinations drive her to stop the train, it becomes clear that the world is once again ruled by plants. The vegetal dominance suggests both a climate-changed future for northern Europe that replaces its previously forested lands with grasslands, but also the ancient past before human beings existed, when plant pioneers conquered and crossed the continents, covering the rocky Earth in green. Plants are avid pioneers and powerful colonizers. As the editors of *The Language of Plants: Science, Philosophy, Literature*, Monica Gagliano, John C. Ryan, and Patricia Viera, write:

> Plants are perhaps the most fundamental form of life, providing sustenance, and thus enabling the existence of all animals, including us humans. Their evolutionary transition from Paleozoic aquatic beginnings to a vegetative life out of water is undoubtedly one of the farthest-reaching events in the history of the earth. It was the silent yet relentless colonization of terrestrial environments by the earliest land plants that transformed the global landscape and radically altered the geochemical cycles of the planet. This resulted in lowered concentrations of atmospheric carbon dioxide and thus set the scene for the emergence of terrestrial animals about 350 million years ago.[20]

Plant life shaped the world and enabled the emergence of larger life forms. Plant philosopher Emanuele Coccia writes in *The Life of Plants*: "For the vast majority of organisms, the world is the product of plant life, the product of the colonization of the planet by plants, since time immemorial."[21] Yet industrialized culture has suppressed much of our sense of belonging to a plant world; the common perception is that plants

---

20   Monica Gagliano, John C. Ryan, and Patricia Viera, "Introduction," in *The Language of Plants*, Gagliano, Ryan, and Vieira, vi–xxxiv, here vii.
21   Emanuele Coccia, *The Life of Plants: The Metaphysics of Mixture*, trans. Dylan J. Montanari (Cambridge: Polity, 2018), 8–9.

are just part of separate wild zones, or aesthetic objects in the background, or lives that we control with petroleum-fueled agriculture or in gardens, parks, and nature reserves. The environmental philosopher, Val Plumwood, writes in *Environmental Culture* of such problematic assumptions: "the dominant forms of reason—economic, political, and ethical/prudential—are failing us because they are subject to a systematic pattern of distortions and illusions."[22] These "distortions and illusions" emerge from the belief that humans rule the world and all life, and that we are independent and separate from ecosystems: that we are not fully dependent on plant life (food and oxygen) or bacterial help to digest our food, and that our intelligence, rationality, and/or spiritual essence not only place us above the world, but make us (nearly) free from such materiality or, at the very least, in full control of it all. Plumwood notes, furthermore, that these so-called forms of "reason" believe in human autonomy from the world: "It is the special form of failure such monological and hegemonic forms of reason are subject to that they misunderstand their own enabling conditions—the body, ecology and non-human nature."[23] I use Plumwood here to emphasize in particular the tendency of industrialized cultures to perceive vegetal life, one essential part of our "enabling conditions," as mere backdrop or passive matter for us to control and manipulate at will. Plants, of course, fuel both our bodies and our wood-burning and/or fossil-fueled cultures (plant bodies transformed through time to make coal, gas, and oil), and they are the co-species on which we depend. Plumwood describes our lack of attention to such crucial facts of life as "blind-spots." Vieweg exposes the vegetal power in *Endzeit*, making it visible, particularly in the scenes about three quarters of the way through the comic when Vivian meets the Gardener.

These significant scenes with the Gardener fulfill the typical fairy-tale requirement of meeting a witch or other dangerous being while on a journey; the encounter takes place after Vivian and Eva have covered much ground and begin to become friends. They fight frequently, though, since Vivian struggles to overcome her hallucinations and refuses to kill any of the zombies even to save their own lives since she fears her sister is now one of the walking dead. Additionally, Eva has been bitten by a zombie in the opening scenes of the novel when she was fighting on the fence with Vivian and Isabelle. She is hiding her infection and eventual doom, but the images show her pulling up her shirt and revealing the signs of roots spreading in her stomach, moving upwards. The girls help each other, fight, separate, find each other again, and continue onwards. During one separation after Vivian almost let Eva die and Eva's vegetal rage starts

---

22 Val Plumwood, *Environmental Culture: The Ecological Crisis of Reason* (London: Routledge, 2006), 16.
23 Plumwood, *Environmental Culture*, 17.

to overwhelm her, Vivian comes across a beautiful field and discovers a plate of cake. She hungrily eats this offering and then is approached by the Gardener, a witch, perhaps, in fairy-tale terms, who saves her from a marauding bride-zombie in full white dress mode, bent on biting Vivian. The Gardener is the most important figure whom the young women encounter: she is a scientist of sorts and is infected but lives as a half zombie/half human with her face literally divided into two sides. She maintains her human intelligence and language but also is friendly with and clearly can direct the local zombies. Inside her compound, Vivian feels at home, safe, and well-fed. The Gardener promises to help with her hallucinations and nightmares, feeding her a strawberry—another key strawberry image, this one, functioning like a magical fairy-tale prop—that will make her forget all the pain. The strawberry may infect her or immunize her so that she will become half plant-zombie but remain half human; again the meaning is not stated but the end of the graphic novel seems to suggest that the strawberry was an immunization/infection of sorts that will render Vivian a hybrid like the Gardener's own half-human, half-zombie state. When Vivian eats the delicious fruits, the Gardener asks her: "Du fragst dich, wie die Tomaten so wunderbar gedeihen? Guter Dünger" (You ask yourself why the tomatoes flourish so wonderfully? Good fertilizer).[24] This blissful state lasts briefly until Vivian realizes that this fertilizer for the beautiful greenhouse where the plants flourish and even appear to speak in human language (water me! Me! Me!) consists of dead human bodies; we see a hand sticking out of the rich soil. In the greenhouse, we also see lab equipment and Petri dishes with the same plant forms growing out of them as are radiating out of the Gardener's face. She is clearly working on the infection, in whatever form. And the focus on faces continues when Vivian stands in the Gardener's garden in her post-strawberry state with shadows of plants across her features, an image that resembles a famous moment in Stephen Spielberg's first *Jurassic Park* film from 1993 as the dangerously predatory velociraptor's faces shine with a reflection of DNA code as they hunt the two children. Here, plant shadows shine across Vivian's face as if revealing her inner core (not DNA but vegetal power). At no point does Vieweg provide any comment on the scientific implications of these images, nor on the Gardener's actual role: is she the actual predator or the creator of the zombie plague, a doctor seeking a cure or a hopeful hybridity, or is she a half-zombie studying her kind? Vivian never asks. But when she shortly thereafter finds Eva buried in the soil as future plant fertilizer, she digs up her now rapidly transforming friend and saves her. The Gardener tries to prevent Vivian from unearthing Eva, but Vivian fights until the Gardener concedes and gives Eva a bright red tomato to help, one that possibly

24 Vieweg, *Endzeit*, 204–5.

transforms her infection into a similarly survivable hybridity. They depart, continuing their journey to Weimar. What we learn is that the Gardener is, in any case, the unstated link between humans, plants, and plant-zombie hybrids.

That Vieweg purposefully contrasts human-word versus plant-image storytelling is not just evident in the text. It also becomes clear in her 2018 interview with Marc Frisch in *The Comics Journal*. Frisch writes:

> In the 2018 edition of *Endzeit*, ... the episode in which Vivi and Eva encounter the Gardener runs 40 pages—four times as long as in the initial version—and ends on a very different note. Also, this time there is a plant-like quality to the decay of the zombie infection—its victims look less like their flesh is rotting and more like it's ivy that's creeping all over them. The Gardener isn't explicitly named as such in this incarnation of the story, and the clues to her background are left for the art to convey, rather than verbalized.[25]

Vieweg's editors requested that she make the role of the Gardener explicit, but Vieweg insisted on leaving the information solely in the images. In other words, the text-image contrast is part of the story; it is also a particularly useful strategy for showing but not commenting on unspeakable trauma, climate change, and vegetal power that still so often remain unstated and backgrounded politically. The encounter with the Gardener also empowers Vivian, who now leads Eva instead of the other way around. They are, however, separated one last time right before the end, but I address that fact later.

First, I want to provide more comments on how Vieweg's *Endzeit* depicts the realm of plants into which we enter when reading. On its inner covers, immediately inside the book before one begins reading, and again at the end, we find a full-page, bright pink vision of thorny plants looking rather threatening, something like what one might expect from the dangerous vines surrounding Sleeping Beauty's castle (*Dornröschen*). This blatant imagery continues; facing the first actual page of the story is a strawberry with a bite taken out of it and red juicy drops next to it; these subtle strawberry drips echo the title page's accompanying image of a thin strip of bright green grass on which a child's toy ball rests, a toy of yellow and blue, but flecked by a few disturbing drops of blood on it and the grass. The story itself then opens with a splash page featuring "Weimar, geschützte Stadt" (Weimar, protected city); one half of the page is bright orange, red, hot sky and the second half is part of the

---

25 Marc-Oliver Frisch, "Angst essen Comics auf: The Twisted Beauty of Olivia Vieweg's Coming-of-Age Tales," *The Comics Journal*, April 19, 2018. https://www.tcj.com/angst-essen-comics-auf-the-twisted-beauty-of-olivia-viewegs-coming-of-age-tales/.

city with many trees and yellow grasslands behind it. What is most interesting about Weimar is that all of the city that we see is now dedicated to cultivating plants as food; indeed, we never witness any human eating anything other than plants throughout the tale. This vegetarian aspect appears helpfully environmental, but may actually highlight the tension between plants and humans in the novel: who is using whom for energy and transportation?

The fairy tale-like journey undertaken by Vivian and Eva includes repeated narrow escapes from zombies, all of whom feature horrific roots and leaves emerging from their faces and wounds. Only the Gardener, Eva at the end, and, finally, Vivian have pretty green leaves and/or flowers emerging from their bodies. It is as if the battle has changed and the two young women, for they have transformed from girls into young women by the end, will begin a new life with the seeing-eye dog named Ghost whom Vivian found during one of her solo days. They begin as a new, queer, hybrid family, one that incorporates the non-human with vegetation in their bodies and with Ghost in huge flower fields covering the final pages from top to bottom. In order to get to this final, multi-species conclusion, however, several other transformations have to occur. Eva's infection continues so that her flowers emerge and her eyes go white—a zombie sign. And yet when she reunites with Vivian, she does not attack nor does she speak. Vivian, too, must transform. Briefly on her own again, Vivian loses an eye while battling against a zombie—who is Ghost's, the dog's, former person; using an antler horn to protect herself, her eye gets pierced and destroyed. This loss of one eye replicates the Gardener's face with one zombie white eye and one human eye. The next day, Vivian's transformation continues when she finally comes across her sister's corpse and lies down beside her to spend the night at her side. When she awakes in the morning, she is sprouting pretty green leaves from her eye and other wounds, which she rips out. Vivian then leaves her pink asylum dress behind to cover her sister's little dead body. Now Vivian wears only a black slip, her clothing indicating her inner transformation away from trauma and grief and into a new, adult strength, ready to accept the loss of her sister, shed her guilt, and embrace the multi-species reality that has always been with us but has now become blatant and visually all-consuming. Transformations are crucial to most fairy tales; Vivian's and Eva's transformations into adulthood status are also bodily transformations into hybridity. We are, however, always already hybrid beings, bodies with teeming multitudes of bacterial and other lives co-sharing every surface and the interior of our bodies. Vieweg's *Endzeit* closes with a revelation of hybridity that appears new but is as ancient as multicellular life itself.

I read the novel as a plant story, a story of the vegetal reconquering of the world, but also a story of multi-species entanglements revealing themselves. In terms of the latter, I refer to Ed Yong's 2016 book,

I Contain Multitudes: The Microbes Within Us and a Grander View of Life, which describes how our bodies, like all large, multicellular bodies, are co-occupied by innumerable bacteria, viruses, fungi, and archaea.[26] We are large, moving islands, Yong writes, of microbial life. The idea that we are born alone and die alone not only discounts our mothers but also our life companions, the microbial beings that shape all life. As Plumwood says, overlooking and misunderstanding our enabling conditions (or enabling beings, I would note) like bacteria who help us digest, and plants who feed us, is a typical weakness of industrialized, pseudo-rational societies. The editors of *Arts of Living on a Damaged Planet*, Anna Tsing, Heather Swanson, Elaine Gan, Nils Bubandt, dedicate much of their volume to considerations of our multi-species bodies. The book has two sections, one beginning at each end of the text and meeting the other, upside down, in the middle: the "Ghosts" section on the persistent imprint of the co-evolutionary past and ongoing hybridity of our lives with microbes, and the "Monsters" section on these complex entanglements so often overlooked in the (modern, Western) philosophical concepts of individuality and subjectivity. In the introduction to the monster section, the editors write that "our bodies contain more bacterial cells than human ones."[27] We are, in short, a blended form of being. They also note that "Life has been monstrous almost from its beginnings. In ancient times, prokaryotes (bacteria and archaea) gave birth to monsters in which one organism engulfed others or joined immoderate liaisons, forming nucleated cells and multicellular organisms called eukaryotes. Ever since, we have muddled along in our mixes and messes. All eukaryotic life is monstrous."[28] In this monstrous form of hybridity, symbiosis, and bodily integration, life is entwined disturbingly, and disease-spread is not so distinct from life-spread. In her chapter "Noticing Microbial Worlds: The Postmodern Synthesis in Biology," Margaret McFall-Ngai clarifies that "Microbes don't just 'rule' the world; they make every life-form possible, and they have been doing so since the beginning of evolutionary time. …It turns out that most animals and plants have coevolved in and with microbial-rich environments and have relied on the microbial

---

26 Ed Yong, *I Contain Multitudes: The Microbes Within Us and a Grander View of Life* (New York: Ecco, 2016).

27 Anna Tsing, Heather Swanson, Elaine Gan, and Nils Bubandt, "Introduction: Bodies Tumbled into Bodies," in *Arts of Living on a Damaged Planet*, ed. Anna Tsing, Heather Swanson, Elaine Gan, and Nils Bubandt (Minneapolis: University of Minnesota Press, 2017), M1–M12, here M5 ("M" is for the Monsters half of the book; "G" is for the Ghosts section that begins also with page 1 from the other cover, flipped upside down).

28 Tsing, Swanson, Gan, and Bubandt, "Introduction: Bodies Tumbled into Bodies," M5.

world for their own evolution and health."[29] In other words, Vieweg's bodily portrayal of human-plant hybrid zombies makes visible the actual "monstrous" aspect of our lives.

Arts of Living on a Damaged Planet offers another important insight that helps with interpreting Vieweg's *Endzeit*, specifically the issue of contamination as a means of making clear our relations to plants and other species. The editors note in the Monsters Introduction that: "Contamination often acts as a 'tracer,'—a way to see relations. We notice connections in part through their ruination."[30] The zombie infection is the "tracer" that reveals hybridity and brings new insights into our relations with the world and the vegetal. In the "Ghosts" Introduction to *Arts of Living on a Damaged Planet*, the editors also speak of extinction, a problem currently facing a huge percentage of animals and plants on Earth, but one that human beings are apparently facing in the graphic novel of plant-zombies. Tsing et al. worry that "we might lose a majority of all species by the end of the twenty-first century. The problem is not just the loss of individual species but of assemblages, some of which we may not even know about, some of which will not recover. Mass extinction could ensue from cascading effects. In an entangled world where bodies are tumbled into bodies (see our Monsters), extinction is a multispecies event."[31] In Vieweg's rather optimistic version of an entangled world, with plant bodies tumbled into human bodies, the extinction of human beings is at stake, though this "extinction" may actually be a fairytale transformation into something else.

The Gardener specifically addresses this issue of transformation rather than extinction. This is a crucial moment in which the real situation in the novel is addressed directly, just this once. Just after giving Vivian the strawberry so that "du wirst nie wieder traurig sein" (You will never be sad again),[32] the Gardener says that she is going to share a secret with her as they look at a lizard: "die Dinosaurier sind auch nicht ausgestorben. Sie sind noch unter uns. Vielleicht werden wir keine Herrscher mehr sein, aber immer noch ein Teil dieses wunderschönen Gartens" (the dinosaurs also didn't go extinct. They are still with us. Perhaps we will not be the rulers anymore, but we will still be part of this wonderfully beautiful

---

29 Margaret McFall-Ngai, "Noticing Microbial Worlds: The Postmodern Synthesis in Biology," in *Arts of Living on a Damaged Planet*, ed. Tsing, Swanson, Gan, and Bubandt, M51–M69, here M59.

30 Tsing, Swanson, Gan, and Bubandt, "Introduction: Bodies Tumbled into Bodies," M8.

31 Anna Tsing, Heather Swanson, Elaine Gan, and Nils Bubandt, "Introduction: Haunted Landscapes of the Anthropocene," in *Arts of Living on a Damaged Planet*, ed. Tsing, Swanson, Gan, and Bubandt, G1–G14, here G4.

32 Vieweg, *Endzeit*, 106.

garden).³³ Thus Vieweg does finally, at least in this scene, allow a character, the Gardener herself, to reveal a verbal truth: we will transform as the dinosaurs did (actually they became birds rather than lizards, but the idea is the same). Immediately thereafter is the abovementioned scene replicating the "Jurassic Park" moment of the velociraptors with DNA code reflected on her face as Vivian stands fully surrounded by trees and plants and flowers with their shadows reflecting on her face. Transformation into new forms of hybridity, of vegetal-human multispecies bodies and beings is implied in Vieweg's *Endzeit*, though its pop-culture zombie theme may cleverly distract readers. Distraction is typical though, as Plumwood writes; we are always distracted by ourselves and frequently denying our entwined dependencies, claiming (at least in industrialized cultures) instead a hyperbolized autonomy from the rest of the ecological systems.

The fact that the graphic novel's final images are of Vivian's and Eva's newly hybrid surviving bodies, together with Ghost the dog among the lush flower field as plant-human mixes, still needs additional attention. As Matthew Hall writes, advocating against harm to plants in his 2011 *Plants as Persons: A Philosophical Botany*: "As well as sharing an interdependent kinship, it is clear that plant, animal and human bodies also interpenetrate. This is another strong reason for only committing harm to plants where necessary."[34] This philosophical claim relates to Hall's argument for the proper treatment of plants and to encourage awareness of human responsibility for our vegetal "kin." Interestingly, we must turn this vision on its head when writing of Vieweg's *Endzeit* since she has clearly reversed the roles so that the plants now harm humans and use their bodies instrumentally, instead of humans abusing plants. The humor of such reversals is strong, but it can also shock a viewer or reader into re-thinking our fundamental relationships to our ecological co-species specifically in terms of kinship and power. Hall dedicates much of his discussion to "non-Western" cultures, including indigenous peoples of Australia who conceive of the connection to non-human lives as cooperation rather than subject-object relationships. The Gardener suggests that the transformations of human bodies will lead to a similar re-emergence of cooperation even if most of the domineering humans will no longer reign. Many other scholars, such as Kimmerer in *Braiding Sweetgrass*, write of similar traditions of indigenous peoples, other non-Western or ancient cultures that have or had reverence and more aptly ecological knowledge of plants based on the assumptions of essential relationships among species instead of placing humans as the apparent rulers over mere material objects. Indeed, as Katherine E. Bishop's introduction to *Plants*

---

33 Vieweg, *Endzeit*, 107–8.
34 Matthew Hall, *Plants as Persons: A Philosophical Botany* (Albany: State University of New York Press, 2011), Kindle edition, loc. 1562.

in Science Fiction: Speculative Vision claims, in reference to Anna Tsing's work: "the way we think about vegetation is not simply central to the way we think about ourselves or even humanity; the way we think about vegetation may also be key to our continued existence."[35]

Vieweg ends her graphic novel with a song, one that appears to share its lyrics at least in part with what one can find in German online as "the stone speaks," identified as a "prayer of the Hopi"; in *Endzeit* it is the favorite song of Vivian's little sister, one she always played when anxious, and to which Vivian listens repeatedly throughout the text. This strategy of leaving unsaid what comes next and providing a song instead is shared by Goethe's infamous *Novelle*, which describes a hunt, wild plants retaking a ruin, and the peaceful recapture of an escaped lion under a tree by a little boy playing music and singing a mysteriously repeating song.[36] Vieweg's version concludes with part of the lyrics from "Ich bin ein Felsen" (I am a Stone):

Ich bin ein Felsen.	I am a Stone.
Ich habe Leben und Tod gesehen.	I have seen life and death.
Ich habe Glück erfahren, Sorge und Schmerz.	I have experienced happiness, anxiety, and pain.
Ich lebe ein Felsenleben.	I live a stone-life.
Ich bin ein Teil unserer Mutter, der Erde.	I am part of our mother, the earth.
Ich habe ihr Herz an meinem schlagen gefühlt.	I have felt her heart beat with mine.
Ich habe seine Geschöpfe gesehen, meine Brüder,	I have seen her creations, my brothers,
die Tiere, die Vögel,	the animals, the birds,
die redenden Flüsse und Winde, die Bäume,	the talking rivers and winds, the trees,
alles, was auf der Erde,	everything, that is on earth,
und alles, was im Universum ist.	And everything that is in the universe.
Ich bin mit den Sternen verwandt.	I am related to the stars.[37]

---

35 Katherine E. Bishop, "Introduction," in *Plants in Science Fiction*, ed. Bishop, Higgins, and Määttä, 1–8, here 4.

36 Johann Wolfgang Goethe, "Novelle," in *Johann Wolfgang Goethe: Die Leiden des jungen Werthers; Die Wahlverwandtschaften; Kleine Prosa; Epen*, ed. Waltraud Wiethölter (Frankfurt am Main: Klassiker, 1994), 531–55.

37 Vieweg, *Endzeit*, 283–85. The song is found repeatedly in the graphic novel, but the final partial lyrics on the last pages include changes to emphasize the idea "Ich schlafe nicht" (I do not sleep), suggesting a vibrant consciousness beyond one individual. German sources are few, but one can find the song as part

Whatever its origin, the song "I am a Stone" reads as a kind of ecological, seemingly indigenous declaration of interrelations and connections. Rather than making an overt statement, Vieweg uses the images of plant-sprouting Eva and Vivian together with Ghost the dog among the full-page-covered purple fields as we "hear" the lyrics of this song declaring that "I" am a multi-species existence among animals, birds, plants, rivers, winds, trees, and stars.

---

of a longer prayer on this website, for better or worse: https://welt-der-indianer.de/verschiedenes/indianer-weisheiten-zitate/, accessed March 20, 2021.

Part II

Rethinking Race

4: Born into Trauma? The Interplay of Biologism and Social Paradigms in Trauma Theory and Graphic Novels

Aylin Bademsoy

BIOLOGICAL REDUCTIONISM IS constitutive of the dominant ideology in the contemporary Western metropolitan world and, often undetected, pervades all spheres of human life.[1] The contemporary obsession with DNA—manifest, for example, in the increasing popularity of genetic hereditary testing—is only one of many phenomena indicative of the triumph of positivism in the social sphere.[2] In the world of academia, this triumph is reflected negatively in the steady decline of the humanities, which conventionally do not produce positivistic knowledge, and in the anguished attempt of Digital Humanities scholars, amongst others, to extract quantifiable "value" from culture. As the culture industry perpetuates an ideology that undermines its foundations, making claims about the *conditio socialis* on the basis of quantifiable data has become a common practice. Thus, idiosyncratic hereditary material is thought to determine not only hair or eye color, or "roots" that purportedly lie in a physical location identified with some faraway ancestors, but also social categories, such as ethnic or racial identity. The persistence of racial paradigms originates in a mechanism inherent to positivist discourses, namely the conflation of social and biological elements: race, a social category, appears as a quantifiable, biological fact, derived from hereditary transmission. As such, the concept of race seems indubitably rooted in the

---

1 Heather Looy discusses the contemporary popularity of biological reductionism, which represents an attempt to fully rationalize "humanity." Heather Looy, "Losing our Humanity: Biologism, Bad Reduction and Father Brown," *The Midwest Quarterly* 54, no. 3 (2013): 263–78, here 263–65.
2 "Finding out about your heritage through at-home DNA testing has become a popular American pastime. In fact, according to one forecast, the DNA testing market generated more than $487 million in revenue in 2019, and projections for 2026 push those numbers even higher." Jessica DiGiacinto, "5 Best DNA Testing Kits of 2023," *Forbes*, February 22, 2023, https://www.forbes.com/health/body/best-dna-testing-kit/#footnote_1.

impeccable realm of "positive" knowledge. Biological reductionism collapses history into biology, thus transfiguring social relations into nature. Positivism and biologism are intertwined when, under the pretense of scientific inquiry, our understanding of what is human is reduced to measurable categories, in the modern period pertaining to, for example, genetics. After a brief discussion of trauma theory's situatedness within or relation to such discourse, this essay elucidates how the fundamental vocabulary of graphic narratives can both reinscribe and undermine ideological epistemes elemental to biological reductionism. A comparative analysis of two popular examples of the comic genre, Art Spiegelman's *Maus* (1980–91) and Nora Krug's *Belonging: A German Reckons with History and Home* (2018), illuminates the antithetical use of multimodality in these two works: in *Maus*, the anthropomorphic mask ultimately unmasks the social conditions that underlie essentialist concepts of ethnic/racial identity, whereas in *Belonging*, the aesthetic and textual composition of the narrative reinforces the notion of a natural and immobile identity.

The permanent tension between history and biology, as well as the collapse of these notions into an indistinguishable and undifferentiated ontological totality, is perhaps nowhere as evident as in trauma narratives. Even though the hypothesis of trauma transmission is widely accepted today, how trauma is transmitted, and whether such transmission constitutes a biological or social phenomenon—or both—remains controversial. Irrespective of how one answers these questions, the concepts of lineage and genealogy figure prominently in trauma narratives. At times this relation is unmediated; for example, when the narrative presents a genealogical investigation, oftentimes in the form of a so-called search for roots. At times it is established via mediation, for example, when extradiegetic narratives recount the stories of ancestors, who are more or less known to the author.[3] The underlying concept of the family tree naturalizes the social construct of family, while the metaphor of the tree unequivocally transposes social reproduction into mere nature. The tree's buried, invisible roots suggest permanent immobility, the existence of an immutable essence. The biological interpretation of race and ethnicity, today often concealed by pseudo-culturalisms, too, is linked directly to such naturalized conceptions of intergenerational transmission, albeit not of trauma but of "racial makeup."[4] In Spiegelman's text, the symbolic mask in particular counteracts such essentialism by denaturalizing race and unveiling in the meta-narrative its social origination.

---

3   While *Maus* and *Belonging* fall into the first category, Barbara Yelin's *Irmina* (2014) would be exemplary for the latter, mediated form.

4   The aim is not to promote "color-blindness" but to emphasize that race does not exist apart from the social context.

While theories of intergenerational trauma assume that ancestral or parental traumata are transmitted to the child—and thus evoke theories such as Lamarck's theses on the inheritance of acquired characteristics—it is unclear how much biology the concept of memory incorporates and, furthermore, how many generations such trauma transmission can span.[5] In the context of the biological family, the concept of transmission in and of itself suggests an isomorphic relation between the transfer of trauma and other physical and quantifiable properties, such as genes. Such blurring of social and biological factors can have uncanny consequences. Tellingly, contemporary DNA tests often assume the function of highly individualized horoscopes; they identify not only physical markers, such as allergies, but also claim at times to reveal information about attributes such as temper. It would not be all too surprising if in such tests the predicted degree of temper, linked to the idea of the Other's intrinsic irrationality and proximity to nature in Orientalist discourse, correlated directly with the ascribed "racial" makeup of the tested subject. Moreover, much like genealogical inquiry, these tests are frequently utilized for "self-discovery."[6] Even though one might argue that WWII perpetrators' guilt is mediated not only via the familial realm but culturally, in an attempt to banish the specters of the past, narratives of intergenerational trauma often regress to the realm of the biological family.

Biologism, the modern epistemology par excellence, is prevalent in the culture industry of advanced capitalism, where the modern myth of biological reductionism marks a myriad of textual and visual narratives. The concepts of trauma and particularly of trauma transmission prove particularly suitable for the ideological reproduction of biologistic reductionism, and graphic narratives, in turn, are said to be particularly suitable for representing trauma.[7] Yet, as I show, graphic narratives do not only reinscribe but also bear the capacity to resist such reductionism through

---

5   "There is a marked need to integrate quantitative, qualitative and mixed methods findings in order to develop a more nuanced understanding of what is transmitted across generational fault lines and the process and mechanisms by which transmission occurs." Flanagan et al., "Crossing Borders: A Systematic Review Identifying Potential Mechanisms of Intergenerational Trauma Transmission in Asylum-seeking and Refugee Families," *European Journal of Psychotraumatology* 11, no. 1 (2020): 1–13, here 2.

6   Or, like the function of astrology that Adorno points out in the "Theses Against Occultism," they become substitutes for old myths in times of the dialectic of late capitalist Enlightenment. Theodor W. Adorno, "Theses Against Occultism," in *The Stars Down to Earth: And Other Essays on the Irrational in Culture* (London, New York: Routledge, 2001), 172–80, here 172.

7   Hillary Chute, *Disaster Drawn: Visual Witness, Comics, and Documentary Form* (Cambridge, MA: Belknap Press of Harvard University Press, 2016), 35–36.

genre-specific techniques. To illuminate this contradistinction, I will discuss the representation of trauma and ethnicity against the backdrop of a field of tension between biologistic and social paradigms in Spiegelman's *Maus* and Krug's *Belonging*. The traumata of war and genocide and their cross-generational repercussions are central to these graphic memoirs, even though they present distinct accounts of descendants of victims and of bystanders and perpetrators, respectively.[8] The inclusion of the latter—the accounts of perpetrators and bystanders—calls into question the false association of trauma with victimhood, an association that does not align with the Freudian origins of trauma theory, but that is nevertheless prevalent in popular discourses on trauma.[9]

Serialized initially in the underground comic magazine *RAW*, Art Spiegelman's *Maus: A Survivor's Tale* narrates in two volumes the story of the survival of Art's parents Vladek and Anja. *Maus* operates with two storylines and dual temporalities: the memories of Vladek, which constitute the main plot, are periodically interrupted by panels that visualize the family's post-war condition in the present. The traumatic reverberations of the Holocaust are manifest in the continuing presence of the narrator's deceased brother Richieu, his mother's suicide, and in the troubled father-son relationship. By means of sophisticated visual-narratological techniques, *Maus* challenges concepts such as "heritage" and "ethnicity" and ultimately unmasks the social processes at work in the construction of such categories. In a key panel, the narrator's unexpected gesture of taking off the mouse mask and revealing his face highlights anthropomorphism's primary function in the text: to underscore the making of racial difference.

While Spiegelman's narrative critically interrogates categories such as race and ethnicity, Nora Krug's visual strategies reify the biologistic interpretation of guilt transmission via nationality and ancestorial ties.

---

8   For example, Andrew J. Kunka discusses exclusively works written and drawn by those who identify as victims and descendants of victims in his chapter on trauma in *Autobiographical Comics*. Andrew J. Kunka, *Autobiographical Comics* (London: Bloomsbury, 2018).

9   Although Freud includes soldiers returning from WWI in his trauma theory, the traumata of perpetrators or bystanders have often been neglected by post-Freudian trauma theories and by popular discourse. An exception to this trend in cultural studies is, for example, Cathy Caruth's reference to Freud's reading of Torquato Tasso's Tancred in *Unclaimed Experience: Trauma, Narrative, History* (Baltimore, MD and London: Johns Hopkins University Press, 1996), 1–9 and 63. Sigrid Weigel, in turn, provides a sophisticated critique of Caruth's reformulation of trauma theory in "The Symptomatology of a Universalized Concept of Trauma: On the Failing of Freud's Reading of Tasso in the Trauma of History," *New German Critique* 90, special issue on "*Taboo, Trauma, Holocaust*" (2003): 85–95.

Belonging narrates the author's quest to recuperate the German notion of *Heimat* along with her attempt to restore a "healthy" patriotism untainted by Germany's recent past. National Socialism and its afterlife haunt the protagonist's adult life: she feels shame when asked to raise her right arm in a yoga class; she feels guilted when she encounters a Holocaust survivor on a rooftop in New York; and she laments feelings of discomfort when waving the German flag during a parade. In Krug's graphic memoir, the repression of guilt manifests itself first and foremost in the narrator's visual disembodiment, accompanied by a bizarre, corresponding emphasis on objects associated with the homeland; among others, a file holder, a Hansaplast patch, an acorn, and Uhu glue. These objects epitomizing *Heimat* are drawn in meticulous detail and pose a stark contrast to the two-dimensional icons representing humans. The visual supremacy of the object world, however, is in this particular case not a "postmodern" parody of the commodity fetish; rather, it is exemplary of the manifestation of the reified consciousness in the sphere of culture.

Biological Determinism and Social Paradigms

The term biologism describes the transfer of biological concepts onto non-biological, for example, historical and social, contexts. In the *Encyclopedia Britannica*, the kindred notion of biological determinism is defined as "the idea that most human characteristics, physical and mental, are determined at conception by hereditary factors passed from parent to offspring."[10] A prominent earlier version of such a biologistic conception of humans can be found in the theorems of Hippocrates (460 to 370 BC), who correlated human mental states, which he referred to as temperaments, with the composition of bodily fluids, the four humors. In spite of such early theorizations, the emergence of eugenics and scientific racism presupposed a technology that was fully developed only during the long nineteenth century. Gregor Mendel's botanical observations of the transmission of hereditary traits had to be rediscovered in order to be transposed onto the conceptualization of humankind, a transposition exemplary of the logic of biologism. Not coincidentally, during the same period the ideologies of white supremacy, Social Darwinism, and *völkisch* nationalism simultaneously mushroomed across the Western hemisphere.[11] The transfer of scientific findings to humanistic inquiry was

---

10 Kara Rogers and Garland Edward Allen, "Biological Determinism," *Encyclopedia Britannica*, October 17, 2013, https://www.britannica.com/topic/biological-determinism.

11 While Social Darwinism was advocated, most famously, by Herbert Spencer and Thorstein Veblen, the two founding fathers of *völkisch* thought were Paul de Lagarde and Julius Langbehn. George L. Mosse, *The Crisis of German*

of particular importance for the positivist re-conceptualization of race and formed the basis for the idea of the *Volk* as a national-racial collective rooted in a specific geography with a distinct natural environment, which in turn is reflected in the specific set of characteristics attributed to the members of each *völkisch* collective.

In turn, the formulation of an extensive, rigorous critique of positivism was fundamental to many major philosophical schools of the twentieth century, including French existentialism, the Frankfurt School, structuralism, and post-structuralism. The reduction of the human disposition to a quantifiable, biological essence pertained not only to racist tropes but also to conceptualizations of womanhood that justified women's subordination to the patriarchal hegemonic order and stalled emancipatory struggles. As a response to such biologistic reductions of women, in *The Second Sex*, Simone de Beauvoir famously proclaimed that "one is not born, but rather, becomes woman," thus laying the foundation for unveiling mechanisms inherent in the "social" interpretation of biological factors, which are fundamental to patriarchal ideology and the justification of the perpetual oppression of women.[12] Although in English the notions of gender and sex seek to distinguish the social from the biological, this dichotomy is itself hardly natural, but rather a product of a positivist ideology that professes the supremacy of biology. Similarly, in the context of categories such as race or ethnicity, the dividing lines between social and biological factors are far from clear. After all, biological facts do not exist for themselves, and their (seemingly objective) interpretation is invariably social. In other words, a biological fact that has not already been interpreted and established as a fact does not exist. Consequently, all these categories constitute social interpretations of biological facts and as such are contingent upon socio-historical conditions.

Perhaps the most notable debate that arose from the tension of the above-mentioned epistemic dilemma was the *Positivismusstreit* (positivism controversy).[13] The *Positivismusstreit*, whose most prominent representatives were Theodor W. Adorno and Karl Popper, was largely confined to the German-speaking intellectual world, particularly within the discipline of sociology. Even so, Adorno's critique of the "fetishized principle of

---

Ideology: Intellectual Origins of the Third Reich (Madison: University of Wisconsin Press, 2021), 33.

12 Simone De Beauvoir, *The Second Sex*, trans. C. Borde and S. Malovany-Chevallier (New York: Vintage Books, 2011), 283.

13 Theodor W. Adorno, Karl Popper, Ralf Dahrendorf, Jürgen Habermas, Hans Albert, and Harald Pilot's discussions of positivism are compiled in *Der Positivismusstreit in der deutschen Soziologie*, ed. Heinz Maus and Friedrich Fürstenberg (Neuwied and Berlin: Luchterhand Verlag, 1972).

immanent logic"[14] is pertinent to the context of the *Geisteswissenschaften* as well, notwithstanding their predominantly non-quantifiable objects of study. For although the "specters" of the humanities conceive of themselves and their subject matter as non-quantifiable in essence,[15] they are all too capable of reproducing positivism by making claims that underpin the "absolute independence of science and its constitutive character for all knowledge."[16] Positivism goes beyond limiting *Erkenntnisgewinn* (cognizance) to the sphere of quantifiable data; as a comprehensive ideology of knowledge, it also permeates humanistic inquiries. The prime humanistic epistemic quest—investigating the conditions of the production of knowledge—is inseparable from a specific ontological position: the determination of the substance of *conditio humana*. The fetishization of the factual pertains, however, not only to interpretations of the individual but to social totality:

> That society does not allow itself to be nailed down as a fact actually only testifies to the existence of mediation. This implies that the facts are neither final nor impenetrable, even though the prevailing sociology regards them as such in accordance with the model of sense data found in earlier epistemology.[17]

Although biologistic conceptions of race and theories of racial hierarchy, such as Gobineau's famous treatise "On the Inequality of Races" (1853), were fiercely contested and critiqued early on, their theoretical foundation—genealogy—appears today categorically as indisputable as the force of gravity. Furthermore, claims that rest on such genealogic "positive" data pertain to much more than the quantifiable: from behaviorism to trauma theory, categories such as heritage and genealogy predominate attempts and processes of interpreting the universal human condition. Within these ideological parameters, society and everything that is social, including history, appear merely as a derivation of the predetermining biological foundation.

But how much biology is contained in the notion of trauma (and its transmission)? In literature and the fine arts, social and biological presuppositions are often subtext, and more often than not, they are vague. This vagueness is manifest, for example, in family narratives, where the lines

---

14   Theodor W. Adorno, "Introduction," in *The Positivist Dispute in German Sociology*, trans. Glyn Adey and David Frisby (London: Heinemann, 1976), 1–67, here 2.
15   Digital Humanities, which quantify narrative structures and find an "objective" basis for knowledge production, arguably pose a challenge to this conception.
16   Adorno, "Introduction," 4.
17   Adorno, "Introduction," 12.

between family as a social construct and family as a genealogical unit are blurred.[18] In *Fun Home: A Family Tragicomic*, for example, comic artist Alison Bechdel differentiates between "spiritual" and "consubstantial" fatherhood in order to interrogate the diverse modes of paternal inheritance.[19] The term "consubstantial" here serves as the concrete, material antithesis to the metaphysical, spiritual realm, and implicitly reinforces the notion of a human substance.[20] It is unclear whether education, socialization, and other social, institutional, and symbolic structures, all of which are antithetical to the notion of essence, are spiritual entities, or whether they lie outside this dichotomy. The dualism of consubstantial and spiritual parallels the dualism of essence and appearance and of abstract and concrete, which also yields the false separation of content and form. For Adorno, it remains the task of art to aestheticize their dialectical mediation.

Traumatic Wounds: Bodies and Families

But if in fact DNA is the substance that carries all necessary information to encode humanity, then how long until humankind can discern and quantify the traumatic wound inscribed onto the human body? In *Unclaimed Experience: Trauma, Narrative, and History*, Cathy Caruth elucidates the trajectory of the concept of trauma in relation to the dichotomy of abstract and concrete via Torquato Tasso's epic poem *La Gerusalemme Liberata*:

> As the repeated infliction of a wound, the act of Tancred calls up the originary meaning of trauma itself (in both English and German), the Greek trauma, or "wound," originally referring to an injury

---

18 In his theses on family, Adorno describes the ambivalent situatedness of "family" in modernity as follows: "The family is both: natural relation and social relation. It is based on social relations and biological descent, often without consciousness of duration, but it becomes something permanent, objective, independent—an 'institution.'" Theodor W. Adorno, "On the Problem of the Family" (1955), trans. Jacob Blumenfeld, *Endnotes*, https://endnotes.org.uk/posts/theodor-adorno-on-the-problem-of-the-family-1955, accessed December 3, 2024.

19 Alison Bechdel, *Fun Home: A Family Tragicomic* (Boston, MA and New York: Mariner Books, 2007), 231. An implicit inquiry in this narrative is, furthermore, whether sexuality is inherited.

20 The philosophical discourse on "substance" ranges from pre-Platonic theories of one definite or indefinite element as the basis of all being to the Platonic anti-materialist theory of substance as form and ultimately to Empiricist, Rationalist, and Enlightened re-conceptualizations of the term. Howard Robinson and Ralph Weir, "Substance," *Stanford Encyclopedia of Philosophy*, published October 3, 2004, revised May 6, 2024, https://plato.stanford.edu/entries/substance/.

inflicted on a body. In its later usage, particularly in the medical and psychiatric literature, and most centrally in Freud's text, the term trauma is understood as a wound inflicted not upon the body but upon the mind.[21]

According to Caruth, psychoanalysis severed the term from its original, biological denotation, and instead shifted the focus onto the metaphysical realm of the spirit or mind. However, Caruth's reading suggests a dualistic constellation of body and mind in Freud's trauma theory, which seems untenable particularly in the light of his early work on the cases of "hysteria" (similar to Sándor Ferenczi, Freud argued that his patients were victims of sexual abuse) and of shellshocked soldiers coming back from the battlegrounds of World War I. Freud's trauma theory can be read as a dialectical corrective to positivist currents of his time as it—in Cartesian fashion—purports the entwinement of body and mind, the unity of these two seemingly separate realms.

Even so, Caruth's work too ultimately upholds a dialectical entanglement of the material and metaphysical, of body and mind. Caruth stresses the temporal distance between the moment of infliction and the belated narrative as "the story of a wound that cries out," and thus frames trauma narratives as literary accounts in which the dialectic of traumatic temporality manifests.[22] Trauma representation is for Caruth always a response to formerly inflicted wounds and is thus by its very nature "belated." In Caruth's reading of Tasso's *Liberata*, the traumatic wound's origin is the accidental murder of Clorinda by Tancred. But rather than highlighting the physicality of the bodily injury ultimately resulting in death, Caruth derives her trauma theory from the aspect of "not knowing," recuperating the concept of trauma ultimately for the realm of the mind. While Caruth's theorization of trauma representation leaves the question of transmissibility open, myriad trauma narratives written (and drawn) by the second and third generations demand clarification: can the repressed, the "unknown," be imparted to the next generation and elicit a belated intergenerational response?

In turn, Marianne Hirsch's notion of *postmemory* investigates the "inter- and trans-generational transmission of traumatic knowledge and experience."[23] In "The Generation of Postmemory," Hirsch suggests that the transmissibility of trauma is not limited to the sphere of family and differentiates between *familial* and *affiliative* postmemory. This differentiation, however, reifies the familial and stresses its particularity via the

21 Caruth, *Unclaimed Experience*, 14.
22 Caruth, *Unclaimed Experience*, 15.
23 Marianne Hirsch, "The Generation of Postmemory," *Poetics Today* 29, no. 1 (2008): 103–28, here 106.

negative image of "non-familial" relationships. Similarly, in reference to Aleida Assman's concept of group memory, Hirsch notes that "'group memory' in [Assman's] schema is based on the familial transfer of embodied experience to the next generation."[24] The notion of "embodiment," which plays a significant role in Hirsch's theory and appears in various contexts, highlights the physical facet of the incorporation of transferred experience. On the one hand, it seems self-evident that "family" is conceived as the "privileged site of memorial transmission,"[25] as early developmental experiences are typically mediated by the family and thus appear restricted to the confines of the "familial sphere." On the other hand, it is important to stress that they may merely "appear" to emerge from the familial sphere—as every family remains embedded in a social totality, and the private only seemingly constitutes an opposition to the public. Furthermore, one must ask what "embodied experience" refers to in such theoretical considerations of trauma, and if such terminology could potentially contribute to a biologistic interpretation. Hirsch remarks that the familial transmission does not necessarily implicate biological bonds—and yet the rationalization of the familial frame's distinctiveness is almost mystical: "The language of family, the language of the body: nonverbal and non-cognitive acts of transfer occur most clearly within a familial space, often in the form of symptoms."[26]

Marianne Hirsch's concept of postmemory conceives of the "family" as a privileged locus of trauma transmission due to experiences the descendants "'remember' only by means of the stories, images, and behaviors among which they grew up."[27] It is very likely that such mechanisms of conscious and unconscious transfer apply to the experiences of many descendants of genocide survivors. Such exposure to stories, images, or behaviors would then fall under the rubric of experience. Yet in many contemporary German WWII narratives, we encounter a scenario where the third generation (the grandchildren's generation) seeks to reconnect to an ancestry that is not known or familiar at any rate. Nora Krug, for instance, seeks to restore the familial bonds to her ancestors and estranged family members that were deliberately severed by her father. A conversation with her father reveals that he severed his ties with his (biological) family and avoided talking about his family's history. In Krug's case, it is less the stories or images with which she grew up that motivate her interest in her ancestors' past, but rather the desire for closure that is in the

---

24 Hirsch, "The Generation of Postmemory," 110.
25 Hirsch, "The Generation of Postmemory," 110.
26 Hirsch, "The Generation of Postmemory," 112.
27 Hirsch, "The Generation of Postmemory," 106.

narrator's imagination linked to the restoration of the biological family.[28] It is her lack of knowledge, the absence of memory, or with Caruth the "unknown," which prompts her attempt to overcome an identity crisis by recuperating lineage. Such return to the roots often features narratives euphemistically known as tales of self-discovery. In trauma narratives by descendants of bystanders and perpetrators, the "bonds" between generations often do not have any basis but biological linkage; such works restore, at least on a symbolic level, the bonds within the biological family.

Krug's title is revealing: the question of *Belonging* or not belonging is central to her narrative. Both family and ethnicity refer to forms of collectivity that may hold the potential to foster a sense of belonging—something that in Krug's case, however, is complicated by the Nazi past.[29] And in spite of contemporary attempts to relieve these notions of their reductive definition, to this day both rely predominantly on positive, biological factors. It is moreover of utmost importance to note the structural intersection of the notions of ethnicity and family; both are social constructs that conceptually incorporate biological, quantifiable components, such as lineage. Thereby, their proximity to the realm of nature seems plausible, and any attempt to contest them controversial.

Family, Race, and Mask in *Maus*

Art Spiegelman's *Maus*, which has recently been banned from public school education in Tennessee, is widely recognized as one of the most prominent post-generational graphic narrative accounts on Holocaust trauma.[30] Central to the narrative is the process of working through a familial trauma, and such traumatic family histories have been a recurring topic in graphic memoirs of the post-WWII period. Trauma and family are arguably conceptually entwined from the very beginning of trauma theory: The bourgeois family is central to Freud's theory of the Oedipus complex, and as Sándor Ferenczi, Karl Abraham, and Ernst Simmel noted

---

28 This is also true for Barbara Yelin, who works through the German past through her grandmother's World War II experience as a female bystander in *Irmina*.

29 Mithu Sanyal superbly parodies the identity-formative (and often interchangeable) aspect of socially construed collectives such as family and ethnicity. Mithu Sanyal, *Identitti* (Munich: Hanser, 2021).

30 Kunka notes that *Maus* is the most frequently discussed comic in academic articles. Kunka, *Autobiographical Comics*, 175. The scholarly discussions of *Maus* focused, unsurprisingly, primarily on questions relating to the representation of trauma. Interestingly, Rosemary Hathaway reads *Maus* as a work of postmodern ethnography but avoids engaging with the notion of "ethnicity." Rosemary V. Hathaway, "Reading Art Spiegelman's *Maus* as Postmodern Ethnography," *Journal of Folklore Research* 48, no. 3 (2011): 249–367.

during the Fifth International Psycho-Analytical Congress, even psychoanalytic considerations of war neuroses did not supplant the development and repression of sexuality as the cornerstones of psychoanalysis.[31] The intersection of family and war, specifically World War II and the Shoah, constitutes the basis for Spiegelman's account of a secondary experience of trauma. At the same time, as discussed above, the notions of family and (racially coded) trauma, are conceptually inseparable from both biological and social determinants and are thus particularly prone to reproduce biologism. Especially in the context of the "passing on" of trauma, the demarcation line between biological and social, or nature and society, vanishes quickly.

In *Disaster Drawn: Visual Witness, Comics, and Documentary Form* (2016), Hillary Chute characterizes the comic as a unique medium specifically in regard to its relation to trauma narratives. In particular, Chute conceptualizes the gutter (which McCloud considers an unparalleled feature of the comic in *Understanding Comics*) as a distinctive space where trauma and history materialize.[32] Yet, what distinguishes Spiegelman's comic is not only its working through World War II trauma in a form marked as "infantile," but the visual strategies it employs to construe race as a mask in order to ultimately unmask the concept of race. Adolf Hitler's statement that "the Jews are undoubtedly a race, but they are not human" prefaces the first volume of *Maus*,[33] emphasizing that race and racialization are focal points in this graphic memoir.[34] The banning of *Maus* in Tennessee is likely not due to "swear words" but motivated by the centrality of race to this graphic novel. However, apart from a few instances, including Vladek's anti-black rant against a hitchhiker and the difficulty of categorizing Spiegelman's wife Françoise, the discussion of race is confined to the visual plane and not explicit in the linguistic landscape of *Maus*. Its subtextual omnipresence reflects the overall discourse on race in the second half of the twentieth century. In the United States, the fact that race has become a subtext is seen as perhaps more dangerous

---

31 Nolen Gertz, "Blood/Lust: Freud and the Trauma of Killing in War," *Formations* 1, no. 1 (2010): 65–79, here 65. Nolen Gertz's argument, that more "proper training and discipline" could help avoid war traumata, however, is highly questionable.

32 Chute, *Disaster Drawn*, 35–36.

33 Art Spiegelman, *Maus: A Survivor's Tale Vol. 1, My Father Bleeds History* (New York: Pantheon Books, 1986), 3.

34 David Mikics discusses the epigraph to emphasize the severity of the topic Spiegelman deals with, and to which he responds with theriomorphic characters. David Mikics, "Underground Comics and Survival Tales. *Maus* in Context," in *Considering "Maus": Approaches to Art Spiegelman's "Survivor's Tale" of the Holocaust*, ed. Deborah Geis (Tuscaloosa and London: University of Alabama Press, 2003), 15–25, here 20.

than overt references to race, which is why the paradigm of "race" is now used equally, if not more, by the anti-racist left, while in right-wing discourse its subtextuality is recognized as an advantage. However, pointing out the race paradigm's continued subtextual persistence and its oppressive consequences inevitably leads to its reproduction. As a result of this dilemma, the question of the authenticity of racial identity is now being posed equally by groups that we can provisionally describe as left-identitarian and by right-wing discourse. Especially in the German-speaking world, the taboo of the race paradigm after 1945—as Nora Krug lamentingly mentions—has by no means led to its categorical deconstruction, but only to its sublimation via the category of culture, below the line no less biologically determined. Spiegelman's Orwellian narrative offers a distinct, if not groundbreaking, means to dismantle the relationship between social and biological paradigms discussed above: here, the drawing of a mask serves to unmask the purportedly biological dimension of race as a "social" interpretation. It illuminates thus—on the visual plane—the deconstructability of race.

It is not surprising that much of the secondary literature on *Maus* concentrates on trauma and trauma representation. The past haunts both parents of the narrator, who interviews his father Vladek, a Polish Jew, about his life before the camps and his survival. Art's experience as a *Nachgeborener*, the lingering presence of his dead brother Richieu, and the suicide of his mother Anja, are undoubtedly central to *Maus*. Yet, as Michael Rothberg points out, *Maus* is also concerned with the artist's historical condition in late capitalism, which is characterized by the permanent and systemic commodification of his work.[35] The irreconcilable conflict, then, arises from the artist's failure to both represent trauma *and* resist its commodification.[36] The entanglement of these two distinct origins of trauma is manifest specifically in a panel that depicts the artist as he is working on this graphic novel sitting on top of a heap of dead bodies, the victims of Auschwitz. Not coincidentally, precisely here Spiegelman exposes the "mouse" identity—hence race—as a mask.[37] It is a mask, however, that reiterates a core aspect of the logic of the fetish: in

---

35 As Tarkovsky points out, film is subject to this condition to an even greater extent. Andrey Tarkovsky, *Sculpting in Time: Reflections on the Cinema*, trans. Kitty Hunter-Blair (New York: Alfred A. Knopf, 1987), 228.

36 The public circulation of or the "postmodern" demand on history has been, most prominently, discussed by Michael Rothberg in *Traumatic Realism: The Demands of Holocaust Representation* (Minneapolis: University of Minnesota Press, 2000), 7–10. See also Michael Rothberg, "'We Were Talking Jewish': Art Spiegelman's *Maus* as 'Holocaust' Production," in *Considering "Maus,"* ed. Geis, 137–58.

37 Art Spiegelman, *Maus II: A Survivor's Tale Vol. 2, And Here My Troubles Began* (New York: Pantheon Books, 1991), 41.

the meta-narrative, the author can take off his mask and unveil its contingence on social rather than "natural" history. This realization, however, remains deconstructive solely in the ideational realm; any such unveiling of false consciousness represents a mere gesture.

Along with challenging notions such as "objectivity, truth, and authenticity,"[38] *Maus* thus resists biologism insofar as the so-called "substance" of inheritance, genetics, is not reinscribed, but rather unmasked as a reflection of a false consciousness. Although Chute's theses on the entwinement of comics and trauma are remarkable, what renders Spiegelman's graphic memoir unique is also (and perhaps most importantly) the appropriation of the visual domain for the dismantling of racial essentialism. What the mask, symbolic of the realm of appearance, appears to conceal is the "essence": an essence that Spiegelman seeks to disintegrate. The initial response a mask elicits from the viewer is the desire to strip it off, to unveil the truth that lies beneath. Instead of providing us with the truth, however, the mask in Spiegelman's *Maus* reveals the false opposition of essence and appearance in the context of race: here, race only exists in the realm of appearance. Given that the realm of appearance can only subsist insofar as it represents a derivation from an essence, this visual technique thus subverts the category of race *in toto*.

Inherited Guilt in *Belonging*

In contrast to Spiegelman's dismantling of the biological interpretation of a social category, Nora Krug's *Belonging: A German Reckons with History and Home* reifies genealogy. The essentialist conception of national or ethnic identity, both of which are closely linked to genealogy, is manifest first and foremost in its supposed immutability. Written from the perspective of a descendant of perpetrators and/or bystanders, the recuperation of *Heimat* implies exonerating the nation's past, which is, in turn, mediated through ancestorial history.

In *Belonging*, the narrator, a German émigré, feels "more German than ever before" after twelve years living in the United States, and yet she is not comfortable with her German accent, with raising her right arm in her yoga class, or waving the German national flag at the New York City Steuben Parade. As a self-identifying émigré, Krug capitalizes on her status as a migrant, which enables her to express longing for the *Heimat* without being attacked as a right-wing nationalist, as she might be if she lived in Germany. As a German living or traveling abroad, she feels marginalized and discriminated against, haunted by her nation's history. Consequently, she confronts Germany's "troubled" past by returning to

---

38 Hathaway, "Reading Art Spiegelman's *Maus* as Postmodern Ethnography," 251.

her homeland and investigating her (predominantly male) family members' roles in the National Socialist murder machinery. While the narrator attempts to reconcile German identity and patriotism with Germany's "troubled" past, exoneration is posed as contingent upon proving the innocence of her grandfathers. The quest for closure is directly linked to the desire to recuperate patriotism and nationalism in Germany, sentiments that were long overshadowed by the National Socialist past and that certainly have a great appeal to the masses of Germans who today vote for the AfD (Alternative für Deutschland; Alternative for Germany) and blare xenophobic anthems—such as, most recently, "Ausländer raus, Ausländer raus, Deutschland den Deutschen, Ausländer raus" (Foreigners out, foreigners out, German for Germans, foreigners out)—in public. Thoughts of offsetting inherited guilt by "marrying a Jew"[39] only underpin the supremacy of genealogy, nonetheless, the narrator laments that "not even marrying a Jewish man has lessened my German shame." The narrator is frightened by the possibility of passing on her inherited guilt. Hence, having children with a non-German appears as a means of freeing her progeny from the guilt, or shame, that has tormented the narrator throughout her entire life. Identity with its varying subcategories (gender, sex, race, ethnicity, etc.) is here clearly conceived of as a phenomenon determined by natural, biological, and hereditary conditions.

It comes as no surprise that Krug's *Heimat* narrative is preceded by and ends with comic-like reproductions of a family tree. The montage of actual headshots of Krug's family members onto bodies drawn in typical German attire not only prepares us to engage with a real family history but also aims to engender nostalgic sentiments in Germans by evoking endearing images of a shared collective phantasy of a bygone past. It is furthermore by no means coincidental that the first family tree is situated on the inside of the book's cover, which depicts our heroine facing a genuinely German landscape. The cover alludes to Caspar David Friedrich's famous *The Wanderer above the Sea of Fog*, which recurs throughout the narrative in various shapes and can be interpreted as the second *leitmotif*—in addition to the self-victimization that pervades the entire text. The guilt the narrator suffers from is contextualized via the "concept of inherited sin" which for the narrator means "having to bear the consequences of another generation's actions." In Krug's cover, the sublime mountain view in Friedrich's probably best-known painting is tellingly replaced by green hills and forests, the Ur-locale of Germandom par excellence. To underpin the deep connection between the forest and Germandom, the narrator critically engages with the importance of the forest for German identity in the second entry for the catalog of "Things German." Clearly,

---

39 Nora Krug, *Belonging* (New York: Scribner, 2018). This book is not paginated.

the image of the family tree is deeply anchored in this image of a German forest as a locale for the preservation of *völkisch* purity. The symbolic relationship between the search for roots, the family tree, and the forest that indexes the unity of a *völkisch* collective remains, however, unspoken.

The trope of suffering that pervades Krug's narrative is closely linked to the narrator's national-ethnic identity as a German, which, in turn, is mediated in a *völkisch* fashion via ties determined by the biological family. The self-victimizing begins on the first page comprising the first entry of the catalog titled "From the notebook of a homesick émigré," which depicts a Hansaplast patch. It is no coincidence that the first entry of the catalog alludes to a "traumatic wound" that is sought to be healed via the recuperation of "roots" that were thought to have been lost. Significantly, the cathartic closure is heralded by the notebook's final entry, which depicts a Uhu glue advertised as strong enough to patch any hole even though it "cannot cover up the crack."

The first image of a traumatic wound evoked by the Hansaplast patch is followed by a conversation with a Holocaust survivor in New York, which the narrator leaves feeling victimized (because guilted). On the next page, we see a photograph of the narrator sitting in a middle-class, fenced backyard in West Germany in 1980. We learn that the narrator as a child felt threatened by the allied US Air Force "hissing and roaring like dangerous animals." It is very likely that the child, at this stage, was not able to rationalize that the threat was not directed at her, but it is also very telling that the adult narrator decides to avoid mentioning that these allied forces did certainly not target her family idyll in Karlsruhe. Instead, the self-victimization continues with a juxtaposition of the uncanny feeling the narrator experiences when confronted with the Holocaust, which she compares to the threatening appearances of an alleged pedophile man, who comes to the family's porch to gift her and her brother balloons and candy when their mother is not present. The narrator's childhood memory of wanting to sew a yellow star as a sign of solidarity is also testimony to her strong desire to belong to the group of victims and to bask in the victim identity instead of confronting historical responsibility. The narrator thus implicitly aligns herself with the German women who, on another page, distort their faces with suffering, disgust, and horror as they are confronted with their participation in crimes against humanity.

To point out the successful rehabilitation of Germany, the narrator claims that her country, unlike other belligerent countries, now refuses the idea of initiating wars but doesn't mention Germany's role as one of the major exporters of military equipment ever since the FRG joined NATO in 1955. Under photographs showing fellow students after a visit to Birkenau, the narrator notes: "Here was the evidence of our collective guilt." This comment not only seeks proof of collective guilt in the horrified faces of her classmates but implicitly questions the concept of collective guilt. Why, after all, do Germans have to be confronted with such guilt, while other nations proudly keep waving their flags? The idea of the deep rootedness of such collective guilt in the "genetic" and hence biological makeup, is explicitly expressed in a section that laments that, again, unlike others, Germans have to "delete words such as "HERO, VICTORY, BATTLE and PRIDE" along with "ZUSAMMENGEHÖRIGKEITSGEFÜHL" (sense of belonging), "RACE," and "ETHNIC" from their vocabularies, "yet [they] felt that history was in our blood, and shame in our genes." At the end of the section, tellingly, the narrator feels the need to point out what Germans growing up in the FRG in the 1980s and 1990s were not informed about: anti-Nazi resistance movements and the 150,000 Jews who fought for the Wehrmacht. The reader is left wondering whether knowing more about the German resistance or Jewish soldiers in the Wehrmacht would have disburdened the narrator, and by implication, all Germans who felt forced to take responsibility for a war that not only cost six million Jewish lives, but encompassed the attempted destruction of Roma and Sinti, massacres of Soviet Prisoners of War, and much more. At the same time, rhetorically, the narrator's collective affiliation and sense of belonging are reinforced linguistically throughout these passages that express yearning for a collective identity troubled by genocide: "we learned," "we didn't learn," "we associated the word JUDE strictly with the Holocaust," etc. In the West Germany of the 1980s, one wonders whether the emphasized "we" comprised Turks, Kurds, Greeks, etc., or if the narrator's "we" indexes a collective exclusive to ethnic Germans. On the following page, against the backdrop of another idyllic green German landscape—an image of Berlin Neukölln or Hamburg Altona would not have conveyed the correct sentiment—such nationalist rhetoric continues to transition into lament: "We never learned the lyrics to our national anthem," "We never learned old folk songs," "We struggled to understand the meaning of HEIMAT."

Unsurprisingly, the abovementioned section also comprises a reference to German victimhood and German suffering, for example, with references to the postwar displacement of Germans from Eastern Europe. The lamented "hatred against the Germans," mentioned on a homework sheet from April 1991, which provides the background for a panel on the Star of David, is central to the narrative and the pervasive trope of self-victimization. Here and elsewhere, Krug employs montage to combine an actual *Zeitdokument*—her homework as a fourteen-year-old—with the handwritten commentary of the contemporary narrator on pastel-colored panels. Repeatedly, the composition and, specifically, the use of montage elicit the question of whether the montage as a fragmentary aesthetic form is necessarily subversive, or whether it cannot also serve to underpin reactionary tropes, such as the trope of German victimhood, so elemental to contemporary *völkisch* thinking. The deeply problematic provenance of many such narratives of self-discovery is fully revealed on the last page of the first section, on which another replica of Caspar David Friedrich's painting features the quote: "How do you know who you are if you don't understand where you come from?"

Krug's graphic memoir features an aforementioned series of images of objects that the narrator associates with *Heimat*. A catalog entitled "From the notebook of a homesick émigré" provides detailed drawings of a Hansaplast bandage, a forest, mushrooms, a hot water bottle, a file folder of the brand Leitz, a bar of ox-gall soap, and Uhu glue. These (predominantly inanimate) objects, which function as a structuring principle of the narrative, shrink the distance between the voluntary émigré and the idea of *Heimat*, a romanticized locale of belonging. The vividness of the objects, stressed in the detailed execution of the drawings, presents a stark contrast to the amorphic, two-dimensional humans, whom the narrator encounters during her journey. Significantly, the narrator herself is for the most part excluded from the realm of visual representation, which symbolically frees the narrator from having to confront the Nazi past and any attendant responsibilities or guilt, since, within these ideological parameters, guilt too presupposes a biological body in which inheritance materializes. Instead, the identity of the narrator is defined through ancestral ties, through which she seeks to cleanse herself of collective guilt, and is mediated by objects that simultaneously personify and reify *Heimat*. The richness in detail in the depicted objects can be read as an attempt to bring to life dead commodities. In turn, the crafting of identity as a phenomenon both contingent upon genealogy and mediated through commodities reinforces the immutability of the concept of identity. In contrast to Spiegelman's visual tactics of unmasking essentialism as a symptom of false consciousness, in the linguistic and visual realm, Krug's graphic memoir reifies an essentialist notion of identity.

The discrepancy between the visual strategies of *Maus* and *Belonging* can be read along with Adorno's distinction between the dialectical method and positivism: "Not the least significant of the differences between the positivist and dialectical conceptions is that positivism, following Schlick's maxim, will only allow appearance to be valid, whilst dialectics will not allow itself to be robbed of the distinction between essence and appearance."[40] This dualism manifests itself in Spiegelman's visualization of the chasm of appearance and essence on the one hand and Krug's collapsing of this chasm on the other. The graphic novel as a genre is particularly suitable for the application of both methodologies to narrative strategies: the image, in its immediacy, conceals its mediation in a way that the word cannot. Comics' distinctiveness arises from the idiosyncratic relationship between text and image, which is characterized by

---

40 Adorno, "Introduction," 14.

tension, belatedness, distance, congruence, contradiction, disintegration, and more. For example, a panel illustrating a figure walking in heavy rain could contradict the narrator's claim that it is a sunny, bright day. In this situation, viewers are likely to trust the image (and implicitly, their own eyes) instead of the words of an "unreliable" narrator, even though such privileging of the visual image arises from a false dissociation of word and image. Although in his long essay on Magritte's painting, Foucault claims that images and words cannot refute each other due to their diverging modalities,[41] in processing them we translate images into words: "This is a pipe," or "It is a rainy day." It is only after the image has been processed that the claim "This is not a pipe" appears as a contradiction.[42] Magritte thus brilliantly illuminates this divergence of word and image and the viewer's quasi-automatic but misguided inclination to link the concept of "truth," first and foremost, to vision. This tendency—which may be symptomatic of the "modern" condition rather than universal—and the thereby generated tension between the written word and the image are central to the workings of the comic genre. Graphic narratives, however, can operate within this field of tension in two distinct ways: they can ideologically underpin the superiority of the eye—as Krug does when she removes herself as the narrator from the visual realm of the narrative, thus positioning the reader as the "seer"—or they can, following the lead of movements such as surrealism, cast doubt on this supposed superiority, and instead point to the dialectics of essence and appearance, or even subvert the notion of essence altogether.

Conclusion

In his discussion of autobiographical comics, Andrew Kunka distinguishes between "historical" and "personal" trauma narratives. And yet, as indicated by the famous parole of second-wave feminists, one might argue that the separation of the historical from the personal is as false as the division of the personal and political. In response to feminist critiques of the

---

41   Foucault suggests that it is not the contradiction between word and image, but rather the failure to connect the specific text to the image, that brings about this "uncanny" effect: "What misleads us is the inevitability of connecting the text to the drawing (as the demonstrative pronoun, the meaning of the word pipe, and the likeness of the image all invite us to do here)—and the impossibility of defining a perspective that would let us say that the assertion is true, false, or contradictory." Michel Foucault, *This is Not a Pipe: With Illustrations and Letters by Rene Magritte* (Berkeley, Los Angeles, and London: University of California Press, 1983), 20.

42   In *On Photography*, Sontag makes a similar claim about the "reading" of photographs. See Susan Sontag, *On Photography* (New York: Rosetta Books, 2005), 58 and 65–88.

centrality of the bourgeois family and maternal figures in trauma narratives, Marianne Hirsch claims that "the generation of affiliative postmemory needs precisely such familiar and familial tropes to rely on."[43] Hirsch adds that such tropes, however, are "no more than performative."[44] But does performativity that is grounded in biological premises undermine or reiterate the "corruption of facts into ideology"?[45] The question that arises is whether "performing" family deconstructs or reifies family, and a similar question pertains to "performances" of all kinds, including gender or race/ethnicity. Indeed, performativity in and of itself might not call into question social constructs, such as family, gender, or ethnicity, but rather reify and reproduce them. Performance then only obscures the *Trümmerhaufen der Geschichte* (wreckage of history),[46] which in its complexity and amplitude lurks behind the racial trauma that appears to originate in the realm of the family.

According to Adorno, the fetish of quantifiable, factual knowledge is retained only at the expense of a liberated society:

> Ultimately it is positivism's most profound moment of truth—even if it is one against which positivism rebels as it does against the word which holds it in its spell—that the facts, that which exists in this manner and not in any other, have only attained that impenetrable power which is then reinforced by the scientific cult of facts in scientific thought, in a society without freedom of which its own subjects are not masters.[47]

Reification, as the subject's becoming an "object," is immanent to the modern form of subjectivity, which in turn is closely linked with the predominance of positivist epistemology and connected to the compulsive quantification of life. It is characteristic of this process of modern subjectification that not only external objects of study are quantified, but the subjects themselves, who at once become the objects of their (self-)study.

Attempts to work through familial and racial traumata are central to both graphic memoirs discussed in this essay, *Maus* and *Belonging*. While Spiegelman's work unmasks the social constructedness of notions such as race, in Krug's *Belonging* the attempted exoneration from guilt

---

43 Hirsch, "The Generation of Postmemory," 124–25.
44 Hirsch, "The Generation of Postmemory," 125.
45 Theodor W. Adorno, "Soziologie und Empirische Forschung," in *Der Positivismusstreit in der deutschen Soziologie*, ed. Maus and Fürstenberg, 81–112, here 101.
46 Walter Benjamin, "Über den Begriff der Geschichte," in *Gesammelte Schriften*, vol. 1.2, ed. Rolf Tiedemann and Hermann Schweppenhäuser (Frankfurt am Main: Suhrkamp, 1991), 691–704, here 698.
47 Adorno, "Introduction," 64.

is mediated by the ultimate return to genealogy. The predominance of genealogy as an explanatory model for the *conditio humana* illustrates nothing but the triumph of positivist epistemology and identitarian logic in the twenty-first century.

5: Birgit Weyhe's *Rude Girl* (2022): Comics, Blackness, and Transnational Dialogue: A Conversation with Priscilla Layne, Birgit Weyhe, and Elizabeth "Biz" Nijdam

Elizabeth "Biz" Nijdam

Birgit Weyhe is *a key figure in contemporary German-language comics and her work has sparked a number of conversations on race and representation in recent years. Her graphic novels include* Ich weiß *(2008),* Im Himmel ist Jahrmarkt *(2013),* Madgermanes *(2016), and* German Calendar No December *(2019). Dr. Priscilla Layne is a Black professor of German at the University of North Carolina. This following conversation between Weyhe and Layne took place in the Goethe-Institute Montreal on October 6, 2023, as part of the GSA Comics Studies Network's programming at the 47th Annual Conference of the German Studies Association in Montreal, Canada. The hybrid discussion, which was moderated by comics scholar and UBC professor Dr. Biz Nijdam, provides insights into the lives of these two women, their lived experiences, and how they came to work together on a comic about Layne's life as a Black woman living and working in predominantly White spaces. It also sheds light on Weyhe's creative process and issues around race and representation in her comics.*

This hybrid public event was cosponsored by the Goethe-Institut Montreal, the German Studies Association's Comics Studies Network, and the UBC Comics Studies Cluster. Weyhe and Nijdam participated on site in Montreal and Layne participated via Zoom from Italy.

Introductory Remarks by Biz Nijdam

Biz Nijdam: In 2018, Birgit Weyhe joined a room of German Comics scholars at a GSA panel on diversity and inclusion in German-language comics to bear witness to a presentation that openly criticized her graphic novel *Madgermanes* for its representation of Blackness. While unanticipated, this commentary marked the start of Weyhe's reflection on the role of her work in discourses of race and representation prompting a journey in re-evaluating her power and privilege as a comics artist. Soon thereafter, Weyhe met Dr. Priscilla Layne, then an Associate Professor of German Studies at UNC Chapel Hill. Over the course of the next few years, Weyhe and Layne collaborated on the graphic novel *Rude Girl*, which was published in 2022 in German and is currently set to be published in English translation in April 2024, translated by Layne herself. This graphic novel explores Layne's life growing up in Chicago, her experiences of racism, and her path to German Studies, all the while interrogating what it means for a White artist to represent Black lives.

Birgit Weyhe was born in Munich in 1969. She spent her childhood in East Africa and studied literature and history in Konstanz and Hamburg. Since graduating from art school, Weyhe has been working as a comics artist in Hamburg. Her graphic novels have been nominated for several prizes in Germany, France, and Japan. *Madgermanes* received the Berthold Leibinger Stiftung Comic Book Prize in 2015 and the Max und Moritz Prize in 2016 as the best German-language comic. In 2022, Weyhe was awarded the Lessing scholarship of the city of Hamburg. Her book, *Rude Girl*, was shortlisted for the Hamburg Literature Prize as "Book of the Year" and was the first comic ever to be nominated for the Leipzig Book Fair Prize in 2023.

Dr. Priscilla Layne is Professor of German and Adjunct Associate Professor of African Diaspora Studies at the University of North Carolina at Chapel Hill. Her first book, *White Rebels in Black: German Appropriation of Black Popular Culture*, was published in 2018 by the University of Michigan Press. She has also published essays on Turkish German Culture, translation, punk, and film. She translated Olivia Wenzel's debut novel *1000 Serpentinen Angst*, which was published in June 2022. Her two most recent books, *Out of This World: Afro-German Afrofuturism* (Northwestern University Press) and a critical guide to Fassbinder's *The Marriage of Maria Braun* (Camden House), both appeared in 2024.

Birgit Weyhe's Life in Pictures

Following Nijdam's opening remarks, Weyhe presented her life and work in a combination of words and images drawn from Ich weiß (2017) *and* Madgermanes (2016), *the transcript of which is transcribed below.*

Birgit Weyhe: Where do I come from and what is my job? Let me try to explain. My hometown is Hamburg. Well, it's where I live anyway. But is it my home? I'm not sure. I was born in Munich. As a child, I had to move often, sixteen times altogether. There was a big, black case, my toy box. Everything that fit into it was allowed to move with me. Back then the box seemed rather big, but it was always too small. Only one toy managed to stay with me the whole time. Why? You never know what's going to happen in this world. In 1973, when I was three years old, my mother and I moved from Munich to Kampala, the capital of Uganda. What does memory feed on?

My most formative early memory is moving to Uganda or, to be precise, arriving in Entebbe. The flight was boring. The heat bounced back off the runway. The air was soft and humid. So many new sounds. A very special mix of sensory perceptions that would accompany me throughout my childhood, first in Uganda and then in Kenya. Uganda had been governed by Idi Amin since 1971. As supreme commander of the armed forces, he satisfied his thirst for revenge by brutally eliminating all of his opponents in the military. In the following years, Amin's dictatorship increasingly deteriorated into an anarchic form of despotism. To begin with, torture and murder were primarily used on politicians, intellectuals, and members of the elite, but it soon mutated into senseless violence exerted against all groups of the population.

Memories travel for free. What does the child remember? There was a big bush in the yard of my primary school. It was very popular among us children as it was full of chameleons from time to time. During the school breaks, our goal was to pick up as many as possible and put them on our arms, heads, and shoulders. Whoever had the most was the lucky winner. Seven, eight, nine; most of the time, it was me. As a child, I was capable of nearly anything. The teacher said the chameleon changes its color to camouflage itself. It adopts the color of the current surface. This makes it nearly invisible to its enemies. We invented a new game. We placed the chameleons on different surfaces to watch their colors change, but they had limited abilities. They could only do some shades of green, brown, and yellow. Red, they couldn't do at all, and with patterns they failed as well. They were only able to do some stripes and irregular spots. At some point, they would always get very dark, nearly black, and then they would stay like that. "Mine is broken, mine too." "You changed the surface too quickly." Now they are trying to do all the colors at the same time. That's why they are so dark now. But that's not true. Black shows irritation and is a sign of submission.

One year the bush stayed empty. There were no more chameleons. And then they closed the school because of the escalating political situation in Uganda. Maybe they returned. Maybe. But I couldn't check because we left, too. In 1978, we moved to the Seychelles, an archipelago in the Indian Ocean. I was homeschooled and often lonely. Visitors brought me the latest craze from Europe: slime, a strictly fun toy. Every day we bought fresh fish at the beach. One of the fishermen saw me playing with my new toy and wanted to touch it. The slime was passed from hand to hand. When I got it back, it was full of fish scales and worse.

Above all, it reeked horribly of fish. Despite all my efforts, I had to say goodbye. I buried it in the sand. I spent the year 1979 in Munich. I was very homesick. When I heard we were moving to Kenya, I eagerly began counting down the days until our departure. For me, it was crystal clear. We were never going back to Europe.

Six years later my opinion had changed completely. Kenya was definitely the end of the world. It was now quite the opposite. Europe was totally cool. At the age of nineteen, I returned to Munich without my family. I felt a bit like the chameleons of my childhood. I had been set down in a different place once too often. Adapting to a city like Munich just didn't seem to work. It was too orderly, too rich. And I had no idea what to do. I first studied literature and history. I obtained my master's degree in Hamburg. Ultimately, I fell in love with the harbor, the sounds, the smells, the comings and goings, the roughness. There's constant change. My restless history has found a home because a harbor is a chameleon. We go well together. I found where I belong, but I still lacked a voice. I studied illustration and started to draw comics. Suddenly it was easy. I could tell my stories. I found my way.

Forty years after I arrived in Uganda as a child, on a visit to the north of Mozambique, I'm greeted by the same blend: the boiling hot runway, the buzz of an unfamiliar language, the extreme humidity. I've never been to Mozambique and yet it feels so familiar, more like a homeland than Hamburg in any case. I feel at home here instantly. What is home? In Pemba, I run into former East German contract workers. "Muzungu donde vem? Eu sou alemão. De Hamburgo." "Ah, Sie sind aus Deutschland! Do you know Ilmenau? I lived in Thuringia for nine years." There were twenty thousand Mozambiquans in East Germany from 1979, often doing very unpleasant jobs. After years of absence, they had to return home in 1990. Strangers in their own land. They faced fundamental questions of belonging and where to call home. The "Madgermanes," as they call themselves, have a close network. Some of them were willing to tell me their stories. "Regis," "this was in Karl-Marx Stadt." "I was in Hoyerswerda." Back in Hamburg, I was still fascinated by the subject. I began to do research and held more interviews. Many thanks to all my interviewees for all their patience and cooperation. Together their stories make up the fictional characters of José, Basilio, and Annabella.

Biz Nijdam: How did you come to the *Rude Girl* project? Why did you decide to expand it into a full graphic novel?

Birgit Weyhe: Maybe Priscilla can start because she reached out to me.

Priscilla Layne: Yeah, this was fall 2018. I was in Berlin for a few months on a fellowship at the American Academy in Berlin, and I was going to present at my first comics conference in Cologne. I'd read *Madgermanes,* and I'd really enjoyed it and ended up reading Birgit's other comics because I wanted to get an idea of where it fit in the context of her work. And then I realized she lived in Hamburg, and I thought since I'm in Germany, I might as well reach out and see if I can come and interview her because I thought it was interesting how much her comics related to her life experience. But when I contacted Birgit, she told me she was in America, in Pennsylvania, at the moment. We met for the first time at the GSA in Pittsburgh. There were several panels and one on Birgit's work. We got to say hi briefly, and when Birgit got back to Hamburg, I went and spent an afternoon with her. I went to her atelier because I was on my way to Denmark for a conference. So, I spent a day with her and had a bunch of questions about *Madgermanes* and her other works. The funny thing was: she was walking me to the train after I had spent the day interviewing her, and she started asking me about myself. How did you start learning German? Where did your interest in German Studies come from? I thought it was funny because I'm used to asking all the questions, but I like to be self-reflective about the work we do in academia. I do feel like it can be easy to always be the one in control asking the questions and not really being exposed. And so, for me the fact that Birgit was flipping the lens onto me felt like an invitation to an interesting feminist undertaking—this idea of "let's interview each other." Based on our talk on the way to the train, she was working on her series *Lebenslinien* [Lifelines] in the newspaper, and she said "can I do a page about your story for that"? And that's really where the idea started and then grew into something larger.

Birgit Weyhe: And then I went to Berlin to interview Priscilla and spent the day with her talking about her. I had the idea of a short piece because when I asked Priscilla where the idea for German came from, Priscilla said: "from Indiana Jones." And that was so funny that I thought it had to be in the newspaper. And then this day in Berlin was so packed with information and so interesting that I said as a joke at the end of the day: "This is so much material, I could make a book out of it and now I just have sixteen little panels to stuff your life into." And then Priscilla said: "Why don't you do a book?" And then I was confused.

Priscilla Layne: The funny thing is that, on the one hand, I have always liked the idea of writing a memoir of sorts—and I hope I don't come across sounding super full of myself—but I remember being a kid and wanting to film my life. I never told Birgit, but when I was twelve, I said Macaulay Culkin will play my friend and Harrison Ford will be his dad. I wanted to take my story and fictionalize it. I proposed the idea of a book because I realized that I went through a lot of struggles and hurdles in my life. And I feel that, growing up, there weren't a lot of stories reflected back at me that depicted specifically Black girls in a complex, diverse way. There were only a few representations. And I thought it would be great if we could do a project together that could be something that could be helpful for young people, other people who deal with being told "You're not Black enough" or "You're bad because you're a tomboy." A lot of my life has been people trying to fit me into categories and me resisting that. And I feel that's still a problem for a lot of people in the world. So, I thought this could be a cool fun thing for us to do. And hopefully people will like it. That's why I just kind of rolled with the idea of a book. And I've always loved comics, and I loved the idea of drawing my life as a comic, but I'm a terrible artist. So, I thought if I do this with Birgit, then I don't have to draw anything. So, it worked out really well because we collaborated, and I got to tell her all these stories, and then she worked her magic and created the scenes. While I'm translating it into English, I am still amazed at some of the stuff she came up with to convey my thoughts on the page.

Birgit Weyhe: It was actually really hard for me to find a way to tell Priscilla's story because it was immediately after this *Madgermanes* cultural appropriation issue, which I totally understand on one level, but I hadn't figured out what the consequence is for me as an author or as a person. Do I stop telling stories, and where do I stop telling stories? Am I only able and allowed to tell my own story? Or can I tell stories about younger people or people of a different sex or gender? Or from a different time? Suddenly I felt very limited in my range of storytelling. And now I had to—no, I wanted to tell Priscilla's story, and her story was so different in so many ways from my experience growing up and from my pop cultural context. It was so different in every way that it took me nearly a year to find a way of dealing with all the material. I had all these moleskin notebooks full of handwritten excerpts from the interview. And I had some ideas, but I couldn't find a voice. It worked when I had the feeling "I'll do my job and then I'll send it to you and ask you can you please comment on it—positively or negatively." I was really glad that you were willing to do this.

Priscilla Layne: I would just add that there is an interesting thing that you and I have in common. You were struggling with the question: "Can I represent people of a different gender, different age, different race?" For me, as an academic, I get asked: "Why don't you study the literature of Caribbean women? Why don't you do Black Studies?"—although I do a kind of Black Studies, Black German Studies. Often my response was: "I study German literature because I find it interesting." That just happens to be what I became interested in. I think this is all tied to my interest in cross-racial empathy and interculturality. I like to think there is a way for us to work together, to come together, and to learn from each other's stories while also being aware of our privileges. For me, this collaboration was a way to reflect more on that.

Biz Nijdam: Many of the questions that I was hoping to pose have just been foreshadowed in this opening conversation. I thank you for that. In the context of this journey that you were on, Birgit, this is your third graphic novel—in not quite a sequence—exploring intersections of belonging and Blackness, a graphic novel that emerged in dialogue with another journey embodied in work, exploring what it is to tell other people's lives. Could you talk a little bit about why you're drawn to this particular intersection of Blackness and belonging? I think maybe it touches on your own biography and the story of the chameleon, but I find it really fascinating that you can engage this theme over and over again—in *German Calendar No December*, *Madgermanes*, and now *Rude Girl*.

Birgit Weyhe: It definitely has something to do with my biography. That's also why I wanted to preface this conversation with these remarks about my work, which are actually from my books. I didn't draw new stuff. I just took it out of the books and wrote a new text. For me, it took a long time to adapt to Germany when I came to Germany, and I still don't really feel at home in Germany even though it's my cultural context and my language. And also coming to Germany in 1988—before globalization and computers and everything—I had a very limited cultural and pop cultural knowledge. And it took me a long time to catch up. Even now, people my age talk about what they watched on TV, and I never saw *Heidi* or *Vicky the Viking* or *Lassie* or *Biene Maya* or whatever they watched in Germany at the time. And when I said that I came from Kenya or Uganda, people said "Oh, Africa." So, it was always this continent, and nobody knew anything. So, I had the feeling I wanted to share something, I wanted to tell stories, I wanted to open it up a bit, make it more precise. And then it changed; the discussion changed. Now it was about "why do I tell these stories from my perspective?" Can I tell them? And since I've been working, the discussion has changed a lot. And my way of doing things has changed. Now, I wouldn't draw comics like I drew my first comics, like *Ich weiß*, which is also part of this because the skin color is completely black, but at that point I only had black and white, color or no color. But I found it wasn't appropriate, so I started to mix. It's a long process in every way, in the way I drew. I was trying to draw how I tell stories, and it is still a process because there is this context, this discussion going on, which is good.

Biz Nijdam: Priscilla, do you want to talk a little bit about how you engaged in the conversation that Birgit was having through her work reflecting on what it meant to represent Blackness as well as on what it meant to represent Black skin in consultation with you and how these processes shaped the graphic novel that we see today?

Priscilla Layne: I know that we specifically talked about the issue of skin color and representing skin color in comics. This is something I've thought about a lot in other contexts regarding blackface and different iterations of that, and comics' connection to that, or even animation with Mickey Mouse as a minstrel. I remember asking Birgit what went into her decision-making for how Black people are represented in an earlier text like *Ich weiß* compared to *Madgermanes* where she is working more with greens and oranges, and the same in *German Calendar No December*. One of the things we disagreed about was that in some of her *Lebenslinien* comics she just used no color for everyone, including people of color. And I remember saying that I don't think that's a good solution. It just reminded me of the discussions about post-race after Obama was elected—this whole idea that we're in this post-racial era. I just felt like that's not really honest. The reality is we do look different from each other. And some people deal with structural, institutional racism because of that. And so, for me, it was really important that Birgit use some color in *Rude Girl*. And I like the way she did that, starting out without the color and then me making this point and then introducing the color.

Birgit Weyhe: And I found it so clever that I left out the color—I thought: "We're all the same." And then it was really good to have this comment from Priscilla: "No, it's necessary to have the color in it."

Biz Nijdam: What I admire about your book is the level to which it was co-created, which is something that is really important to me in my work and also sets this graphic novel apart from other social-justice-oriented projects. And this is such a powerful element of *Rude Girl*; it's a comic about making comics—which is my favorite kind of comic. I wanted to pose two more questions before I open it up to the audience. The first one touches on what you, Priscilla, shared about how you have always wanted to have a story or a movie about your life—but fictionalized. There is this tension in the book between its relationship to Priscilla's lived experience and the fictionalized elements—which is really only in the sense that Priscilla's name is changed. Despite this name change, however, it's very clear that you, Priscilla, are Crystal, and if anyone were to google any of the specifics of Crystal's life, it would be clear that you are the person the protagonist is based on. So, I wanted to ask you a little bit about the decision to change your name in the book and then also what it feels like to be such a public persona now with regards to this particular project. What is it like to have your colleagues at a conference in your field participate in thinking about your contribution to this book? I also know you teach material from *Rude Girl*. So, I wanted you to speak about all of this in the various contexts of your life—the fiction and the facts.

Priscilla Layne: I went back and forth about whether or not I wanted it to be so clear that this is based on my story. Birgit had asked me: "Do you want me to name you or not?" And first I thought: "no, no, don't" and I think that's because in the past, actually anytime I've been interviewed for punk stuff or skinhead stuff I've used a pseudonym because I thought that's separate, that's my life in the subculture and then there's my academic life, and I don't want those things to mix." But then I realized that this is silly. I've come to a place in my life where I accept all the parts of me, all of my story that led me to where I am now. I am not ashamed of anything. The mistakes I've made are part of growing and changing. I did think "oh, this is weird." Suddenly, colleagues are going to know super personal things about me, which I think most people would be uncomfortable with. But that's me trying to live my feminist praxis, this idea of "the personal is political," you can't separate the two, all of that is me, me now as a scholar. And deep down I hope maybe some of my colleagues will now understand why I'm so weird and socially awkward. This all leads into why I can be really uncomfortable at parties. I like that this is all based on my memory of events, of how things happened. And I understand that my narrative is not the universal narrative; it's not the truth and there is only one perspective. My mother will have a totally different story of what really happened, and so will my friends. But I like the idea that Crystal is this fictional person based on my narrative but also Birgit's interpretation of my narrative, and then there is me, the actual person. I like the idea of keeping those separate.

Birgit Weyhe: For me, this was really important because I selected from all the interviews we did, and only two scenes are invented. In all of the chapters, the material is taken from different conversations and put into one scene. So, again, it's fictional. As Priscilla said, it's my interpretation of her life.

Biz Nijdam: So, how do you feel about teaching *Rude Girl* and about having your colleagues have a concrete sense of your life story? What kind of teaching space does that cultivate? What are the outcomes of that kind of pedagogical engagement?

Priscilla Layne: So far, I've only assigned one excerpt of the text. I teach this Berlin class for upper-division students of German in German, and I shared the chapter of me studying abroad in Berlin with them as extra reading. We didn't spend a session on it, but I said if you want to talk about it, let me know. But they didn't bring it up, it was too weird for them. Next semester I'm teaching a class on graphic medicine and we're going to talk about trauma. I'll use it in that context. I'll see how it goes, but, for me, it's also about me trying to be open and vulnerable since I'm asking the students to be the same. In a class where we're reading about mental and physical illness and trauma, students are going to feel connected to that in different ways, and it's only fair for me to be honest about what my connection is. Also, for me, in my work on Black German art, I've interviewed a lot of Black German people in theater, art, and literature, and I feel I ask them personal questions all the time, and about how their lives are reflected in their work. So here is me saying "this is me" because sometimes people will say "Who is this African American woman coming to Berlin to interview me about this performance I did?" People always had a lot of questions about how I got to this work and so I feel this is my way of saying "look, this is my story, if you want to know more about me, I'm grateful for you being open to me about your life and your work."

Biz Nijdam: I know you're in the process of translating the book into English, which will make it available to a broader audience. I have two questions about that but first I wanted you to expand on this. You mentioned that there are all these moments in the translation where you're in awe of how Birgit has transformed your life experience, and I wanted you to share one of those moments where you felt that Birgit captured a particular moment in your life in a really powerful way.

Priscilla Layne: I think, for example, of the orange scenes where I'm responding to the chapter and telling Birgit what she got wrong or right. There are a few moments in the book where I'm talking about politics, my positionality as the child of Caribbean immigrants, living in America, dealing with anti-Black racism but in a different way than African Americans and all the complexities of that. Those were particularly hard parts to illustrate because there's not any action going on. These are just my thoughts, and so Birgit came up with images, such as scenes from protests or scenes of the Black Panthers and really did her research to find the symbolism that goes along well with what I'm saying. I'm particularly struck by those moments in the text.

Biz Nijdam: Did looking at your life through the lens of this comic force you to see it differently? *Rude Girl* is constructed based on your memories. Did the graphic novel recast some of those memories, reveal elements of your own life, patterns that you might not have noticed independently until it was represented to you as a graphic novel?

Priscilla Layne: Not necessarily. For me, this was such a long process. Our conversations happened over a long period of time and then there was the whole drawing of the graphic novel, so that by the time I was translating it I had forgotten a lot of the things that happened. And so, I'm like "Oh I said that" or "oh this story is in there." So, it's funny. I don't necessarily know the whole thing by heart. There have been a few moments of embarrassment while translating.

Biz Nijdam: My last question is about your reading public, your audiences. There are two audiences for this book. One audience consists of German-language readers in Europe and the other audience is the North American audience that will have access to the English translation. Can you talk about what you think your German audience is drawn to and might get out of this book? What is the reception in Germany like? And what will your North American audience be drawn to? What do you think they'll get out of this book?

Birgit Weyhe: I'm doing the readings in Germany. The German audience is very interested because there is a big insecurity about this topic of cultural appropriation. For them, it's about rethinking the topic but without having this sense of "you're not allowed to." And it's about my way of trying to maybe find a way of dealing with it. This makes it easier for the German audience to deal with this topic. And it's still quite a new topic in Germany. There hasn't been the same discussion that the United States has had for such a long time. In Germany, it has just come up very recently, so it's very cutting-edge.

Biz Nijdam: I like how you frame it as an invitation into a conversation that would otherwise be very hard to engage with because it hits too close to home. Observing your journey helps your readers reflect.

Birgit Weyhe: This refers only to the German audience. The book is coming out in France now, then Poland, then the United Kingdom, and then in the States.

Priscilla Layne: I have my oldest son in mind as an ideal reader. He's ten, but he reads comics all the time. He loves *Dog Man* and *Captain Underpants* and all of that stuff. I think it would appeal to young people who are struggling with identity issues, feeling like an outsider, exploring their identities and different subcultures. The book could be helpful for that. It's a good representation of trauma and dealing with trauma, moving through it, and, I hope, also about exploring the world, and about how going abroad can impact your life in a positive way. I have to say, while translating it, I thought this would be perfect right now when all of these books are being banned in America, like the graphic novel of Anne Frank's diary. I thought this book doesn't have any explicit sexual content, so I thought this would be perfect. This won't get in trouble. But then I read the conversations I had with Birgit about race and class, and

I think this could get flagged for Critical Race Theory, so I don't know. If it's able to fly under the political radar, it could be, as Birgit said, a good conversation starter around these issues. I love the idea of this being translated into French and Polish. I feel it's my punk swan song. A few years ago, I got rid of all my old punk shirts, which I'm still sad about. I donated them to a girls' rock organization, so I know they're in good hands, but I still miss them. I like the idea of me living on in these different countries in this version thanks to the graphic novel.

Biz Nijdam: *Punk Swan Song* can be the title of your next graphic novel, which will be about the reception of this graphic novel.

Birgit Weyhe: Now, you can be the heroine of so many people, Priscilla. You're mine already because you opened up and let me do the book.

Priscilla Layne: I'll let my son write the song. He's about to be in a band. He plays the keyboard.

Birgit Weyhe: He is also so good at drawing. He should do the next comic!

Priscilla Layne: That's true. He can do the *Swan Song* comic!

Christophe Koné: What really struck me is this idea of Priscilla telling her story that becomes fictionalized and that fictionalized story is an interpretation by Birgit. This is a multi-layered story and, on top of that, in a different medium. Through these multiple layers, we are getting at something—I hate to use the word "truth"—that approximates some authentic truth and captures someone's life. And someone's life is also—I hate the term "universal"—something that is out there in the world and that's going to concern or touch so many people. That fascinates me. If Priscilla had written her life story and somebody had recorded her or filmed her, that would be completely different. There's something to be said about the multi-layered interpretation, the different format, and also the translation.

Birgit Weyhe: When I do readings, music also comes into it because, in good punk tradition, I used YouTube and recorded the "kchhhh" with my cellphone. So, when I do readings, I have this "kchhh" sort of music for each chapter, and it works well because some people immediately connect with the music.

Biz Nijdam: One of those layers for me, when thinking about comics that are about making comics, is that these kinds of comics are authentic about their own inauthenticity. They are always remarking on their constructed nature, which allows readers to access this level of truth because it's all a combination of fiction and fact. Your observation is really poignant: it gets at a truth by way of its fictionality.

Michelle Gonçalves: I'm from Sao Paulo, Brazil, and a professor in a German conversation class at my university presented *Madgermanes*, and I think the impact was really positive. Because of this, I wanted to read another book and *Rude Girl* appeared for me.

Onyx Camille Henry: I don't know much about the creation of comics. Obviously, your story comes first and the conversations you had; but since it's a graphic novel the images carry the story really profoundly—but obviously so does the text. So, I'm wondering about the process of creating those two together, melding those two. Which one came first? I'm assuming that they probably influenced each other, that you go back and forth with it, but I just wanted to hear about your process, how that all went.

Birgit Weyhe: I went to Berlin two or three times when Priscilla was still there and always stayed for the day. And I asked a lot of questions and wrote the answers down by hand in my notebooks. And then I started to form ideas of topics that I found important. At first, the idea was telling an even longer story up until the present day actually. That's what I had agreed on with Priscilla. But then it would have been even closer to her. And I had the feeling that this is getting too close, also the place where she's teaching now. So, I said I would like to end it earlier. I came up with my interpretation completely alone based on the text I had written down. I sent chapters to Priscilla only after I had finished drawing them. And sometimes I had questions while I was drawing to get something more precise. Did I get it right? Was it this? But I invented scenes based on the interviews and then sent each chapter, one by one, to Priscilla, and then I waited for her comments. And often her comments were quite short, and I used them as she sent them to me. In fact, sometimes, if the comments were very long, I sometimes made them a bit shorter. Priscilla sent me the comments via email. And when I had drawn the comments, Priscilla also commented on them. And I changed it until Priscilla said it's ok now. Otherwise, it would have been an endless process of commenting. And then I started the next chapter. So, for me, this was the first book where I had no idea how it would turn out; I didn't know what the skin color would be. I changed it after Priscilla mentioned it. I had no idea where this book would end. For me and for my publisher, it was very hard to accept that we had no idea how long this book was going to be and how it would end. For me, it was a very interesting process. I do remember having a conversation about how long graphic novels tend to be, and we didn't want it to be too long, so we decided which parts to leave out.

Priscilla Layne: It's interesting how the format shapes the content. I remember having a conversation about how long graphic novels tend to be and we didn't want it to be too long, so we decided which parts to leave out. Other than that, the book revolves around our conversations. I sent Birgit a bunch of photos from my childhood and from high school. I just sent her album covers of different records that I have and explained which bands I was listening to at different points in my life. Everything came together.

Birgit Weyhe: It was really funny: the first or second time I went to Berlin I read through what I had written on the train back and transferred it to my computer with a better structure. I wrote to Priscilla from the train, asking her to please give me a music piece or album or song that was important to her for each year of her life. And I asked if this is too much work. By the time I was home, I already had them. I couldn't use them all because the book doesn't depict every year of Priscilla's life. I tried to use them all and then I had the idea that I would take these covers for the chapter title pages. There is a playlist at the end. And sometimes when I'm invited to readings, they play songs from the playlist while the audience is arriving.

Priscilla Layne: I have a funny story to add. On the plane over here—I'm in Italy right now—they had the latest *Indiana Jones* movie, *Indiana Jones and the Dial of Destiny*. At first, I was not going to watch this—*The Crystal Skull* was already terrible—but I ended up watching it and all those feelings came back, why this character was so exciting to me, cracking codes, speaking Latin, traveling the world, fighting Nazis. I felt that it was just yesterday that I was becoming enamored with this character.

Biz Nijdam: Many people have asked about the TED talk that you are presenting in Italy.

Priscilla Layne: I haven't mentioned it much to people because I'm afraid I'm going to choke and it's going to be terrible. The TED talk is fifteen minutes, it's a summary of the graphic novel, it's me talking about how I got into German, why I felt that studying a foreign language and literature was important, and how that builds empathy and makes you open to the world and other ideas. But it's framed as a letter to my sons because it's so hard to do this kind of public speaking in academia. We are used to having a text in front of us, speaking fast to get through the conference paper. In this case, I'm thinking about slowing down and pausing, so I reframed this as a letter to my sons and that helped me to really connect with the text. But the way I framed it, I thought about the fact that when I'm gone my sons will inherit an obscene amount of books, and they'll wonder "what do we do with this, why did mom have all these books?" So, I'm explaining why, that's the gist of it.

Biz Nijdam: I wanted to conclude with an anecdote about the title. Could you speak about the title? I think it connects to some of the conversations we've already had about music etc., but it wasn't the original title.

Priscilla Layne: I wanted the original title to be *Oreo* because that's what I got called in school. The kids would say: "Oh, you're Black on the outside, White on the inside." And it was really painful to me. Often when I recall it, I still get tearful and choke up about it. I just remember that I didn't understand why people were singling me out. I just knew I was different, and people didn't understand me. For me, calling it that was a way of saying "I'm over it," of reappropriating it, saying it doesn't upset me anymore. But there's already a book called *Oreo*, a novel by a Black author, Fran Ross. At first, we thought "oh, this is a graphic novel, it's different." But Birgit's publisher said we can't have two titles that are the same. It'll be confusing to people. So, Birgit asked me: "what do you think could be an alternative title." I thought of this other book I really love, a memoir by the singer of the British ska band Selecter. It's called *Black by Design*. Her name is Pauline Black, and I thought that's such a great title, and that got me thinking about ska and rude girls and I thought that's a good one because it shows my connection to ska culture, which was very important to me because of my Caribbean background, and it's how I got into punk. But I also like the idea of being a rude girl. My relatives were not very happy with me most of the time. I wasn't doing what they asked me to do. I like the kinds of different meanings that the title conveys.

Birgit Weyhe: It was my publisher who said he wouldn't publish the book with the title *Oreo* because people won't remember my name or the name of the other author, but everybody will remember Oreo and those who want to buy the novel will get the graphic novel and vice versa. He said this is not good for anybody. I said maybe we can have *Oreo* with a subtitle, and he said no. But I like the title *Rude Girl* very much.

Part III

Countering Violence

6: On the Making of *But I Live*: A Conversation between Miriam Libicki, Gilad Seliktar, and Barbara Yelin

Charlotte Schallié

But I Live: *Three Stories of Child Survivors of the Holocaust* (New Jewish Press, 2022), a collection of three graphic novellas, renders oral testimonies into distinct visual narratives. For each of the three novellas, a Holocaust survivor was paired with a graphic artist to co-create a graphic narrative drawing on the survivors' lived experience before, during, and after the Holocaust (in one case: one artist was paired with two brothers who survived together in hiding in the Netherlands).[1] The testimony-gathering sessions between artists and Holocaust survivors took place both in-person and online between late summer 2019 and early 2022. The graphic novelists and survivors were supported by an arts-based participatory action research project (https://holocaustgraphicnovels.uvic.ca) that included scholars from various disciplines, archivists, and community partners from six countries (Canada, Germany, Israel, the Netherlands, the UK, and the US). In close creative partnership with the survivors, Miriam Libicki, Gilad Seliktar, and Barbara Yelin developed preliminary sketches, storyboards, and, ultimately, published an award-winning collection of three graphic narratives (2022), honoring the testimonial voices of Emmie Arbel (Kiryat Tiv'on, Israel), Nico and Rolf Kamp (Amsterdam, the Netherlands), and David Schaffer (Vancouver, Canada). Given the project's focus on research creation, the three artists were also invited to document their artistic practice reflecting on their collaborative work with the survivors, scholars, filmmakers, and community partners. Libicki, Seliktar, and

---

1 Miriam Libicki and David Schaffer, Gilad Seliktar and Nico and Rolf Kamp, and Barbara Yelin and Emmie Arbel, *But I Live: Three Stories of Child Survivors of the Holocaust* (Toronto and London: University of Toronto Press, 2022; paperback 2024). The three stories are: Libicki and Schaffer, "A Kind of Resistance"; Seliktar, Kamp, and Kamp, "Thirteen Secrets"; and Yelin and Schaffer, "But I Live."

Yelin opted to forfeit a written contribution and, instead, jointly drew a ten-page "Behind the Art" graphic essay.

In my role as book editor and project lead, I guided and facilitated this collaborative work. Once I began receiving the first sketches and storyboards in early 2020, it became apparent to me that comics-drawing was an effective and powerful tool for trauma-informed testimonial inquiry and storytelling. I also observed during this initial phase that our arts-based approach was not just a means of turning personal memories into visual testimonies; it encompassed so much more. Our first research findings revealed that art as a critical tool of exploration and understanding illuminates the creative dimensions of witnessing and (hi)storytelling. Moreover, the process of co-creation—bringing artists, survivors, and scholars into this joint research endeavor—sheds light on the entangled web of history, memory, life story writing, and lived experience. As we continued being engaged in this team-based approach, we started to pay close attention to the shared labor informing collaborative testimony collection practices. The artists decided early on in the project that they wanted to foreground the artist/survivor relationship rendering the process of co-creation visible as part of the artists' storytelling work. This interpersonal focus conceptualized memory transmission not as a one-directional knowledge transfer but as an evolving relational process. Memories are not created in a vacuum; we always remember in relation to others, or with others, in their company, or with their presence in mind. We share our life stories and memories differently each time we encounter a new listener, a new interlocutor, or a different storytelling environment (unless it is a rehearsed or scripted commemorative speech/performance). Thus, the idea of relational memory or relational testimony became key to our understanding of arts-based testimony gathering. This ongoing process and commitment to being in relationship with one another, to co-creating the graphic narratives together, necessitated a willingness to build trust-based relationships with our participating survivors. Following in the footsteps of Henry Greenspan's groundbreaking work,[2] we created a fluid research design that gave the artists and survivors leeway to connect with each other on their own terms. Their work was supported by community liaisons, historians, archivists, and research assistants (please see the acknowledgment section in the book for all contributors). Each of the three teams created its own workflow centering the work of the artist and survivor throughout the project. From the onset, we abandoned regimented sets

---

[2] See Henry Greenspan, *On Listening to Holocaust Survivors: Recounting and Life History* (New York: Praeger, 1998); and Henry Greenspan, "Collaborative Interpretation of Survivors' Accounts: A Radical Challenge to Conventional Practice," *Holocaust Studies* 17, no. 1 (2011): 85–100.

of interview questions and standardized testimonial interview protocols. Instead, we adopted an emergent practice that afforded space and time for the artists and survivors to get to know one another, feel comfortable with each other, and make it possible to trust the unfolding process. Throughout the project, the three artists scheduled virtual check-in meetings to compare their notes and drawings, discuss challenges, and find creative solutions for roadblocks. Such sustained in-depth memory work was only possible because the comics artists and survivors were invited to join the project as partners in research. The artists were given agency, creative license, time and space to develop their working routine, their individual style, and their approach to problem-solving and conflict resolution. In the same vein, our survivors participated in the conversations not only as knowledge holders but also as experts in the experience of testimony documentation. This close collaboration and cooperation yielded many insights and revelations, but it also presented unanticipated hurdles and obstacles (some of these will be discussed in the artist conversation). For example, honoring reciprocity in survivor-led testimony-sharing practices required that we held space for subjectivity and emotions. It was impossible *not* to be drawn into these relationships, *not* to care for the well-being of the survivors and artists and all members of the research team—including our research assistants who were tasked to transcribe hours of recorded interviews containing scenes of extreme dehumanization and degradation. For this reason, it became paramount to develop a comprehensive ethics of care framework with the aim of advancing ethical practices that reduce harm wherever possible and centering the insights of our participating survivors at all stages of our work. Lastly, an important—and in many ways unexpected—research outcome was the realization that we had to dismantle hierarchies in our team's governance structures and, instead, enable mentorship-based forms of collaboration. Working closely with artists and survivors over the course of three years, we could no longer ground our work in relational ethics without espousing and practicing an ethos of kinship, solidarity, shared authority,[3] and mutual care.

The following conversation, which was edited and condensed for clarity and conciseness, took place online on May 10, 2021. It was intended as a first brainstorming session to facilitate and coordinate the artists' work for the graphic essay.[4]

---

3   Michael Frisch, "Sharing Authority: Oral History and the Collaborative Process," *Oral History Review* 30, no. 1 (2003): 111–12; Steven High, "Sharing Authority: An Introduction," *Journal of Canadian Studies/Revue d'études canadiennes* 43, no. 1 (2009): 12–34.

4   This conversation was not originally intended to be published or shared with a broader audience. We decided to do so, as a team, with the intent of making

The Narrative Art and Visual Storytelling in Holocaust and Human Rights Education project gratefully acknowledges that Miriam Libicki, Gilad Seliktar, and Barbara Yelin gave permission to publish the interview and the accompanying artwork (interspersed throughout the conversation and reproduced with New Jewish Press's permission). The project also owes gratitude to Janine Wulz, who completed the labor-intensive work of transcription.

Telling the Truth—The Responsibility of the Artist

Miriam Libicki: I'm very into the idea in my story that you can't ever get the whole truth or the completely objective truth. And in my nonfiction, that's something I've always been interested in. I hope that people will be able to see that this is just one side of the story and that you could have drawn it in a completely different way. You could have portrayed people completely differently. And it would be just as accurate as what I have.

Barbara Yelin: These are wise words.

Miriam Libicki: Barbara, how do you see your responsibility towards the survivors?

Barbara Yelin: To tell the story in the right way. It's the biggest responsibility because we have only thirty-five pages to do so. Telling Emmie's story and working with her, I also felt that there was a risk that by asking Emmie, by showing her my drawings, I would hurt her again. I'm not sure if this happened. A drawing can be very powerful as a means to tell a survivor's story. I also feel a responsibility because I worked very closely with her. Once our creative collaboration comes to an end, it won't be the end of our relationship. Emmie is really kind to me, and we became close to one another. If you work with people in the present, you develop a relationship with them. We have now a story together. And the three of us, the artists, also have a story together.

Gilad Seliktar: I think that in my case, after I had met Nico and Rolf [in Amsterdam in December 2019], we didn't Skype or Zoom or talk

---

the collaborative creation process transparent. In 2023, we were invited to discuss our arts-based collaboration and creative practice at the Cherie Smith JCC Jewish Book Festival Vancouver (February), the *HistorioGRAPHICS: Framing the Past in Comics* Conference (Munich), and the German Studies Association Annual Conference (Montréal). Moreover, a joint webinar presentation was hosted by the Consortium of Higher Education Centers for Holocaust, Genocide, and Human Rights Studies in April 2023 (https://consortiumhgh.org/media/).

for a long time because I needed time to get away from the immediacy of the storytelling. I was so close to the brothers in Amsterdam.

Miriam Libicki: To get a bit of a distance.

Gilad Seliktar: To get a little bit of perspective. Because when I went to Amsterdam and spent time with Nico and Rolf, it was too real. I needed to give it time to transform into a story, into my version of their story, so Nico and Rolf could become characters in their own story. During the last few days, they returned to being the persons whom I met in Amsterdam. Now that I am in the process of finishing the story, I'm slowly starting to feel that I am getting close to them again. Suddenly, I become very emotional, which is unusual because most of the time, I don't get emotional when I create a story. I talk about emotions, but from a distance. But, of course, everything in this project is a big responsibility. As artists, we have a responsibility toward the story that we create. We tell a story, and it's like our soul is inside the story. It is a piece of us.

Miriam Libicki: I think it's important to mention that all of us are writers as well. We have all created our own books. Sometimes, I think there is a mistaken impression of a graphic novelist as an illustrator. It's like, you get the story, and you translate it into pictures, but I hope it will be clear in *But I Live* that we are all creating the story, and we're creating the story in collaboration. But we're also authoring this story. We're authoring something new.

Barbara Yelin: Yes. As an author, I'm using somebody's story, so I'm doing something with it. I create something new. And I hope that I'm doing the right thing. Emmie and I, we were in continuous dialogue with one another. I showed her the drawings and the evolving story, and I took in her feedback. Of course, we are also using written sources and visual materials. And we are working with people. It's both.

Gilad Seliktar: It's interesting that the process—from the first sketches to the final work—starts when you meet the survivors. The layout starts to appear during these meetings because you hear the story in your mind. And you start to sketch. You see the survivors, you see the story. You start to create the story from the moment you meet the survivors.

On Meeting the Survivors

Miriam Libicki: In my first meeting with David [in January 2020], there was an arts writer [Marsha Lederman] from one of the big newspapers in Canada [*The Globe & Mail*]. And so, they had asked me to do sketches before the meeting. I had barely read the other transcript that David had done because I wanted to be in an open mindset when I met him for the first time. But I read through the transcript, and I did some sketches. And then when I met David, I was like, oh, I can't keep these sketches. These are not right even though they were based on a lot of the same things that he was telling me. But actually meeting him, seeing what he talked about, seeing the emotion on his face when he would talk about different things, it really changed my idea. In the second meeting, one day after the first meeting, Marsha Lederman was also there. After David and I had the interview with each other, Marsha Lederman did an interview with us, and she asked me: what do you think the art is going to be like? I said, it's very early to answer that. But I already said that I was getting an image of the trees as characters, like the trees are going to be powerful figures. It's going to be a really dark fairy tale. And that did end up being one of the big anchoring themes, trying to infuse the woods themselves, the forest itself with life. From the first meeting with David, that kind of started coming to me.

Gilad Seliktar: I went to Amsterdam [in December 2019], and I met Rolf and Nico Kamp. I had a week, and I don't remember now the full story, but the first meeting was at Rolf's house. I thought that it would be very intimate, but there were a lot of people in the room. It was very weird for me. Suddenly I started to get the idea that this was a group effort. The partners [Jan Erik Dubbelman, Dienke Hondius], Charlotte, and we were in Rolf's home and then Nico arrived. Nico brought the family album. He sat near me and started to show me everything and tell me the story. I wasn't ready, and I didn't record anything. It was very weird because they threw me into the water. Nico gave me the family album, so I could take some pictures. He and Rolf were very kind to me. After the interview, we went to the childhood home of Rolf and Nico in Amersfoort [Utrecht], where I interviewed Rolf. And again, I wasn't ready. And suddenly, they filmed everything. There was the director [Anna Bucchetti] and the cameraman [Friso Pankonin]. I understood that they would film me in the interview, but I wasn't ready for that. They were all looking at me, too. I felt that I did someone else's job. I'm not an interviewer. It was weird for me. But again, everyone was very kind and easy-going. And the interview went very well. Rolf was very emotional. And after that, Nico came and then we went to the farm where they were hiding [in Achterveld, Utrecht]. I interviewed Nico a few days later. And we had a different interview because they are brothers, they are different. I remember it was a straightforward interview with Nico. He told his story, and I didn't get to ask my questions. It was fine by me, by the way, because it was very informative. Nico told it very, very clearly. But maybe I was looking for something less clear, maybe I was looking for more of the little moments, maybe I wanted to get more conversation and less interview. And, you know, sometimes it's hard with people who are used to telling their story again and again. This is their story. This is what they remember. And then I interviewed Nico again at his home a few days later. We had a very good conversation. Barbara, how was your interview?

Barbara Yelin: I met Emmie first at the Ravensbrück Memorial site in August 2019. This was only for two hours. I first saw Emmie when she was talking to the young adults who were there to learn. And I was very touched to see her telling her very tough and very sad story. And all these young people, they didn't know what to ask afterward. They were so horrified and a little bit in shock, but also ashamed. They didn't know what to ask. Emmie was sitting there; it was visibly exhausting for her. And I thought how strong Emmie must be to speak to people who can't even respond. Afterward I met her, and then I was relieved to speak with her one-on-one. It was not only the two of us, but there was one of her very kind daughters and also a young man who was helping her at Ravensbrück. We had two or three hours together, and she already told me her memories during this short time. I recorded our conversation. That was the beginning. Then I went to Israel for several days; this was several months later [in February 2020]. It was an intensive meeting at her house. We spoke for many hours each day. It was hard work and very personal and also very intimate for both of us. Emmie answered all my questions. We also met Gilad and he listened to parts of Emmie's story. And that was really the foundation of everything that came afterwards because I worked with all these recordings. What Emmie told me, and how she told it to me, was very clear and very intense.

Miriam Libicki: You got to hear Emmie's lecture version of her story, her performance of it, and the story she told you in her home, where sometimes it was just the two of you and sometimes it was you and her family. What was the difference between these two versions? What struck you most?

Barbara Yelin: The story was the same, but when we were alone, she told me some parts that she didn't tell in public. Emmie is telling her story as she remembers it. But sometimes, she tried to remember more details. And then her daughter [Orli] said something. The interactions between the daughter and her made Emmie remember more details. In Israel,

Emmie told me about her life after the war and about her family life. She was also showing pictures of family members who did not survive. What became clear to me was how hard it was for Emmie to deal with the fact that she remembered some parts of the story and other parts, she could not remember. We all know that silence is part of a Holocaust survivor's story. It's part of Emmie's story that she is silent in between moments of remembering. There is silence in the room, maybe when she cannot talk about her experience, or maybe when she doesn't remember because it's not there anymore.

Gilad Seliktar: I think that you need a lot of courage to talk about trauma. Each person has his or her own trauma. We are strangers to them [Emmie, David, Nico, and Rolf]. I think you need a lot of courage to talk about trauma in public, and I'm not sure that I have this courage. I call it the trauma of the Holocaust. The survivors talk about it, and they talk about it with us. The survivors trust us. I think that in my case, when I talk with Nico and Rolf, it's a conversation. Then we start again to talk with each other. We have a conversation and not an interview. And I think that's the time [in conversation with Nico and Rolf] when I work on the project. It's something that I understand much better now. The way Nico and Rolf decide to share the story, it's something very important.

Miriam Libicki: Following the survivors' emotional cues while listening to them allows us to be able to communicate the painful things while not being exploitative. We don't have the same trauma to draw on when we are creating the stories. But I think that one thing we all drew on was our fears. It's very interesting to me that all these stories are of children. And it turns out we are all parents of small children. And I think in a certain way, all of us did start imagining our children in these situations. And, of course, that's the worst fear.

Gilad Seliktar: In my last conversation with Nico, he told me about one of his parents. And then he said, it's like your son and you. It was very hard for me to imagine it. Suddenly, I was shaking. I was away from my son, away from Jonathan. And, you know, Nico and Rolf were children. They didn't know what was happening around them. They didn't understand it the way we understand it now. And we, as parents, see it in our children's eyes because we are explaining everything to them. We teach them. We experience everything again through them. To hear the stories of Nico and Rolf as children, it was something that I could identify with. As a parent.

Barbara Yelin: Yes.

Gilad Seliktar: And, by the way, did you tell your kids about it? The project?

Miriam Libicki: When I was drawing most of the project, I was in COVID-19 lockdown in Vancouver. My kids were not doing any kind of school, not even remote schooling, because we just didn't bother. And so, we were home all the time. I was working on this all the time. They started to see my pages and they were asking a lot of questions. I remember that my son, who was just about to turn five at the time, was running through the neighborhood shouting "Holocaust." This kid has seen our meetings and my meetings with David. He was hearing that word over and over, and I'm like, "oh dear!" So, I didn't have too many conversations with him about it. But my older child was seven, turning eight. She was asking a lot of questions. Every day I was trying to figure out what to tell her and what not to tell her.

Gilad Seliktar: As I am always looking at the images, I tape the pages onto the wall in my studio. Every time Jonathan gets into the studio, he looks at the pages. I tell him this is the story of the survivors. I tried to explain it to him, but I didn't find the right words. I think that for him, it's like someone else's story, he doesn't understand it completely.

Barbara Yelin: I didn't tell my son about Emmie' story because he's not yet four, so he's really young. But I told him about Emmie, and he knows Emmie, but I didn't show him the drawings. There was one situation when I opened my laptop because he wanted to see a short film. And then I had photos from the liberation of Bergen-Belsen. He saw them and he asked me some questions. I don't remember what I said, but that was not good. When I started the project, he couldn't even speak, and now he is talking all the time and he's asking me questions. I'm sure that there will be a point when I have to tell him something about the story. Emmie was four when she was deported. And he's going to be four soon. And like you said, this view of a parent, imagining their own child in a situation like this, this goes on and on in my head.

Story Creation and Composition

Gilad Seliktar: What was the most difficult experience you had with the creation of the story? Did you have a moment when you needed to crack or solve something that was in the story, or in the creation of the narrative?

Miriam Libicki: I think that in some of the scenes, I was trying to figure out how violent to make them. Sometimes, I think, I was too much on the side of implied violence, and not actual violence. Sometimes I worry that the story I was creating was too rosy. It was too nice. I remember one scene, the scene where they were being loaded onto the train cars. And so partly it was just the extreme violence of that scene, and partly it was the fact that I kind of felt that's somewhat of a familiar scene, something that you see depicted often. There are lots of photos, there are lots of movie scenes depicting similar events. And so, I was kind of downplaying that at first. And then David told me that he really wanted that scene in the graphic novella. And his character ended up being a bigger part taking up half a page rather than taking up a quarter of a page originally. That's one time when I didn't do a Google image search because we had research assistants. And I asked the research assistant [Betsy Inlow]: can you get me pictures? Can you curate some pictures of what this would have been like? She sent me the pictures and I could see little written notes on them to give context, and that helped me get in a more analytical mindset looking at them. Also, another moment was when I had to draw some bodies hanging. And again, I didn't want to google that. I think that those were difficult moments for me when I actually came across violent imagery. I had to decide whether to depict it or not. I also had to decide whether the feelings I was having about not wanting to depict the scenes were valid creatively or not.

Barbara Yelin: In one of the scenes, David Schaffer talks about his father who is carrying a child on his back. I thought about this again and again. Carrying one's own child and realizing: how long could I do that? For how long could I do that if I had to? I'm just realizing it now, that I thought about this scene. The hardest part, that's a good question. How about you Gilad?

Gilad Seliktar: I think everything was hard for me. I think the hardest part is to keep the balance within the story, not to fall for clichés, not to tell too much, but also not to miss things and to keep the focus. I think the hardest part was to focus on the important things. You want to tell the story and try to balance it with emotional moments. It's very hard because you need to use all your muscles. You need to find these moments in the interviews, catch them and then glue them together in order to create the narrative. The most difficult thing is to find the balance and the flow and the rhythm. Why is the rhythm so important? Because when you notice the rhythm, you need to find a way to move from scene to scene. I tell the story in pieces, you know, it's like a mosaic. The way I tell my story, it has to make sense. There are a lot of pieces that I still try to figure out. I have two pages that I still don't know what I'm going to do with them. It's part of the process. It's like a riddle.

Miriam Libicki: What was the hardest for you, Barbara?

Barbara Yelin: I would say it was a difficult project from the beginning to the end. I think it was the hardest work I ever did. It was very challenging to avoid clichés, unsettle reader expectations, or irritate the reader. But also, I did not only want to show the dark side of Emmie's life, but also show her humor and her strength. I tried to avoid making it easy or simple. It took me a very long time to find a style and a balance between showing the brutality and leaving space for the imagination. And so I reworked the pages again and again—not only rethinking them, but also drawing them again and again. Normally, I like big atmospheric panels. I still did a few of those, but I needed small panels about mostly very sad and horrible scenes. That was difficult to do. Also, I really wanted to include Emmie's words and find out how to render them in Emmie's clear and strong voice. How can I find a rhythm, what is the rhythm of the language within the panels?

Collaborating during the Pandemic

Miriam Libicki: I think it's not obvious to the readers that this is a collaboration between the three of us. And I don't know if it was Charlotte's plan or anybody's plan that this should happen. But when the pandemic struck, and we were stuck, and all three of us were in three different time zones, we started skyping. Sometimes every week, sometimes every other week. And it really was something that kept me sane at that point. It was something to look forward to, to check in. And it was something that gave me goals. I think we decided to do that on our own. And then I think it really did influence my work and influenced my work for the better. Barbara, you were saying that you had to cut down a lot of your atmospheric panels. I think you forced me to not just rush through things. I was like, I want to be more like Barbara, I need to slow down and let things surround the reader. You guys would give me really good critique. I know several times I felt there was something wrong with a page, but then I thought maybe that's just me, and they probably won't catch it. And then I would send you the pages, and you guys would say, no, that page, that's wrong. And I was like, oh, they know.

Barbara Yelin: I absolutely share that experience. Miriam, we have met once or twice in the past before, but never for very long. We didn't know each other so well. But then we were here, suddenly, in this project together. And then the pandemic came, and that created an intimacy somehow. I also would say, normally, I exchange work with colleagues, but this was a special time because we were part of the same project looking to do the story together, influencing each other, helping each other, and that was really special. I didn't experience this before.

Gilad Seliktar: We were lost together.

Barbara Yelin: Yeah, we were lost together. Thank you! This is the point! Excellent point, lost in space!

Gilad Seliktar: I was depressed for a month and a half, I think, until we started meeting on Skype. And immediately after that I started to shine. You know, I thought, OK, let's move on. Every day was the same, and suddenly, there came the day we talked, and it wasn't the same anymore. And then it changed. Suddenly, there it was again, the rhythm of the project. And again, because we are creators, we understand each other.

Miriam Libicki: Yeah. And I think this was different than just peers talking about projects because we were really talking about the same project. We were all having issues. What do we do with the small number of pages? We were all having issues with how to start and end. We were all having issues with how much we could change the text to make it into a narrative. And because so many of our issues were the same, we could really give each other advice. Seeing your stories emerge and seeing themes of stories emerge also helped clarify my path. Gilad, both you and I often like to do photo-based things. Some time ago I used to trace photos and reference the photos very closely. And when I saw the really amazing things you were doing with monoprints, I was, wow, that's great, and now I have to do something different. So, I went more into a fantasy direction.

Gilad Seliktar: Both of your reactions sometimes got me into another direction. In long graphic narratives you always have moments when you crash. And I think the way we worked with one another helped me to be always there, not to go down or hide too much because we shared our thoughts, we shared our feelings about the creation of things. And this keeps you on track.

Barbara Yelin: I also would like to add something about the group process. This project is not three single stories, but it's a group work between the three of us, between the survivors and us, and also with a bigger group. This already started, I think, in Leicester [a workshop in late February/early March 2020]. For me, that was very challenging, and I had some problems understanding everyone. But also, I realized at that moment the luxury of working with so many experts in so many fields who are actually listening to Miriam, Gilad, and me and looking at us as experts, and this was really a fruitful connection between us. I am not sure if there are many projects like this in the comics world. Probably not.

Miriam Libicki: Because, again, it was not like an assembly line. It wasn't like the historians delivered to the writers and the writers delivered to the artists. It was really all about keeping it open and just keeping the flow of ideas open. That was really the experience of the Leicester workshop. And it really felt like they were being inspired by us and we were being inspired by them and each other. And it was really wonderful. I came away with a lot of new ideas. Tim Cole, I remember him talking about finding commonalities and common metaphors in the way that survivors would tell their own stories. And he talked about people hiding in the woods and he talked about people talking about becoming animals. And then, I think it was either Kobi [Kabalek], or it was a discussion between Alex Korb and Kobi, where they were talking about Anne Frank. The fact that they said that it wasn't a triumphant story actually made me change the ending of my story. In my original ending to the story, David got married and ended up in Canada. That's how the interviews ended with David. But I asked myself, what if we stopped it at a place where he's still a child and he's also still really vulnerable, a place where you don't know if he is going to be OK or not? So, listening to the historians in Leicester really changed a decision that I had made about the storytelling structure.

Gilad Seliktar: There are times when you know the ending before you know the words. Sometimes you understand the final scene of a story only the day before the book goes to print. Each time it's different. I only found the ending for "Thirteen Secrets" [Gilad's contribution to *But I Live*] about three weeks ago when I watched the short movie again [*The Making of Thirteen Secrets: A Graphic Novel* by Anna Bucchetti]. The movie finishes with Nico saying: "With this, I would like to close my story." This is where he wants to end it. And this is the last panel of the book, the moment when the boys' mother came back. She was alive. She found them. They found her, it's like a new start. And the first panel in my book is when I ask Rolf if I can start the interview or conversation. And this was before I realized that I would end the story with Nico's words.

The Drawing Process

Barbara Yelin: First, there is the recorded material of my conversation partner Emmie. And then I create a storyboard. I start with a small storyboard, trying out several scenes, and putting them together in different ways—working from storyboard to storyboard until I have a version for my colleagues—you and everyone else who wants to read it—then I will incorporate all the input I get. And then, at some point, I start with the panels, which doesn't mean that I know everything. And then I just have to color the panels. During the process of coloring there's still a thought process going on. Sometimes I have to change the images again. And again. I keep changing images, reworking them, sometimes removing images or putting new ones in, until there's a final version, when I would say: OK, this is it now.

Miriam Libicki: I think that I was the only one who scripted really heavily. I did a full script; it's almost a screenplay script. I scripted things first because I find it easy to outline that way—to see my pages and to see the structure. And then it also helps me because I can see when my pages are getting too long. Images will come to me as I'm writing, even if I can't draw them right away. And then I was doing all my layouts digitally. When we were stuck at home in Canada, my partner bought me a much bigger Cintiq [digital graphic drawing tablet]. I would say that I really became much more comfortable with digital drawing when I was doing it intensely for this project. If I had some photo references I would do some tracing of backgrounds. And then I did character designs as I was going for a storybook look because David was going through different stages. He is going through puberty and he is also going through starvation. I wanted to depict David in these different stages. I remember that I was doing it layer by layer, so I would do the background in brown digital pencil. I decided that I was going to outline David and his family in red all the time, they were just going to have red outlines on their watercolor figures. And then the other family was turquoise and then the enemies were green, and then also the inanimate objects were green. I think at first you might not even pick up on it. I use that tool to say these are the protagonists of the story and these other people are more peripheral. And then there are the Romanian fascists who think that they're the humans and everyone else is not human. In my outlines, I reverse that. David's family are the most human and soldiers have this green outline, which is the same outline the trees have, because they're just forces on the people. After the digital thumbnails, I print the page, and I trace it, and I do it in watercolor. In some ways, it's a very methodical process, but the fact that I use watercolor at the end stage means that I can't ever have complete control. Things would happen when I'm doing watercolor. Things that I couldn't control, including my kids spilling water all over one of my pages, and then I just have to work with it.

Gilad Seliktar: Control. It's something that you need to find. With too much control there are surprises that you might miss. With watercolor, there are a lot of unknowns; you need to stay focused. It's very hard to work with watercolor because you need to find a way to control it, and you can't control water. Going back to Nico and Rolf: After the first day of interviews, I started to see the layout. I knew what the first ten pages would look like. When I got the transcripts, I figured out each theme. Once I decided on a theme, I wrote down all the sentences from all the interviews that connected to this theme. And then I focused on each scene. How do I present each scene before connecting it with other scenes? Next, I started the first ten pages. And then I decided on the color palette. I wanted very few colors, so I could have control. Most of the time when I work with a lot of colors, it starts to be a mess, and I try to control the process as much as I can. I try to find different solutions, such as blending colors. Sometimes it takes me a few months to get from one scene to another. At other times, suddenly everything is connected. I am always waiting and thinking about that moment. So, I try to create a layout and use a lot of references. I had asked Charlotte in Amsterdam to take pictures of everything. And she took pictures of everything. But I also needed to find references for children. One day at Jonathan's school, I saw one of his friends and his brother. Suddenly, I saw Nico and Rolf when they were young. I said that's it; I found Nico and Rolf, the children, in real life. I asked the parents if I could take pictures of the two boys, and they said: no problem. I had one session with them. And all of a sudden, the connection between the present and the past was complete. So, this is the book. I am sitting near the computer and I'm looking at the narrative all the time. I am trying to figure out how things are connected, and I need to see the whole story. We need to give the story the respect, I think. And we need to be very gentle with our decisions.

Working Across Languages

Barbara Yelin: This is also a project about languages, about Hebrew, English, Dutch, German. We are also an international group of people. I think the issue of language was also part of Emmie's story; she told me her story in different languages. And we communicated in different languages. We speak in English, of course. But also, I speak German with Charlotte—she comes from Switzerland. Recently, I wrote a text [for "But I Live"] in English and I tried to translate it back to German; I was not able to do it. It didn't work at all. It's really strange. I'm interested in what the translator will do about it. Because there is now a translator [Rita Seuß], who will translate "But I Live" from English to German for me. I thought of the story in English, which was interesting because my English is not very good; but in my mind, the story was in English from the beginning.

Miriam Libicki: There were a couple of times where I've stood up to the editors for awkward language. I really like the fact that this is a work of translation, and I think translation is a really powerful metaphor for the survivors who are working with us. None of the survivors are speaking in their native language with us. There were times when the editor at New Jewish Press wanted to smooth out the syntax. And I was like, no, I really want to capture how David speaks. That's him. And that's our relationship together. But the fact is that this book was also conceived as being translated from the very beginning. We were going to translate it into Hebrew and into German and hopefully into other languages as well. I wonder how to deal with that. I think it will be a challenge for translators.

Gilad Seliktar: Most of my books were first published in France. So, I work all the time from left to right. I got used to it. I am still working left to right. For "Thirteen Secrets" I tried to translate the interviews into Hebrew. But it was a failure. When I got back to the English text, it suddenly worked out, but I'm still editing the text. It's similar to what happened with Art Spiegelman's *Maus*. The first publisher in Israel corrected the way his father speaks. In the second edition, they keep the mistakes, the way the father talks. And I'm still not sure if I can do it here. I still haven't found a solution for the text yet. But it will come.

Biographies

Barbara Yelin: You both have Holocaust survivors in your families, and you told me that there have been people in your families who did not survive. You know that my family is from Germany. I was shocked when I found out many years ago that my grandfather was a member of the SS. He died in the war, so I never knew him. My grandmother didn't speak about this time until shortly before she died twenty-five years ago. I feel a responsibility to reflect on this history. It is also clear that, regarding the political shift to the right all over Germany and Europe, it is an urgent responsibility for everyone: to remember and never forget, to learn about the past to shape the future. This is one of many reasons why I wanted to be part of this project. The exchange with Emmie and the group is such an important, good, and touching experience.

Gilad Seliktar: My grandmother and almost her entire family—parents, brothers, and two of her sisters—survived. One of them passed away a few months ago. She was 101, I think. I didn't have a good relationship with my grandmother. Before I went to Amsterdam, my sister gave me interviews she had done with my grandmother. I had asked for them to get another perspective before I hear someone else's story. But I have to say that I still didn't connect with my grandmother. Maybe, it's an emotional thing. And maybe it will change.

Miriam Libicki: My grandfather and my grandmother, on one side of my family, were both survivors. My grandfather died about five years ago, and I was really close to him. And I miss him a lot. I dream about him a lot. He was the one who was a lot more open about his story and he was in the camps. He had a shtetl upbringing. He was quite traditional. And then he was in a labor camp. His story really matched the things that I was learning at school. I think maybe for that reason, my grandma, who was, for most of the war, under Soviet occupation, had a hard time identifying as a survivor. I think she had a fraught relationship even with that term because she wasn't in the camps. But her story really is a lot like David's story. Basically, they were just dumped somewhere. But in his personality, David reminded me of a lot of my grandfather, because my grandfather was also an engineer, and he had a great sense of humor. When I met David, I just heard his voice and I wanted to hug him. And so we hugged each other as soon as we met. The way David was, he really reminded me of my grandfather. But when I was talking to my grandmother on the phone about this project, I wasn't sure how much she wanted to talk about it—she never wanted to read books about the Holocaust, like my grandfather would. She never wanted to go to Yad Vashem, and she never wanted to see the memorials. But when I started talking about this project, she, all of a sudden, started telling me stories. She started saying that for her it was the feeling of dehumanization. She just knew at a certain point that she was not human to these people. She said that this was the moment when she knew that she was a Holocaust survivor and that what she went through was an attempted genocide. Working on this project opened up my grandmother and me to all these conversations we never had before. And I really wasn't expecting that to happen.

Gilad Seliktar: It was like a time machine when I met Rolf and Nico and their wives for the first time. It was like suddenly my grandmother and my grandfather were alive. It was very emotional. Once the book is published, it will be interesting to see how the survivors feel when they see themselves in a book. You connect their lives together and they can carry forward their story.

Barbara Yelin: It was difficult to create a good portrait of Emmie. It took me a long time to find her. I'm still not sure if I found her. But—

Gilad Seliktar: But you know her. You saw her laugh, you saw her angry, and suddenly you know how her nose moves when she laughs.

Barbara Yelin: Yes.

Gilad Seliktar: These are the nuances that we catch …

Barbara Yelin: Drawing an older person's face … these are really rich faces with a lot of expressions and a lot of traces. And to catch all of that with all the beauty and all the history in it … I am still looking for ways to show that.

The Making of the Cover Pages

Miriam Libicki: For the cover, I wanted to illustrate a scene that was strong in David's mind but I was not able to fit it into the narrative. I made a digital layout first, creating the forest setting, the soldier, child David, and the text all as different layers. David approved the first sketch (fig. 6.1), so I painted it in watercolor, scanned it, and prepared to re-design the text for print. However, on seeing the finished painting (fig. 6.2), David felt strongly that the fear and violence of the actual experience—specifically, that the fascist soldier had pierced the backpack David was holding with a sword to try to find "contraband"—was not clear. After discussing it, I submitted a new sketch (fig. 6.3) and began working on a new painting. At this time, also through some heartfelt discussions between David, myself, and our editors, we decided to change the title of the entire story from "If We Had Followed the Rules I Wouldn't Be Here" to "A Kind of Resistance" (fig. 6.4). I feel that the current title works better with the heightened fear of the final image. Young David is clearly being victimized, and his life is in imminent danger, so the idea that what he is doing in this scene is also "resistance" creates a tension and a seeming contradiction that works to engage the reader.

Gilad Seliktar: The image of Nico and Rolf holding the rabbits (fig. 6.5) came to me during the first conversation I had with Rolf. I wanted to create a portrait of both of them that would capture their innocence, in a natural way. As they look straight at us, without fear, we begin to sense and know what is happening around them—there is a dissonance and restlessness created in the viewer. That first sketch managed to capture the feeling and ambiance I wanted for their story. From that first moment together, all that was left to do was to hone the details of their experience. Nico was easy to draw from the first sketch to the final illustration. Once it was decided that the illustration would be the cover of the book, I returned to the drawing and polished it as much as I could, especially with the lighting: I wanted the light to really penetrate the characters, like they were being lit by fire (figs. 6.6 and 6.7).

Barbara Yelin: My drawings evolve after I have drawn many sketches first. I always use pencils first (fig. 6.8), before I start with gouache and color pencils. My technique is mixing brushes, pencils, water, crayons, and a digital retouch in the end (fig. 6.9). On this page, I wanted to show Emmie in the present. It was a longer process to find the right expression of Emmie's face that shows her inner strength and also her fragility, and to visualize an atmosphere in form and color that was the one that was present when we met. I use photo references. Emmie and I have been in a dialogue about the pages regularly, and at one point, she asked me to show her room and the tablecloth in the drawing brighter, and I did so (fig. 6.10). The dialogue between us about the evolving drawings was always influencing the complexity of the results, in a good way.

Figure 6.1

Figure 6.2

Figure 6.3

Figure 6.4

Figures 6.1–4. Successive sketches and paintings by Miriam Libicki for the cover page of Libicki and David Schaffer's story for *But I Live*, "A Kind of Resistance."

Figure 6.5   Figure 6.6

Figure 6.7

Figures 6.5–7. Artwork by Gilad Seliktar for the cover page of Seliktar, Nico Kamp, and Rolf Kamp's story for *But I Live*, "Thirteen Secrets."

Figure 6.8   Figure 6.9

Figure 6.10

Figures 6.8–10. Artwork by Barbara Yelin for the cover page of "But I Live," Yelin and Emmie Arbel's title story for *But I Live*.

7: Portrait of the Artist as a Young Man: Perpetrators, Postmemory, and Implicated Subjects in Volker Reiche's *Kiesgrubennacht*

Christina Kraenzle

IN 2013, VOLKER Reiche—most widely known for his daily comic strips in the *Frankfurter Allgemeine Zeitung*[1]—published his graphic memoir *Kiesgrubennacht* (Gravel Pit Night), an account of his early life in post-WWII West Germany. In his memoir, Reiche recalls carefree moments with his four siblings, but also constant conflict between his parents and taking refuge in comics, picture books, and drawing. In a visual style reminiscent of children's comics, the memoir documents the familial tensions and violence that structured Reiche's daily existence between the ages of four and nine. As a child of ardent Nazi supporters who remained silent about their wartime experiences, young Volker is only dimly aware of the extent of the atrocities committed by Nazi Germany and oblivious to his parents' complicity. He is, however, a frequent witness to the domestic violence committed by his father. In fact, violence of many sorts—from physical and psychological abuse to violence in popular forms of entertainment—permeates his surroundings.

The confrontation of the postwar generation with their parents, and especially with fathers who committed crimes during the Nazi regime, is hardly new in German-language culture. Thematically, *Kiesgrubennacht* can be classified as another entry in the long-established category of *Väterliteratur*. Moreover, the treatment of the National Socialist past was already a frequent theme in comics. From early works such as Al Feldstein and Bernie Krigstein's "Master Race" (1955) to the wealth of comics on the Holocaust that followed in the wake of Art Spiegelman's groundbreaking *Maus*, reflection on the events and legacies of the Shoah

---

1 *Strizz* was published daily from Monday to Friday from 2002 to 2009, after which it appeared weekly until the final strip on December 31, 2010. The strip was resumed in 2015 under the title *Strizz unlimited*. Since 2018 *Strizz* has appeared in the *Frankfurter Allgemeine Woche*.

has become a major topic in international comics publishing. And while the wide-ranging critical acclaim of Spiegelman's *Maus* did not initially spark a similarly prolific engagement with the National Socialist past in German comics production,[2] by the time of *Kiesgrubennacht*'s publication there had already been several titles in part or wholly devoted to the topic, such as Line Hoven's *Liebe schaut weg* (Love Looks Away, 2007), Gerlinde Althoff and Christoph Heuer's *Der erste Frühling* (The First Spring, 2007), Moritz Stetter's *Bonhoeffer* (2010), and Reinhard Kleist's *Der Boxer* (The Boxer, 2012). Nevertheless, *Kiesgrubennacht* stands out as an early example of a wave of comics—both in German-language and international comic production—that focus not primarily on victims of war and genocide, but on perpetrators. As Laurike in 't Veld argues, within the ever-growing field of comics devoted to mass atrocities and genocide (including but not limited to the Holocaust), only relatively recently have comics participated in "the broader turn in culture, one we have observed in literature and fiction" to include "increasingly nuanced and complex depictions of the figure of the perpetrator."[3] It is not surprising that German artists have contributed to this trend: in addition to *Kiesgrubennacht*, titles such as Barbara Yelin's *Irmina* (2014), Ulli Lust's *Flughunde* (2013; *The Karnau Tapes*, 2014), Nora Krug's *Belonging: A German Reckons with History and Home* (2018, later published in German as *Heimat: Ein deutsches Familienalbum*), and Bianca Schaalburg's *Der Duft der Kiefern* (The Scent of the Pines, 2021) all take up questions of perpetration, complicity, and bystandership.

This chapter considers Reiche's *Kiesgrubennacht* as the culmination of a larger autobiographical project that began with two short comics: the first published in the magazine *Zebra* in 2003 and the second published in 2008 in the *Frankfurter Allgemeine Zeitung* as a response to the German translation of the republication of Art Spiegelman's *Breakdowns*. I argue that *Kiesgrubennacht* takes many cues from Spiegelman's *Breakdowns*, incorporating its attention to dreams, its processing of familial postmemory, and its retrospective look at the artistic impulses that fueled a lengthy comics career. Of course, Reiche's second-generation memories are entirely different in nature from Spiegelman's since they are not of victimhood, but rather of perpetration, guilt, and

---

2   Nijdam and Sterling locate Marjane Satrapi's *Persepolis* (2000) as the catalyst for contemporary German comics' engagement with Germany's fraught past. Elizabeth Nijdam, "Introduction: The Social Justice Work of German Comics and Graphic Literature," *Seminar: A Journal of Germanic Studies* 56, nos. 3–4 (2020): 191–211, here 202; Brett Sterling, "Introduction: The Intersection of Comics Studies and German Studies," *Colloquia Germanica* 48, no. 4 (2015): 233–44, here 236.

3   Laurike in 't Veld, "Introduction," *Journal of Perpetrator Research* 4, no. 2 (2022): 1–13, here 2.

responsibility. *Kiesgrubennacht* contains not only Reiche's reflections on his parents' refusal to acknowledge their role in the atrocities of WWII, but on his own repression of these violent crimes, and his position as an "implicated subject"—a concept explored by Michael Rothberg to conceptualize subject positions inhabited by those who may not be directly involved in crimes but who nevertheless contribute to, inherit, or benefit from acts of violence, repression, or genocide.[4] Reiche employs different visual styles and adult and child avatars to navigate various levels of implication in a violent past and pose self-reflexive questions about the ways in which violence (domestic, state-perpetrated, and pop-culturally mediated forms) have shaped his life and art. Combining various contexts of, and representational approaches to violence (including Reiche's work in painting), *Kiesgrubennacht* also implicates readers, inviting us to reflect on the ethical implications of consuming images of violence. Together, the three autobiographical comics perform multilayered memory work that explores not only the memory of historical and private events, but the memory of the comics medium itself and the transnational impulses of both American and German comics that have informed Reiche's career.

Portraits of the Artist: Early Prototypes

Before the publication of *Kiesgrubennacht*, Volker Reiche published two short comics containing autobiographical material that can be seen as prototypes for his long-form memoir. The first of these is a four-page comic published in 2003 in *Zebra*, entitled "Ein Tag in meinem Leben" (A Day in My Life).[5] The comic depicts memories of a child's fifth birthday in 1949. We learn that the family are refugees who fled East Prussia at the end of the war and settled in a Bavarian village, while visual details of their living conditions inform the reader that financial resources are scarce in this family of five children. Although the comic is not explicitly labeled as autobiography, the title and author's signature appear together in large lettering at the top of the opening panel, suggesting an equivalence between the artist and narrator-protagonist. This equivalence is strengthened in the final panel which reveals the exact birthdate—May 31, 1949—which corresponds with Reiche's.

The material in "Ein Tag in meinem Leben" bears a striking resemblance to the third chapter of *Kiesgrubennacht*.[6] Like *Kiesgrubennacht*, "Ein Tag in meinem Leben" oscillates between happy childhood

---

4   Michael Rothberg, *The Implicated Subject: Beyond Victims and Perpetrators* (Standford, CA: Stanford University Press, 2019).
5   Volker Reiche, "Ein Tag in meinem Leben," *Zebra* 16 (2003): 25–28.
6   There are some notable differences between the two comics: the figures are not drawn identically in the two versions, the siblings' names are changed

memories and troubling scenes of domestic violence. Although the birthday begins well, things eventually take a sharp turn: when the mother complains of the father's frequent absences and his failure to provide for the family, he reacts violently and beats her to the ground as the children stand by, crying (fig. 7.1). Details in the visual and verbal tracks suggest the father was at the very least a Nazi sympathizer: his attire evokes Nazi styles of dress; and, in a passing remark, he bemoans losing the war along with the financial security he believes a victory would have secured for the family. While these visual and textual elements serve to link the domestic violence in the diegetic present with the state-sanctioned violence of the past, the precise nature of the parents' wartime activities and relationship to the Nazi regime are not explored in any further depth.

The family's involvement in the Nazi regime is explored further in a second short comic created in 2008 as a response to a new edition of Art Spiegelman's seminal work, *Breakdowns*. In the wake of the critical and popular acclaim of *Maus*, Pantheon Books republished Art Spiegelman's early volume *Breakdowns: From Maus to Now* (1977), an anthology of short strips that had appeared in various underground publications between 1972 and 1977. Published by Belier Press, the original version of *Breakdowns* contains a wide-ranging selection of Spiegelman's formative work, ranging from formally experimental to autobiographical comics, including "Maus," a three-page prototype of what would later become the longer, serialized *Maus*, as well as "Prisoner on the Hell Planet," which was later reproduced in the first volume of *Maus*. Under the new title *Breakdowns: Portrait of the Artist as a Young %@&~*!*, Pantheon's reprint comprises a facsimile of the original 1977 version along with new material authored by Spiegelman: an introduction consisting of twenty-four pages of full-color comics panels and a prose afterword illustrated with additional examples from his early work. The additional materials chronicle moments from Spiegelman's fraught childhood, offer a fresh assessment of the early work, and trace his artistic development up until 2008: his early childhood encounters with comics, the profound impact of MAD magazine, the origins of *Maus*, and the traumatic familial post-memory that shaped much of his work.

The original *Breakdowns* proved too unusual for its time to garner any commercial success or wider impact.[7] In contrast, the 2008 *Breakdowns*—

---

in the earlier, short version, and the memories in *Kiesgrubennacht* are associated with a sixth birthday in May 1950.

7   As Bob Levin explains, the book was "too ungainly, too expensive, and too odd for bookstores" and had "too little sex, too little violence and too few drugs" for the underground market and not "a single superhero leaping tall buildings to tempt the masses." Bob Levin, "Art," *The Comics Journal*, January 31, 2023, https://www.tcj.com/art/.

Figure 7.1. Scenes of domestic violence in Volker Reiche's "Ein Tag in meinem Leben," *Zebra* 16 (2003): 25.

published in the wake of both *Maus* and *In the Shadow of No Towers* (2004)—commanded considerable attention, including in Germany. To mark the publication of the German translation (2008), the *Frankfurter Allgemeine Zeitung* (*FAZ*) featured an interview in November 2008 with Art Spiegelman and created an online *Themenforum* dedicated to the significance of *Breakdowns* with contributions by comics scholars and comics artists, such as Ralf König, Paul Karasik, and Flix.[8] For the December 2, 2008, issue of the newspaper, *FAZ* editor Andreas Platthaus commissioned Volker Reiche to create a response to *Breakdowns*. The result was a six-page comic that considered the parallels between his own career and Spiegelman's and offered a personal reflection on his own connection to the traumatic history of the Holocaust memorialized in *Breakdowns*.

"Über *Breakdowns*"[9] opens with a visual reference to the cover of Spiegelman's newly released book, which features an older man (Spiegelman's avatar?), slipping on a copy of the original 1977 version—a nod to the slapstick humor usually associated with comics and the high-low cultural mix constitutive of Spiegelman's work. Instead of a man slipping on a book, the opening panel of "Über *Breakdowns*" depicts Herr Paul, the cantankerous cat from *Strizz*, who is slipping on the classic banana peel. Next to Herr Paul, we see an image of Reiche and a speech balloon with the text "Und noch 'n wahrer Traum" (And another real dream), a reference to the three "Real Dreams" comics in *Breakdowns* and a foreshadowing of the autobiographical and self-reflective turn that Reiche's comic will take.

---

8 "Volker Reiche zeichnet seine Lektüre von Art Spiegelmans *Breakdowns*," *Frankfurter Allgemeine Zeitung*, December 2, 2008, 33.

9 Volker Reiche, "Über *Breakdowns*," *Frankfurter Allgemeine Zeitung*, December 2, 2008, 33–36.

Figure 7.2. The opening image from Volker Reiche's "Über *Breakdowns*," *Frankfurter Allgemeine Zeitung*, December 2, 2008, 33.

Subsequent panels depict Reiche in his studio, reading Spiegelman's "Prachtband" (splendid volume) and commenting on the parallels between their contemporaneous careers: he notes their early work in underground comics ("*Breakdowns* kam 78 raus ... Mein erstes Comic-Buch *Liebe* 76" (*Breakdowns* appeared in 78 ... My first comic book *Liebe* [Love] in 76) and the prevalence of sexual material in these early works.[10] Facsimiles of sexually explicit panels from Spiegelman's "Little Signs of Passion" are juxtaposed with the image of a naked, sexually aroused Günter, a figure from Reiche's self-published debut, *Liebe: Ein Männer-Emanzo-Comic* (Love: A Men's Emancipation Comic), which emerged out of the sexual liberation movements of the 60s and 70s and was inspired by American underground comics such as those of Robert Crumb. Despite these parallels to Spiegelman, visual details and the verbal track take stock of obvious differences: Reiche's studio contains

10 The original edition of *Breakdowns* has a complicated publication history, which has led to commentators alternately listing the publication dates as either 1977 or 1978. Originally slated to be published by Nostalgia Press, the publisher ran out of funding and Belier Press stepped in to pick up the remaining printing costs. As Bob Levin notes, for this reason "some copies reached stores as being from Nostalgia Press and some as from Belier. Some bore a 1977 publication date and some 1978." WorldCat lists the publication date as 1977. Spiegelman humorously refers to the confusion over the publication data in the 2008 edition of *Breakdowns*. For more information on the publication history, see Levin, "Art."

filing cabinets labeled "Strizz," "Mehr Strizz," "Dito," "Mecki-Drecki," "Politik," "Noch mehr Politik," and "Finanz-Krise" ("Strizz," "More Strizz," "Ditto," "Mecki-Crap," "Politics," "Even More Politics," "Financial Crisis"), alluding to his strips in the *FAZ* and *Hörzu* and to contemporary political themes that have characterized his work. Looking back on his rodent-like character Günter from "Eines Tages bei Chris in der Küche" (One Day in Chris's Kitchen), one of the comics contained in *Liebe*, Reiche notes that he also made use of anthropomorphized animals, but with an entirely different thematic purpose: "Bei mir kam auch 'ne Maus vor … oder Ratte … weiß nicht mehr … aber ohne KZ … das hat mich zu der Zeit nicht beschäftigt" (A mouse also appeared in my work … or a rat … don't know any more … but without a concentration camp … I wasn't concerned with that at the time). A panel of Reiche as a young child in the 1950s signals that his lack of engagement was not due to a lack of knowledge: the panel depicts him with an older brother who has obtained a copy of Eugen Kogon's *Der SS-Staat: Das System der deutschen Konzentrationslager* (The SS-State: The System of German Concentration Camps) and is showing him photographs contained in the book that document various atrocities. Very little information, however, came from his parents. In contrast to the young protagonist of "Maus," whose father tells him "bedtime stories" about his experiences during the Holocaust, Reiche's parents, who were "stramme Nazis" (avid Nazis) and therefore "Unterstützer des Mordsystems" (supporters of the murderous system), remained largely silent about their wartime activities. His mother told only "schöne" (pretty) bedtime stories and provided sanitized versions of the past. Questioned by her children about the Holocaust, she avoids answering, saying only "War 'n schlimme Zeit" (it was a bad time), followed by the perversely cheerful observation: "Aber die russischen Kriegsgefangenen haben immer schön gesungen, Kinder!" (But the Russian prisoners of war always sang beautifully, children). We learn no further details about his father's role during the war but are told that his mother was a "ziemlich hohes Tier beim Wandervogel […] später BDM … Gauleiterin von Sachsen … Uff! Hört sich gruselig an …" (big shot in the Wandervogel […] later the League of German Girls … Gauleiter of Sachsen … Uff! Sounds creepy) and that she praised Hitler's "magnetischen Blick" (magnetic gaze) well into the postwar years.

Throughout these reflections, Herr Paul is intermittently visible in the panel frames, indifferent to his owner's reminiscences or his reaction to Spiegelman's work. Halfway through the comic, however, after he has been out of view for several panels, Herr Paul reappears, angrily shouting "Ruhe! Jetzt rede ich!" (Quiet! I'm talking now) to a startled Reiche. Not only can Reiche's cat communicate, he also has opinions about Spiegelman's comics. The effect is largely humorous—Herr Paul objects "im Namen aller beleidigten Katzen" (on behalf of all offended cats) to Spiegelman's use of animal metaphors, and especially to his rendering of Nazis as cats, recalling the initial controversy these metaphors caused, while Reiche's avatar defends Spiegelman's artistic choice. As the debate becomes heated, a panel transition shows Reiche jolting awake, revealing that he had fallen asleep; the argument was only a dream. The abrupt awakening from a dream can be seen as a nod to Winsor McCay's *Little Nemo in Slumberland*, which depicts the dreamworlds of the title character, from which he would always awaken in the final panel. But it is also a reference to *Breakdowns*, which features several surreal dream sequences and includes similar intertextual references, to McCay and to the long and varied comics tradition that preceded Spiegelman.[11] Having established the artifice of his dream about Herr Paul, Reiche proceeds to offer "einen wahren Traum! Von mir! Und echt wahr! Ich schwöre!" (a true dream! Of mine! And for real! I swear!).

The "true dream" that Reiche presents takes its cue from the third "Real Dream" comic in *Breakdowns*, which we see Reiche reading in an earlier frame. In a panel depicting the artist and three younger versions of himself at different life stages, Reiche introduces a scenario that he claims he dreamt of repeatedly as a child, an adolescent, and a young man (fig. 7.3). The next panel shows this dream: Reiche, dressed in the same plaid shirt as in previous panels, is in a darkened basement, his hair standing on end as he looks in horror at a pile of coal. A text box elaborates: "Ich soll Kohlen holen. Ich betrete den Keller und sehe den großen schwarzen Kohlenhaufen und weiß sofort, dass darunter tote Menschen liegen, blutig, zerrissen, zermanscht, ein grässlicher Brei und weiß mit Gewissheit, dass es **meine** Leichen sind. Namenloses Entsetzen und überwältigendes Schuldbewusstsein lähmen mich" (I'm supposed to fetch coal. I enter the basement and see the large, black pile of coal and know immediately that dead people are lying underneath, bloody, torn, and mangled, a ghastly mush and I know with certainty that they are my corpses). Pictured back in his studio, Reiche addresses the readers, who, he believes, will interpret the dream as a pictorial rendering of the expression: "Jeder hat seine Leiche im Keller" (Everybody has a corpse in his basement). Reiche surmises that his dreams were likely fueled by books about the Holocaust that he did not fully comprehend, along with his parents' silence, a "Täter Traum ... In der zweiten Generation ... Tja Artie ..." (A perpetrator dream ... in the second generation ... well, Artie ...). With this "real dream" Reiche responds to Spiegelman's explorations of postmemory, a term coined by Marianne Hirsch to refer to the transmission of traumatic

11 Christian Gasser, "Zusammenbrüche, Mäuse und Türme," *FAZ. NET*, December 15, 2008, https://www.faz.net/aktuell/feuilleton/comic-spezial/diskussion/breakdowns-und-oubapo-zusammenbrueche-maeuse-und-tuerme-1739666.html.

Figure 7.3. The "real dream" in Volker Reiche's "Über Breakdowns."

knowledge and experience from one generation to the next, a "powerful form of memory precisely because its connection to its object or source is mediated not through recollection but through representation, projection, and creation—often based on silence rather than speech, on the invisible rather than the visible."[12] In "Über *Breakdowns*," Reiche offers personal, familial memories of his own; however, Reiche's second-generation memories are not of victimhood and suffering, but rather of perpetration, guilt, and responsibility. While Reiche probes his relationship to the crimes of National Socialism in this short comic, the direct familial connection is explored in much greater detail in his long-form memoir *Kiesgrubennacht*.

---

12 Marianne Hirsch, "Surviving Images: Holocaust Photographs and the Work of Postmemory," *The Yale Journal of Criticism* 14, no. 1 (2001): 5–37, here 9.

Kiesgrubennacht: A Childhood in the Shadow of Violence

Kiesgrubennacht builds on the two short comics from the 2000s. Without mimicking *Breakdowns*, Reiche's memoir incorporates some of its components: the autofictional elements, the engagement with the familial past, and a retrospective look at an artistic career-in-the-making. Although *Kiesgrubennacht* consists of one longer narrative unit rather than several shorter self-contained comics, it combines a variety of generic forms and drawing styles, navigating a complex position between entertainment, testimony, memory work, political commentary, and family reckoning in visual genres and styles ranging from modernist expressionism to funny animal comics and kid strips. Reviewer Lars von Törne characterizes it as a book of contrasts, full of real and fictive elements and alternately humorous and disturbing, a "Wechselbad der Gefühle und Perspektiven" (a rollercoaster ride of emotions and perspectives).[13]

The reader is introduced to these contrasts via the front cover which pictures a young Volker, drawn in a clear line cartoon style, contemplating four large panels from Reiche's series "Kiesgrubennacht"—a set of sketches and acrylic paintings from 1999 (fig. 7.4). The boy is drawn in black and white, with his hand on his chin and a slightly puzzled expression as he gazes at the large-format, full-color panels rendered in an expressionist style in palettes of blue, red, and orange. In terms of color and scale, the panels dominate the cover and contrast starkly with the simplicity of the drawing of the boy. The subject matter of the panels is not immediately discernible; they show human figures, one with a gaping mouth suggestive of pain and torment and reminiscent of Spiegelman's drawings of suffering mice in *Maus*. This composition foreshadows the contrasting styles that appear in the book, the memoir's mix of lightheartedness and brutality, and the themes of spectatorship, violence, and the suffering body. The cover image of the young boy who observes but does not fully understand what he sees also introduces the narrative perspective: readers experience events in the family home through the eyes of the young narrator-protagonist between the ages of four and nine.

In *Kiesgrubennacht*, Reiche employs a two-fold narrative structure, embedding memories of events between 1948 and 1973 in a more contemporary frame that depicts the artist composing his memoir between the summer of 2012 and the spring of 2013. The two narrative tracks progress in alternating chapters: after each remembered episode, the artist discusses his work-in-progress with the animal characters from his comic

---

[13] Lars von Törne, "Volker Reiche's *Kiesgrubennacht*: Blick in den Abgrund," *Tagesspiegel*, November 25, 2013, https://www.tagesspiegel.de/kultur/comics/blick-in-den-abgrund-3531757.html.

Figure 7.4. The cover of Reiche's *Kiesgrubennacht*.

strip *Strizz*: the argumentative and domineering Herr Paul, the pensive dachshund Müller, and the gentle guard dog Tassilo. The ongoing conversation with his *Strizz* figures is reminiscent of the dream sequence in "Über *Breakdowns*" where the artist discusses Spiegelman's comic with Herr Paul. But it also draws on a strategy familiar from Reiche's earlier works. In *Liebe*, for example, Reiche appears throughout the work as a cartoon figure, directly addressing the reader, discussing pages contained in the collection with other characters who critique his artistic choices or offer alternative perspectives on the material.[14] A similar technique is used in the first volume of *Erwachsenen-Comics aus deutschen Landen* (Adult Comics from German Lands), where Schnurr, one of the animal figures in the collection, argues with Reiche about everything from his drawing style to his choice of content.[15] These episodes offer a self-reflexive metacommentary on the different interpretive possibilities and reader responses that specific authorial choices may elicit and highlight the constructed nature of the work. The frame also confronts readers with key questions that the embedded material raises and refuses consumption for entertainment value alone. In this regard, *Kiesgrubennacht* shares the pedagogical tone of some representative works of the German alternative and underground comix scene in which Reiche participated with works like *Liebe*, which was fueled by a desire to spur its readership to reflection and potentially to action and social change.[16] While *Kiesgrubennacht* does not issue the same call for activism, the shared technique of the frame narrative is reminiscent of previous works in Reiche's artistic career.

While the memoir's cover foreshadows some of the darker themes that *Kiesgrubennacht* tackles, the opening chapter begins in a deceptively bright and colorful style reminiscent of children's comics. The opening pages depict an afternoon idyll, as the young narrator-protagonist enjoys a picnic with his mother and siblings. He recalls the peaceful natural environment, his delight in listening to his older brother reading Wilhelm Busch to his siblings, and the joy he took in his new yellow overalls. This perfect day sours, however, when he soils his beloved overalls; his mother's promise that, once washed, the outfit will be good as new is not fulfilled. Now a poisonous green, the ruined overalls no longer hold any appeal. The protagonist refuses to wear them and in a private moment,

---

14 Sylvia Kesper-Biermann, "Man erreicht etwas, das an Authentizität grenzt," in *Echt inszeniert: Historische Authentizität und Medien in der Moderne*, ed. Christoph Classen, Achim Saupe, and Hans-Ulrich Wagner (Potsdam: Leibniz-Zentrum für Zeithistorische Forschung, 2021), 241–64, here 46.

15 A figure in *Liebe* disparagingly refers to the technique as "'Zeichner zeichnet Zeichner'-Masche" ("artist-draws-artist" scheme). Volker Reiche, *Liebe: Ein Männer-Emanzo-Comic (??!)* (Frankfurt am Main: Reiche-Comics-Verlag, 1976), 55.

16 Kesper-Biermann, "Man erreicht etwas, das an Authentizität grenzt," 40.

kicks them across the room in anger. The mix of emotional registers—joy, disappointment, and anger—of carefree and troubled memories sets the tone for the rest of the memoir.

This early disruption of nostalgic memories of a bittersweet childhood is further developed in subsequent chapters that offer a disturbing portrait of a child growing up in the shadow of violence: the state-perpetrated violence of the Second World War, which the narrator was too young to experience first-hand, and the ongoing domestic violence in the family home, which he witnessed frequently. These two forms of violence are embodied in the family's tyrannical patriarch, who photographed and documented various atrocities in his role as a war correspondent. The memoir's unusual title refers to one of these atrocities recounted to the narrator-protagonist by his father, who otherwise remained silent about his experiences during the war. The story pertains to a mass execution the father witnessed, which occurred over the course of one night in or beside a gravel pit. A central and ultimately unanswered question in the memoir is whether the father actively participated in these mass murders. This question is conveyed by the memoir's title page in an image of the young protagonist, standing lost in thought against a blank background. A thought bubble shows two figures in extreme close-up so that only their forearms and hands are visible: we see an outstretched hand offering a gun from the left edge of the frame and the text "Auch mal?" (Do you want to have a go?). The forearm and hand of a second figure are visible at the right edge of the frame, but the single image does not reveal whether the offer of the gun is accepted. At this stage readers may not comprehend the significance of this image and may be as puzzled as the young boy on the cover appears to be; it is only towards the end of the memoir that Reiche's adult avatar relays the story of the gravel pit and his father's claim that he declined the pistol, a claim that the artist cannot verify and therefore doubts.

In the lead-up to this episode, readers are offered ample evidence of the father's enthusiastic support for the Nazi regime. A self-proclaimed "Sänger und Künder des Nationalsozialismus" (poet and prophet of National Socialism),[17] he composed and published poetry that glorified Hitler and National Socialism and justified murderous territorial expansion eastward. Despite his fascist past, by 1953 the father holds a position of authority as a magistrate. He is an authoritarian father and domineering husband who is frequently absent, makes important decisions without consulting his wife or considering her well-being, and squanders money while leaving his family without sufficient resources. When confronted by his wife, he beats her brutally in front of the children. Two scenes of

---

17 Volker Reiche, *Kiesgrubennacht* (Berlin: Suhrkamp, 2013), 71. Further references are given using the abbreviation *K*.

physical assault are included in the memoir. While the father does not physically assault the children, they are terrorized by his unpredictable moods, unreasonable demands, and sadistic behavior. A particularly disturbing memory involves the father killing the children's pet hamster as they stand by because he is bothered by the animal's odor and blames the children for "neglecting" their pet.

A committed Nazi and "Familienfaschist" (family fascist),[18] the father's actions are enough to alienate readers. His depiction furthers this alienation, since he is drawn with his eyes obscured, which visually sets him apart from other figures in the comic. The other characters' eyes are rendered with small dots or, in the case of Reiche's adult avatar, Herr Paul, and Tassilo, in greater detail, including pupils and eyelids, whereas the father's eyeglasses are usually opaque, offering no glimpse of his eyes at all.[19] Laurike in 't Veld locates a similar strategy in Joe Sacco's journalistic comics about conflict zones, in which the eyes of perpetrators are not shown. She observes that "eyes form the connection with the humanity of the perpetrators and by not showing them, Sacco can evade the motivation behind their behavior."[20] The invisibility of the father's eyes has a similar effect and serves as a visual metaphor for his son's inability to fully understand or predict his father's erratic behavior, and for his inability later in life to find the truth about his father's participation in mass violence. This strategy risks denying the father's humanity, thus creating a figure readers can easily distance themselves from while avoiding complex investigations of the motivations for or routes to perpetration. A more nuanced portrait is nevertheless offered through the figure of the mother who is a caring parent and a victim of domestic abuse, but also a committed National Socialist. *Kiesgrubennacht* informs readers that she was a regional leader (Gauleiterin) of the National Socialist youth organization Bund Deutscher Mädel. Asked by her children to tell them about the war, she is initially evasive and then recalls the beautiful songs of Russian prisoners of war (*K*, 148); she also remembers once seeing Hitler in person and describes his "magnetischen Blick" (*K*, 149; magnetic gaze). To her, the war was a "schöne Zeit" (*K*, 149; beautiful time), a statement that she qualifies when questioned by her son: "Nein, Spätzchen. Aber ich war jung. Und gesund. Und—lassen wir das" (*K*, 149; No, dear. But I was young. And healthy. And—let's leave it at that). In these panels, the

---

18 Martina Knoben, "Horror in der Lederhose," *Süddeutsche Zeitung*, January 16, 2014.

19 Dietmar Dath, "Erwachsene Kindersicht, unversöhnt wahr," *Frankfurter Allgemeine Zeitung*, November 1, 2013, https://www.faz.net/aktuell/feuilleton/buecher/rezensionen/belletristik/volker-reiche-kiesgrubennacht-erwachsene-kindersicht-unversoehnt-wahr-12642896.html.

20 in 't Veld, "Introduction," 75.

mother is drawn with facial expressions of joy, a rarity in this memoir of otherwise bleak moments. The verbal and visual tracks suggest a woman who looks back on her wartime experiences with nostalgic fondness and who has not assessed her own level of guilt or responsibility. This lack of accountability or reckoning is further intensified in a scene in which the mother makes antisemitic comments that her young son does not understand (*K*, 100–101), but that for readers establish her continued adherence to antisemitic ideology well into the postwar period. These scenes complicate any empathy readers may have felt for her in the initial chapters of the memoir, which recount the mother's experiences of domestic violence and her struggle to care for the family with scarce resources. Reader responses may oscillate between sympathy and revulsion, mirroring the difficult relationship that children may have with family members once they learn of their complicity. Reiche's adult avatar grapples with this complexity in the final pages of the frame narrative, as he recounts his estrangement from his mother, who descended into alcoholism after her divorce. In the figure of his mother, Reiche breaks with simple dichotomies of perpetrator and victim, offering a multifaceted portrait.

Reiche also offers a nuanced self-portrait that does not always place him in a positive light, moving between naïve, childlike perspectives and self-aware feelings of guilt. Employing an "Erwachsene Kindersicht" (adult child perspective),[21] memory sequences show how the young boy is easily manipulated by his father's occasional attention and, in the birthday sequence, how this susceptibility inadvertently plays into his father's emotional abuse. Other scenes show how quickly he forgets and moves on from brutal episodes of domestic violence, unlike his older brother who repeatedly admonishes him for his obliviousness. In the frame narrative, Reiche's adult avatar expresses remorse over the estrangement from his mother, but also acknowledges the difficulty of growing up with her alcoholism and threats of suicide. Reiche includes his memories of his last encounter with his father in 1973, which reveal his inability to confront him about the mass executions he witnessed. After a long estrangement, he visits his father with a view to finally ascertaining his father's involvement. After the first attempt is cut short, he visits a second time with his partner and their child, but when questioned, his father denies any recollection of the story. Taking his agitation out on the young boy, Reiche's father becomes physically aggressive, and the boy's mother abruptly ends their visit. The frame narrative reveals that afterward Reiche broke off all contact with his father; the extent of his father's involvement in the mass executions remains an open question. This episode, along with many sequences in which the young child stands by and witnesses his father commit acts of violence, is contrasted with a memory of the youngest

---

21   Dath, "Erwachsene Kindersicht, unversöhnt wahr."

brother intervening to protect his mother from his father's physical abuse. The sequence closes with an image of the two brothers playing together, the elder allowing the younger to direct their play: "insgeheim hielt ich ihn für einen Helden" (*K*, 196; I secretly thought he was a hero). While not explicitly stated, together these sequences suggest an awareness, if not regret, about his persistent inaction and repression.

The most explicit expression of feelings of guilt, however, comes in the form of a dream, the same 'real dream' already explored in "Über *Breakdowns*," a nightmare in which the young boy makes a horrific discovery amongst the family's pile of coal. The dream is rendered on one page of the memoir in two panels (*K*, 187). The smaller panel shows the young boy asleep in his bed, with a thought bubble revealing the scene of the nightmare: the young boy stands in the basement in front of the coal wondering why he has been sent downstairs on his own. A second, much larger panel comprising two thirds of the page shows the sleeping boy in the lower right corner, now in a fitful state and crying out as the nightmare reaches its climax; a thought bubble fills the panel with an image of the boy discovering bodies hidden in the pile. *Kiesgrubennacht* renders the nightmare in even more gruesome fashion than "Über *Breakdowns*": severed body parts and blood are depicted amongst the coal, not in black and white, but in color with an explanatory text box: "Was unter den Kohlen zum Vorschein kam, war schlimm. Schlimmer war, dass offenbar ich allein Schuld daran war und ich Angst hatte, meine Schandtaten könnten entdeckt werden" (*K*, 187; What was visible under the coals was bad. Worse, it seemed that I was solely to blame, and I was afraid my shameful crimes might be discovered). The nightmare is not given any further explanation, but directly follows a sequence in which the young boy discovers his older brother's copy of Eugen Kogon's *Der SS-Staat*, suggesting that the nightmare is a way of processing information about the atrocities committed by the Nazi regime. Here, guilt and shame mark the protagonist's growing awareness of his implication in historical events. Later he will explore, but never fully uncover his family's direct connections to the Nazi past.

Autobiography, Memory, and the Comics Form

In terms of its content, *Kiesgrubennacht* treads well-worn territory. Martina Knoben argues that the originality of Reiche's memoir lies not in the topic of family complicity in the crimes of National Socialism, but in its treatment in the comics form.[22] Highlighting the obviously mediated nature of the comics form, *Kiesgrubennacht* devotes as much attention to

---

22 Knoben, "Horror in der Lederhose."

reflections on the artist's ability to access and document memories as it does to the individual memories themselves.

Questions of memory are first posed in the book's frontmatter in an image of Reiche's adult avatar who mimics the posture of the young boy on the front cover. Reiche holds his hand to his chin in a contemplative pose, and a speech bubble considers the fictional elements inherent in life writing and relinquishes any claims to verifiable truth. Later in the frame narrative, Reiche's adult avatar explains that his memoir is an exploration of the nature of memory, its reliability, and veracity (*K*, 26). Noting recent research into the workings of memory and the brain's desire to save energy through imprecise versus exact recall, the protagonist-narrator explains that he has not consulted any historical archives or interviewed family members about their memories of the events he wishes to recount, but instead wants to document what his own memories yield (*K*, 69). As a result, the memoir does not present a detailed portrait of any extended period, but relays memories in an episodic manner; each chapter is set in a different year and concentrates on a singular event or short time span, sometimes incorporating flashbacks to earlier time periods. The recorded memories do not unfold in a linear fashion; they leap forward and backward in time and leave many gaps, offering no more than snapshots and fragmented impressions, mimicking the workings of memory. The different degrees of recall are reflected in the varying levels of detail provided in the panel frames: for instance, panels depicting rooms in the family home or the surrounding landscape are often rendered with many visual details, while other panels provide no background details at all, picturing figures against a blank backdrop.

Moreover, the very presence of a frame narrative—which pictures the artist with finished pages from the memoir, making notes, questioning its structure, and discussing the work in progress with other comics characters—draws attention to the process of the graphic narrative's construction. This depiction of the artist at work is a common technique in autobiographical comics, which tend to foreground the split between autographer and subject while rejecting the collapse of author, narrator, and protagonist typically found in other media of testimony. As Jared Gardner has argued, because of their obviously mediated nature, comics cannot easily deny their status as discourse and therefore do not claim evidentiary status in the same way as other image- or text-based forms of documentary media: "the stylized comic art refuses any claims to the 'having-been-there' truth, even (or especially) on the part of those who really were."[23] But this is not to say that comics relinquish their status as evidence or as media capable of documenting the past. Rather than

---

23 Jared Gardner, "Autography's Biography, 1972–2007," *Biography* 31, no. 1 (2008): 1–26, here 12.

disqualifying comics' documentary status because of their unique formal properties, scholars such as Sylvia Kesper-Biermann have shown that it was precisely the decision to foreground, rather than obscure, the mediated nature of comics that led to a shift in the perception of comic art in Germany. Concentrating on German-language historical comics, Kesper-Biermann shows how in the 1950s comics were perceived as an inauthentic medium unsuitable for meaningful explorations of the past. This changed fundamentally in the 1970s with the rise of alternative adult comics, which were prized for their medial qualities.[24] Employing what Charles Hatfield has termed "ironic authentication," these autobiographical comics self-reflexively laid bare their constructed and subjective nature, claiming a "sense of honesty by denying the very possibility of being honest."[25] As Kesper-Biermann, Charles Hatfield, Elisabeth El Refaie,[26] and others have shown, comics that showcase their own artificiality and status as representation through self-reflexive "Offenlegung medialer Prozesse" (disclosure of medial processes)[27] are often perceived as more honest and therefore more, rather than less, authentic.

In *Kiesgrubennacht*, "ironic authentication" is achieved primarily through the discussions that the artist's avatar has with his anthropomorphized animal figures from the *Strizz* universe. Herr Paul and Müller in particular serve to highlight the artists' choices and to point out ambiguities, showing that the form in which the memoir is presented to the reader is one of many potential directions it could have taken. The argumentative Herr Paul takes issue with many aspects of the artist's memoir: he dismisses it as "widerwärtiger Egotrip" (*K*, 26; appalling ego trip) and expresses his suspicion that the artist is selectively presenting the facts to portray himself in a more favorable light, a depiction he finds "wenig glaubwürdig" (*K*, 136; not very credible). Müller voices his concerns over the illustrations that accompany one of the father's poems, worrying that they could be understood as an attempt to exculpate his father from participation in war crimes. These interventions draw attention to the ways in which the memories have been represented and highlight the fact that documentary comics frame past events in such a way as to make a particular argument. As Johannes Schmid notes, documentary film scholar Bill Nichols "likens the role of documentarian to a lawyer: both reconstruct past events in a particular manner in order to make a case for

---

24 Kesper-Biermann, "Man erreicht etwas, das an Authentizität grenzt," 259.
25 Charles Hatfield, *Alternative Comics: An Emerging Literature* (Jackson: University Press of Mississippi, 2005), 125–26.
26 Elisabeth El Refaie, *Autobiographical Comics: Life Writing in Pictures* (Jackson: University Press of Mississippi, 2012), 91.
27 Kesper-Biermann, "Man erreicht etwas, das an Authentizität grenzt," 253.

their 'clients.'"[28] Hillary Chute similarly notes the function of the documentary as "the presentation of evidence" and sees in the architecture of comics, and specifically the unit of the panel, "the inclination to document," while at the same time making visible the comics' framing devices and revealing its own process of making.[29] As Schmid, following Nichols, elaborates, "documentaries may represent the world in the same way a lawyer may represent a client's interests: they put the case for a particular view or interpretation of evidence before us."[30] To build on Nichols's analogy, in *Kiesgrubennacht*, the *Strizz* characters serve up a sort of cross-examination, debating with the artist-avatar the soundness of his case and the strength of his presentation of the facts of his childhood. This is taken a step further in a chapter titled "Das Verhör" (The Interrogation), in which Herr Paul and the artist discuss the nature of memory. When the artist claims that his memoir is governed by what he can remember and that he has no control over which memories surface, Herr Paul stages a mock trial, accusing the author of "perjury," that is, of falsely denying his own role in the selection and framing of his recollections. This sequence underscores the statements made at the outset of the memoir about the fictive elements of life writing. This is not to deny the documentary status of life writing, but to highlight its dependence on narrative to produce meaning and the potential to reconstruct past events—or memories of past events—through different modes of representation.

The *Strizz* characters also serve another purpose in a memoir that repeatedly points to various stations along the protagonist's journey as an artist. Throughout the text, we see the young boy drawing and reading, activities that offer refuge from the ongoing domestic violence. A gift of the children's book *Der Hüter Toni wird Maler* (Toni the Herder Becomes a Painter) mirrors the boy's artistic development while the comics he reads speak to some of the German and American influences in Volker Reiche's career: Wilhelm Busch (whose borderless panels Reiche adopts in much of his work),[31] Micky Mouse, and Donald Duck (the character he drew for the Dutch publisher Oberon). The disputes with Herr Paul remind us of earlier comics such as *Erwachsenen-Comics aus*

---

28 Johannes Schmid, *Frames and Framing in Documentary Comics* (Cham: Palgrave Macmillan, 2021), 31.

29 Hillary L. Chute, *Disaster Drawn: Visual Witness, Comics, and Documentary Form* (Cambridge, MA: Belknap Press of Harvard University Press, 2016), 2 and 18.

30 Schmid, *Frames and Framing in Documentary Comics*, 31.

31 For an excellent survey of the influence of Wilhelm Busch in German and American comics, and the dual lineage of German picture stories and American comics that many contemporary German-language comics artists claim, see Daniel Stein, "The Long Shadow of Wilhelm Busch," *International Journal of Comic Art* 12, no. 2/3 (2010): 291–308.

Deutschland, in which the artist's avatar fights with his fictive character Schnurr, while the presence of the Strizz characters represent a high point of Reiche's success with his daily strip in the *FAZ*. Herr Paul, Müller, and Tassilo also discuss Reiche's paintings, which can be seen in the artist's studio and are used to illustrate one of his father's poems. The *Strizz* characters thus reference Reiche's artistic development, a trajectory that is only hinted at in the memory sequences. In this aspect, *Kiesgrubennacht* circles back to some of the main thematic preoccupations of "Uber Breakdowns," combining Reiche's reckoning with his family's past and a retrospective look at his artistic career.

Representations of Violence

In its self-reflexive examination of its own modes of representation, *Kiesgrubennacht* devotes particular attention to representations of violence. Violence is a central preoccupation of the memoir, most obviously in its depiction of domestic violence and its reflections on the mass violence and genocide of the Second World War, but it also considers more broadly the role that violence and representations of violence play in popular culture. Reiche's childhood memories are replete with violent imagery and the artifacts of war. He and his siblings play war games such as "Stalinorgel" and set up a war museum with discarded objects, such as helmets and a gas mask. A local homeless man is imagined to be a child murderer, the village children trade stories of gruesome accidents involving American tanks, and the family attends a violent boxing match billed as entertainment for St. Nicholas Day at the local inn. Reiche depicts his younger self struggling to distinguish between the various types and contexts of violence he encounters, from the knockabout or slapstick violence in Wilhelm Busch comics or his father's jokes, to the corporal punishment meted out by his mother or other villagers, to the domestic violence in his own home. This is mirrored in the frame narrative, in which Reiche's avatar and his *Strizz* characters grapple with questions about representations of violence across the media landscape, questions that have also preoccupied Reiche in his paintings, for example, in exhibits and catalogs such as *Killing is Fun* or *Friendly Fire*. In his paintings, Reiche cites iconic photographs, the canon of fine art, film, and other popular culture forms to explore what Mark Seltzer has called "wound culture," a public culture in which violence and bodily suffering have become public spectacle and that provides identity through a "convening of the public around scenes of violence ... the milling around the point of impact ... the public fascination with torn and open bodies and torn and opened persons, a collective gathering around shock, trauma, and the wound."[32] We see the artist sorting through these paintings in his studio, as he selects works and makes notes for an upcoming exhibit. Müller expresses surprise that, after having experienced so much violence, the artist would choose to explore themes of violence, while Herr Paul accuses the artist of taking pleasure in creating images of spectacular violence, a charge that the artist rejects. In real-world interviews about these paintings, Reiche has articulated both his uneasiness about and fascination with representations of violence in fine art and popular culture. He acknowledges his own penchant for thriller, horror, and fantasy genres, popular films by Emmerich and Tarantino, TV shows such as *Breaking Bad*, and video games[33]: in fact, readers of *Kiesgrubennacht* first encounter Reiche's adult avatar at his computer, battling virtual demons in the video game *Diablo*. Reiche has nevertheless questioned the function of these representations and the pleasure audiences take in images and simulations of spectacular violence: why do we find representations of violence—in its various forms, from classical fine art (such as the image of Laocoon and his sons that appears in *Kiesgrubennacht*) to Hollywood action films, computer games or murder mysteries—so endlessly entertaining, even humorous?[34] While these questions are explored in his painting, Reiche has commented that he is not interested in infusing his comics with representations of violence. In a conversation with Ralf König and Andreas C. Knigge on the project *Wilhelm Busch und die Folgen*, for which Reiche contributed a comic, Reiche explains that although comics like *Strizz* deal with current events, including war, he rejects the use of violent representations in his own work:

> Für mich gibt es überhaupt keinen Anlass, meine Comic-Figuren in irgendeiner Weise gewalttätig werden zu lassen. […] Ich will noch nicht mal das Busch-Prinzip—nämlich, dass das komisch ist. Das gibt es ja nicht nur bei Busch, sondern das durchzieht ganz breit unsere Medien—nicht nur im Kino auch in Computerspielen etwa. Es ist komisch, Leute zu quälen.[35]

---

32 Mark Seltzer, *Serial Killers: Death and Life in America's Wound Culture* (New York: Routledge, 1998), 1.

33 See Reiche's interview with Andreas Platthaus in Volker Reiche, Dietmar Dath, Andreas Platthaus, and Friedrich Weltzien, *Killing is Fun: Malerei con Volker Reiche* (Frankfurt am Main: Edition Faust, 2015), 16.

34 Alexander Jürgs, "Volker Reiche," *Schirn Mag*, January 29, 2014, https://www.schirn.de/magazin/kontext/volker_reiche/.

35 Andreas Knigge, "Ralph König und Volker Reiche über 'Wilhelm Busch und die Folgen,'" *Comixene* 101 (2008): 27–32, here 32.

[For me there is absolutely no reason to let my comics characters become violent in any way. [...] I don't even want the Busch principle—namely, that it's funny. You don't just get that with Busch; it pervades our media more broadly—not just in film but in video games, for example. It's funny to torment people.]

Of course, *Kiesgrubennacht* does include scenes of violence, prompting a discussion between the artist's avatar and his comics characters about the nature of these representations. Herr Paul reminds the artist that "action sells" (*K*, 71) and complains that the second chapter, which portrays scenes of domestic violence, contains only "eine einzige lausige Ohrfeige" (*K*, 70; one lousy slap in the face), knocking the artist's pencil out of his hand to stress his point. The artist insists he will not produce "eine Superhelden-Klopperei von zehn Seiten ... Das ist meine Mutter, die da verprügelt wird!" (*K*, 70; a ten-page superhero brawl ... that's my mother being beaten there). In fact, the scene of domestic violence is condensed into only three panels: in one, the father hits the mother, in the second we see her bloody and crumpled on the ground, and in the third she examines her bruised face to test whether her nose has been broken (*K*, 57). The events that occur between the first and second panel are not pictured; instead, a text box informs that the father "schlug sie mit gezielten Hieben zu Boden" (*K*, 57; knocked her to the ground with well-aimed blows). Herr Paul's complaint about the lack of violent visual representation is rendered in a panel that echoes the scene of domestic violence. Herr Paul (*K*, 70) is pictured in precisely the same physical posture as the father in the moment he hits his wife (*K*, 57), with comparable facial features (a similarly positioned red, open mouth and eyebrows) and an expression of rage. Both images use the same speed lines and a star to indicate motion and point of impact, while the pencil, in vertical flight, takes up the space occupied by the mother in the earlier panel. This visual echoing is repeated when Herr Paul mocks Müller for the sweater he is wearing (*K*, 131), mirroring the father's mocking of his wife in another display of his domestic tyranny (*K*, 118). This technique risks trivializing its subject matter, rendering the father as cartoonish and therefore benign, but it also may have the opposite effect, rendering the slapstick humor uncomfortable as it evokes memories of the physical and psychological abuse in the home. It also links the temporal levels of the memoir, which otherwise remain strictly separate, and prompts reflection on the ways in which the artist's childhood experiences may have shaped his art, a legacy most noticeable in his paintings.

The inclusion of other, non-comics media both references the multifaceted nature of Reiche's artistic practice and places the memoir within a larger terrain of public displays and spectacles of violence. This is most explicitly achieved in the illustrations that accompany one of the fascist poems written by Reiche's father. The full-page illustrations break with the comics style of the rest of the memoir; with their bold color palette of blues, reds, and orange and visible brush strokes, they are more akin to the acrylic paintings reproduced on the memoir's front cover. They thus mark a different register, and as single images they slow down the narrative pull of the sequential images that dominate the memoir. While the father's poem attempts to justify the eastward territorial expansion and genocide of National Socialism, the images employ contemporary iconography reminiscent of Hollywood action films or video games in which men brandish modern weaponry and slaughter alien, monstrous creatures. It is at this point that Müller objects: in his view the anachronous images that point to virtual—rather than historical—reality could be construed as minimizing the crimes of National Socialism or as an attempt to exculpate his father (*K*, 85). The artist explains that while he in no way means to equate a poem supporting actual genocide with virtual representations of fictional violence, he is still troubled by his own participation in forms of entertainment that facilitate fantasies of murder and mayhem based on a rhetoric of survival against threats of otherness (*K*, 92–94). Their debate remains unresolved, but it serves to implicate readers who have been slowed down in their consumption of the various representations of violence in the text. As Dietmar Dath, writing on the different effects between sequential and single images puts it, comics encourage readers to move quickly through spectacular scenes, as the eye is continuously drawn to the next panel in the sequence.[36] The illustrations thwart this urge to move on to the next image, inviting the viewer to contemplate the scenes of spectacular violence and, prompted by the meta-narrative, to assess their own reactions to these images and to spectacles of violence more generally.

Conclusion

Kiesgrubennacht can be seen as the culmination of an ongoing autobiographical project that began with Reiche's two short comics from the 2000s and that synthesizes the many ways in which Reiche has engaged with themes of violence in his work. Although not mimicking *Breakdowns*, *Kiesgrubennacht* builds on his engagement with Spiegelman's text, and incorporates *Breakdowns*'s preoccupation with dreams, its attention to traumatic family memories, and its retrospective look at the artistic impulses that have underpinned a successful career. Incorporating the "real dream" from his 2008 comic, Reiche's memoir is a reflection not only on his parents' roles in the atrocities of WWII, but on his inability

---

36 Dietmar Dath, "Malen, Töten, Schauen, Sterben: Über den Gesichtskreis des Malers Volker Reiche," in *Killing is Fun*, 71–81, here 75.

to confront his father and his growing awareness of his own implication in this violent past. Adding a frame narrative allows him to examine the ways in which he has processed a family legacy of perpetration and the many forms of violence that have shaped his life and influenced his artistic practice. The memoir moves beyond old debates about the suitability of comics for traumatic subjects, and while discussions about the disturbing nature of spectacular representations of violence may seem to echo the moral panic that surrounded comics in the 1950s—now transferred to concerns around film or video games—the violent imagery found in Reiche's paintings and in the pages of *Kiesgrubennacht* suggest a different line of thought. Combining various contexts of, and representational approaches to violence, Reiche explores how representations of violence are so prevalent that they often go unremarked. If *Kiesgrubennacht* invites us to look at scenes of violence, it does so not simply to entertain, but to look more carefully: to provoke reflection on the challenges and ethical implications of various approaches to representation and to consider our role as witnesses, spectators, or voyeurs.

8: Comics on Display: Conceptual Remarks on *Gewalt erzählen: Eine Comic-Ausstellung* / *Narrating Violence: A Comic Exhibition* (Sigmund Freud Museum Vienna)

Marina Rauchenbacher

THE EXHIBITION *Narrating Violence: A Comic Exhibition* was on display in the Viennese Sigmund Freud Museum from October 22, 2023, until April 8, 2024. The museum opted to organize this exhibition for several reasons. Firstly, the museum's annual 2023 theme was "violence," with a focus on sexualized violence. Second, the museum team, Monika Pessler (director), Peter Nömaier (business director), and Daniela Finzi (research director), sought to explore new media within the special exhibition space of the newly renovated museum as an alternative to the book-based permanent exhibition.[1] Thirdly, the team found the comics medium particularly intriguing for engaging with the theme of violence—above all, of course, from a psychoanalytic perspective.

The team commissioned me with the curation of the exhibition—together with Daniela Finzi, who is an expert in psychoanalysis. From the outset, it was important to assemble a diverse selection (e.g., various perspectives, intersectional questions, different carrier media; see below) and adopt an approach that could effectively explore both the topic of violence and the medium of comics while simultaneously reflecting on how to exhibit violence in its various forms and manifestations (e.g., acts of physical violence, but also forms of structural and epistemic violence; see below).[2] Aligned with the museum's interests, the exhibition was organized into four sections: sexualized and gender-based violence,

---

1 The special exhibition room is located in the former living quarters of the Freud family, see Monika Pessler and Daniela Finzi, eds. *Freud, Berggasse 19: Ursprungsort der Psychoanalyse* (Berlin: Hatje Cantz, 2020), 152–53.
2 Violence has always played a key role in the history of the comics medium. For instance, it was integral to the slapstick aesthetics that defined the early daily strips in the US. Violence is also central to the superhero genre, where plotlines

coming of age, Shoah, and, finally, war, fleeing, and migration.[3] It displayed works from over thirty international artists producing Underground Comix and so-called alternative comics. The exhibition also had a small "creative corner" where visitors could reflect on their experience of the exhibition through drawing and writing. A catalog documents the exhibition and offers in-depth information.[4] The following reflections outline the exhibition concept and provide brief analyses of selected exhibits.

On Display: Violence

The subject of violence, the confrontation with various forms of violence, and, consequently, the experiences of pain, grief, and trauma need to be treated with great caution in museum exhibitions; exhibition practices must be reflected on with care. The exhibition discussed here was initially guided by questions surrounding historical engagements with violence in museums.[5] How can a museum even exhibit violence? To what extent does it need to reflect its potential institutional involvement in violence, and, ultimately, how is a museum, as a socially accredited institution of knowledge transfer, violent itself?

The concept of the exhibition approached these questions from various angles. The four sections of the exhibition room were each accessible separately, allowing visitors to choose which topic they wanted to explore. General introductory texts were affixed to a column in the middle of the room, while separate thematic introductory texts were placed on the outer walls of the individual sections grouped around the center. These texts briefly introduced the comic-historical examination of the respective topics and prepared visitors for each section. Preview images were installed to give visitors an idea of the aesthetics and styles displayed in the respective sections. At the entrance to the special exhibition room, a roll-up banner prepared visitors for the exhibition with a detailed trigger warning and emphasized that the exhibition was open only to visitors aged sixteen and over.

---

often revolve around acts of violence. See, e.g., Jörn Ahrens, *Überzeichnete Spektakel: Inszenierungen von Gewalt im Comic* (Baden-Baden: Nomos, 2019), 13.

3   During the conception phase of the exhibition, we discussed the issue of translation extensively. The German title of the section is "Krieg, Flucht und Migration," which references processes rather than individuals. This is why we opted for "fleeing" instead of "refugees," as it refers to actions rather than individuals.

4   Daniela Finzi and Monika Pessler, eds., *Gewalt erzählen: Eine Comic-Ausstellung / Narrating Violence: A Comic Exhibition* (Vienna: Sigmund Freud Museum, 2023).

5   Zuzanna Dziuban, Stefan Benedik, and Ljiljana Radonić, "Displaying Violence," *Österreichische Zeitschrift für Geschichtswissenschaften / Austrian Journal of Historical Studies* 34, no. 1 (2023): 7–17, here 10.

At the same time, the exhibition was also intended to draw on the potential of the exhibits, in that the feeling of being overwhelmed, repeatedly addressed in the comics, was implemented curatorially: The diversity of exhibits in a relatively limited space, the multitude of experiences of violence, and their heterogeneity should be palpable for the visitors, thereby conveying—in a productive manner—a sense of unease.

As for the exhibits themselves, the spatial design was simple and modest. Reproductions were affixed to the walls without frames, while original drawings were displayed in frameless picture frames to avoid duplicating the panel frame and to steer clear of high-cultural habits and standard art museum conventions. All screens (e.g., for webcomics) were approximately the same size and, like reproductions and originals, they were mounted on the wall. All but two artists granted permission to enlarge the prints to European standard DIN A3 format, roughly corresponding to the US tabloid format. This decision was influenced by a desire to increase accessibility for recipients, such as readability (e.g., for visually impaired) visitors. However, when staging violence, the practice of enlargement must be critically examined so as to avoid a voyeuristic gaze and effect. With this in mind and considering the sensitivity of the topic of violence in general, I adhered to three guidelines regarding the selection and presentation of exhibits: diversity, contextualization, and self-reflection.

Firstly, diversity pertains to the range of perspectives presented, allowing space for both established artists and younger ones who are not as well known. Secondly, although the exhibit was divided into four sections, it was designed around intersectional questions, thereby exploring the topic from various angles and addressing the complexity of violence from the perspectives of those who are victimized by it and those who inflict it. Thirdly, this multi-perspective approach aligns with the diversity of forms of violence itself; the exhibition addressed not only physical but also psychological forms of violence as well as structural and epistemic violence, as I explain below.[6] Fourthly, the display included not only excerpts from stand-alone publications in book format but also shorter works from comic magazines. Additionally, I incorporated five screens featuring webcomics, an excerpt from Vincent Paronnaud and Marjane Satrapi's animated adaptation (2007) of Satrapi's comic *Persepolis* (2000–2003),[7] and the Instagram feed of Pictoric (pictoric.ua),[8] a group of Ukrainian artists who collect illustrations, posters, and comics to educate the public about the situation in Ukraine in light of

---

6 Marina Rauchenbacher, "Gewalt. Eine begriffliche Annäherung / Violence. Approaching a Definition," in *Gewalt erzählen*, ed. Finzi and Pessler, 6–9.
7 Vincent Paronnaud and Marjane Satrapi, *Persepolis* (France, 2007); Marjane Satrapi, *Persepolis. The Story of a Childhood and The Story of a Return* (London: Vintage, 2008).
8 See also: www.supportukraine-pic.com, accessed September 27, 2024.

the Russian war of aggression since 2022. Fifthly, within this corpus, the genres were diverse, ranging from autobiographical and biographical comics, comic reportage to fictional comics. Lastly, reflecting the focus on diversity, the exhibition also presented a variety of aesthetics and styles.

In addition to choosing a diverse selection of artists and artworks, I also emphasized contextualization. Beyond the introductory texts to the four sections, the excerpts from the comics on display were accompanied by object texts that explained the significance of each excerpt for the respective comic and offered contextual knowledge (e.g., cultural, historical, or sociopolitical topics). Furthermore, to contextualize the motifs, scenes, and actions depicted in the reproductions (excluding the webcomics, which could be accessed in full), I selected longer or multiple excerpts from the comics. This approach allows for an examination of the structure of the medium itself: comics is a narrative medium that develops its stories, in addition to other medium-specific strategies, through the interplay of sequentiality and simultaneity. No graphical/textual element exists by itself, but—quite obviously—always in interaction with other graphical/textual elements. At the same time, such extensive excerpts served to elucidate the complexity of the story and prevented individual scenes from being perceived as (voyeuristic) spectacles. Rather, the selected comics narrated violence in an "embedded" manner as they addressed its causes, the ensuing trauma, pain, and fear, as well as the transmission of trauma, and, ultimately, cultural, historical, and socio-political factors along with individual motivations, and their consequences.

As has become evident, the exhibition concept, much like the medium of comics itself, championed self-reflectivity, fostering ongoing contemplation of the narrative form due to its "structural overdetermination." The comics medium unfolds along a complex set of structural characteristics: comics are defined by "hybridity" (word/writing and image), and story development in comics is shaped by the rhetorical figure of repetition, which holds particular significance for the creation of bodies in comics.[9] Furthermore, comics—as already stated—narrate sequentially, yet all panels of a page or two pages are present simultaneously, allowing for a unique spatiotemporal configuration. Finally, constitutive elements of comics include panel structure and the spaces in between panels, the gutter. Drawing from these structural elements, comics demand an

---

9 See, e.g., Ole Frahm, *Die Sprache des Comics* (Hamburg: Philo Fine Arts, 2010); Elisabeth Klar, "Wir sind alle Superhelden! Über die Eigenart des Körpers im Comic—und über die Lust an ihm," in *Theorien des Comics: Ein Reader*, ed. Barbara Eder, Elisabeth Klar, and Ramón Reichert (Bielefeld: transcript, 2011), 219–36; Véronique Sina, *Comic—Film—Gender: Zur (Re-)Medialisierung von Geschlecht im Comicfilm* (Bielefeld: transcript, 2016); Marina Rauchenbacher, "Comics—posthuman, queer-end, um_un-ordnend," *Genealogy + Critique* 8, no. 1 (2022): 1–28.

interlinear, "dispersed" reading, challenging traditional reading conventions. Thus, the works on display not only addressed forms of violence but also, through this overdetermination, shed light on their own structure.

On Display: Comics—The Spatial Arrangement

In developing the exhibition concept, we were acutely aware that visitors of the Sigmund Freud Museum, a biographically and historically oriented museum, would not necessarily be familiar with the medium of comics and might not expect art on display. Therefore, the central area of the exhibition room, as mentioned above, featured brief general introductory texts on the medium of comics, its history,[10] and, though not the primary focus of the exhibition, a brief overview of the connection between the medium of comics and psychoanalysis.[11]

Despite a vibrant international history of comic exhibitions,[12] exhibiting comics may seem counterintuitive, as comics are not primarily made for exhibition but rather for solitary reading,[13] which invites comparisons between comic exhibitions and literature exhibitions.[14] In a comic exhibition, comics are transferred from an intimate reading situation to a public space, from a printed publication or private screen onto a wall and into a room. This fundamentally alters the relationship of the exhibited comic to the surrounding space in terms of proportion and the reader's/visitor's connection to the comic and the surrounding space. When presented as a book or magazine, readers engage in a haptic interaction with comics as they hold them in their hands. In contrast, in the exhibition space, visitors

---

10 Marina Rauchenbacher, "Gewalt erzählen in Comics / Narrating Violence in Comics," in *Gewalt erzählen*, ed. Finzi and Pessler, 10–41.

11 Daniela Finzi, "Psychoanalyse und das Sprechen in Bildern. Ausgewählte Streiflichter im Spiegel der Zeit / Psychoanalysis and Speaking in Images. Selected Spotlights Over Time," in *Gewalt erzählen*, ed. Finzi and Pessler, 42–50; Daniela Finzi, "Dem Unaussprechlichen zur Darstellung verhelfen / Helping to Represent the Unspeakable," in *Gewalt erzählen*, ed. Finzi and Pessler, 50–61.

12 See, e.g., Kim A. Munson, "The Galleries," in *The Secret Origins of Comics Studies*, ed. Matthew J. Smith and Randy Duncan (New York: Routledge, 2017), 226–45; Anna Maria Loffredo and Barbara Margarethe Eggert, eds., *Ran an die Wand, rein in die Vitrine?! Internationale Positionen zum Ausstellen von Comics in der pädagogischen und musealen Praxis* (Munich: kopaed, 2020); Kim A. Munson, ed., *Comic Art in Museums* (Jackson: University Press of Mississippi, 2020).

13 See Barbara Margarethe Eggert, "Für Ausstellungen gemacht? Comics im Spannungsfeld von Kunst, Ausstellungsdesign und Lehrmittel," in *Ran an die Wand, rein in die Vitrine?!*, ed. Loffredo and Eggert, 22–37, here 23–24.

14 Dietrich Grünewald, "Muss das sein? Das muss! Comicausstellungen und Ausstellungskataloge," in *Ran an die Wand, rein in die Vitrine?!*, ed. Loffredo and Eggert, 40–63, here 41.

find themselves "amid unconnected things and can simultaneously place them next to each other, on top of each other, against each other, with each other, to each other, and for themselves."[15] The complexity of this transformation emerges fully when we consider the difference in media. Unlike with print publications, haptic interaction can be retained in webcomics: visitors still have to operate the screen, albeit in a different spatial arrangement. The exhibition incorporated four screens across three of the four sections that had to be navigated by the visitors. These screens featured webcomics, including *Jamie's Story* (2008) from Tab Kimpton's series *Khaos Komix* (2006–2008),[16] Nino Bulling's *Tamgout, Buchenwald, Paris* (2015),[17] and the series *Alphabet of Arrival*, edited by the German Comics Association (2017),[18] and displaying the Pictoric Instagram feed (see above). The only screen that visitors could not interact with played an excerpt from Paronnaud and Satrapi's *Persepolis* animation adaptation.

The approximately 80m² (around 860ft²) room was divided into five areas: starting from the central area described above, visitors made their way to the four section areas, each of a different size and shape. The sections addressed sexualized and gender-based violence, war, fleeing, and migration. Here, the rooms were not immediately visible in their entirety upon entering but needed to be explored gradually. Even so, the diverse aesthetics and styles on display in the individual sections were apparent at first glance. A subtle interplay of gazes and stories would unfold as visitors moved among the many drawn figures in the relatively small section areas. For example, the section on war, fleeing, and migration opened with excerpts from Joe Sacco's *Palestine* (1993–95),[19] a work of particular significance in the development of comics reportage. As it was important to give another perspective on the Middle East conflict, I decided to juxtapose Sacco's work with excerpts from Rutu Modan's *Exit Wounds* (2007).[20] Visitors could thus position themselves in front of this wall and connect two very different perspectives on the conflict, showing diverse

---

15 Heike Gfrereis, "Literatur ausstellen als poetische Forschung," *Jahrbuch der deutschen Schillergesellschaft* 64 (2020): 331–47, here 339, my translation.

16 Tab Kimpton, "Khaos Komix. Jamie's Story," https://www.discordcomics.com/comic/jamies-story-cover/, accessed September 27, 2024.

17 Nino Bulling, "Tamgout, Buchenwald, Paris," https://drawingthetimes.com/story/tamgout-buchenwald-paris/, accessed September 27, 2024.

18 Deutscher Comicverein e. V./German Comics Association, "Alphabet des Ankommens/Alphabet of Arrival," https://alphabetdesankommens.de, accessed September 27, 2024.

19 Joe Sacco, *Palestine*, 18th ed. (Seattle: Fantagraphics Books, 2019).

20 Rutu Modan, *Exit Wounds* (Montreal: Drawn & Quarterly, 2007).

points of view.[21] An interview that Sacco conducted with Modan allowed for a dialogical moment.[22]

In arranging the displays, it became evident, especially through the thematic connections, that comic exhibitions amplify the structural characteristics of the medium. Repetition emerges as the central rhetorical figure of comics as visitors are confronted not with a double-page spread of a comic book, but rather with multiple pages on a wall. This effect is intensified as the structure of repetition is reinforced on a different level when excerpts from various comics are strung together. Additionally, the gutter, a crucial structural element of the comics medium, is referenced by the white spaces between individual exhibits,[23] so that the exhibition setting itself imitates a comic layout. Also, the arrangement in the room demands extensive interlinear reading as the visitors follow different stories in various comics amidst a multiplicity of simultaneously present pages and exhibits. Thus, the three-dimensional exhibition space exposes the materiality of comics, and the reading/viewing of the comics (excerpts) is explicitly set up as a bodily experience. This experience intensifies the feeling of being involved, and with it, in the context of this exhibition, the feeling of unease. The visitor becomes, so to speak, a physical link between the walls and the exhibits on display.

In the exhibition setting, the respective plot of each comic is presented in new and potentially different ways through its arrangement in the room. Una's *Becoming Unbecoming* (2015) is particularly intriguing in this context.[24] It narrates experiences of sexualized violence, even rape, of the autobiographical avatar, delving into various layers of structural violence against women deeply rooted in our patriarchally shaped societies. In order to shed light on these structures, Una connects the individual experience with the story of the so-called Yorkshire Ripper, Peter William Sutcliffe, who murdered at least thirteen

---

21 During the conceptualization of the exhibition, we considered the Russian war of aggression against Ukraine the most recent conflict, incorporating Pictoric and excerpts from Igort's *Quaderni ucraini: Diario di un'invasione* (Ukrainian Notebooks: Diary of an Invasion, 2022), along with Danyl Shtangeev and Borys Filonenko's *Spacetime in Rubizhne* (2022). Of course, as of October 7, 2023, when our concept of the exhibition had already been finalized, this was no longer the case; thus, Modan's and Sacco's comics gained specific relevance. Igort, *Quaderni ucraini: Diario di un'invasione* (Bologna: Oblomov edizioni, 2022); Danyl Shtangeev and Borys Filonenko, "Spacetime in Rubizhne," *Strapazin* 148 (2022): 39–46.

22 Joe Sacco, "Rutu Modan interviewed by Joe Sacco," *Drawn & Quarterly*, February 15, 2018. https://drawnandquarterly.com/press/rutu-modan-interviewed-joe-sacco.

23 Barbara Margarethe Eggert, "Roter Faden und Re-animation. Beobachtungen zu den Funktionen von Horst Steins Museumscomics für das Haydn-Geburtshaus in Rohrau," in *Familie und Comic: Kritische Perspektiven auf soziale Mikrostrukturen in grafischen Narrationen*, ed. Barbara Margarethe Eggert, Kalina Kupczyńska, and Véronique Sina (Berlin and Boston, MA: de Gruyter, 2023), 15–28, here 16.

24 Una, *Becoming Unbecoming* (Oxford: Myriad Editions, 2015).

women between 1975 and 1980. At the core of the reflection are the rape of the protagonist and reflections on how to lead a life in the face of severe traumatization and how to articulate trauma. Her critical conceptual strategy involves a heterogeneous page layout, largely dispensing with panel structures and arranging pictorial and textual elements in various ways on the pages.[25] The decision to forgo a rigid structure visualizes a restless search, as disordered and uncontrollable memories and flashbacks irrupt (on both the protagonist and the readers/viewers), interrupting narrative sequences. In order to understand the transition from the book to the exhibition space, it is particularly intriguing to closely examine the difference between the setting of reading and that of the exhibition. In the reading experience, the reader turns the page and, thus, to some extent, "controls" the unfolding of the story. However, the reader is at the same time subjected to moments of surprise that arise during the act of turning the pages. In contrast, in the exhibition setting, simple linear sequences affixed to the wall made the violence experienced by the autobiographical avatar immediately apparent. Here, the uncontrollable, unconscious experience was not subject to the turning of the pages, but, even so, it was palpably present. Simultaneously, the heterogeneity of the page layouts was evident, highlighting the comic's artificiality and "aesthetic distance." The fact that the pictorial reproduction of the linearly fixed sequences from the exhibition setting cannot be realized in a print book (nor thus in this essay) emphasizes the contrast between reading the book and experiencing the exhibition.

On Display: Comics—Reproduction and Original

Importantly, comic exhibitions must decide whether originals or reproductions from the published comic should be exhibited, a question that first of all addresses the hybrid status of the medium itself: comics is—just like literature—a medium of reproduction, but it is also a medium that originates from the visual arts. Hence, exhibiting originals takes a completely different direction than exhibiting reproductions from the final publications. Furthermore, this question correlates directly with the didactic and educational aims of the exhibition.[26] For a theme-based exhibition, such as the one discussed here, which sought to encourage visitors to engage further with the comics on display and with the narrated forms of violence, we decided to use (high-quality) reproductions, complemented by selected original works. The opportunity to compare the published works with the originals provided additional insight into the artistic process and the genesis of the comics. With regard to the hybrid status of the medium, and thus,

---

25 See also Nancy Pedri, "Breaking Out of Panels: Formal Expressions of Subjectivity in Ellen Forney's *Marbles* and Una's *Becoming Unbecoming*," *Studies in Comics* 9, no. 2 (2018): 297–314.

26 Grünewald, "Muss das sein? Das muss! Comicausstellungen und Ausstellungskataloge," 58.

the hybrid status of a comics exhibition, for future exhibitions, I would exhibit not only original drawings alongside reproductions but also first editions or significant editions of the comics (similar to literary exhibitions).[27]

One prime example of the insights to be gained from a comparison between an original drawing and a reproduction from the final publication was Ulli Lust's *Heute ist der letzte Tag vom Rest deines Lebens* (2009; *Today Is the Last Day of the Rest of Your Life*, 2013).[28] An autobiographically inspired comic, it recounts teenage Ulli and her friend Edi's trip to 1980s Sicily, where they are confronted with a patriarchal society characterized by the objectification of women and structural, physical, and psychological violence against them. In contrast to the book publication, which digitally inserted the color green, the originals are black-and-white, drawn with a fiber pen (figs. 8.1 and 8.2). Here, the addition of color creates a more vibrant dynamic. In the first six panels, color is used discreetly on Ulli's body; subsequently, however, it infuses the panels' background, emphasizing the overwhelming nature of Ulli's experience (figs. 8.3 and 8.4).[29] The comparison between the originals and final publication provides insight into the comic's genesis. In the Lust displays, visitors are not only able to observe the addition of color but can retrace the (digital) changes in the lettering. Some notes, jotted down in the margins of the original drawing, were eventually used for a speech bubble, replacing other text. A crucial textual change concerns the autobiographical avatar Ulli's ultimate experience of violence. She is raped. In the original, Ulli's final realization about the rape is narrated indirectly—"It had to happen"[30]—this was replaced for publication with: "Raped."[31] Other displays showed that pictorial elements were pasted over, that speech bubbles were repositioned, and that some captions were added at a later stage.

Another revealing example of an artistic working process are the displayed works of Anke Feuchtenberger, which included three pages from *Genossin Kuckuck: Ein deutsches Tier im deutschen Wald* (2023).[32] Again, reproductions were accompanied by originals (fig. 8.5). In this comic,

---

27   The relevance of this became particularly evident with Justin Green's *Binky Brown Meets the Holy Virgin Mary*. The first publication from 1972 was printed on cheap, rough paper, corresponding with the comic's underground aesthetic. This character of the first print was lost in the exhibition's high-resolution prints on high-quality paper. Justin Green, *Binky Brown Meets the Holy Virgin Mary* (Berkeley, CA: Last-Gasp Eco-Funnies, 1972).

28   Ulli Lust, *Heute ist der letzte Tag vom Rest deines Lebens* (Berlin: avant-verlag, 2009); *Today is the Last Day of the Rest of Your Life* (Seattle, WA: Fantagraphics Books, 2013).

29   In the black-and-white illustrations in this article, green is shown as light grey.

30   Lust, original drawing for *Heute ist der letzte Tag vom Rest deines Lebens*, my translation.

31   Lust, *Heute ist der letzte Tag vom Rest deines Lebens*, 243, my translation.

32   Anke Feuchtenberger, *Genossin Kuckuck: Ein deutsches Tier im deutschen Wald* (Berlin: Reprodukt, 2023). "Genossin Kuckuck" translates to "comrade cuckoo" with the German "Genossin" in the grammatically female form. The comic has not yet been translated into English.

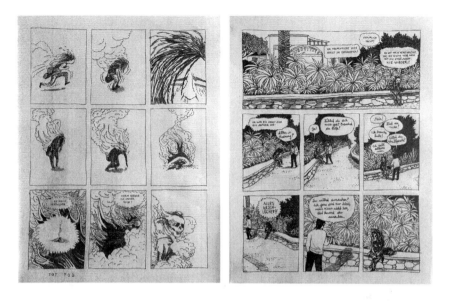

Figures 8.1 and 8.2. Ulli Lust, original drawings for *Heute ist der letzte Tag vom Rest deines Lebens*.

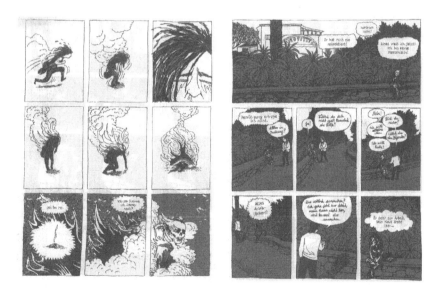

Figures 8.3 and 8.4. Ulli Lust, *Heute ist der letzte Tag vom Rest deines Lebens* (Berlin: avant-verlag, 2009), 278 and 279.

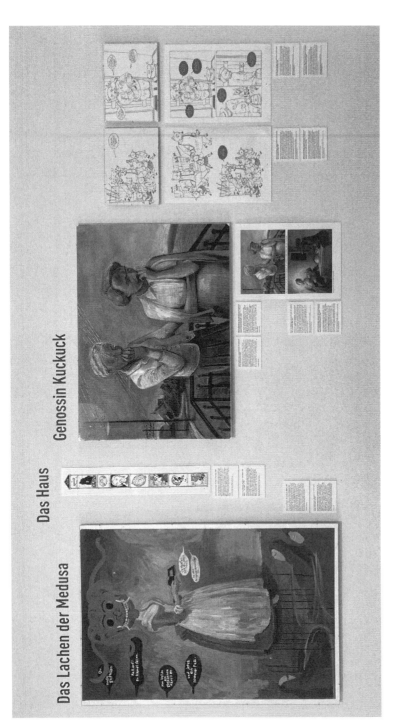

Figure 8.5. Anke Feuchtenberger, exhibition display of: the painting *Das Lachen der Medusa* (Acrylic on paper, 2021); a reproduction of *Die Zunge*, part 1 of *Das Haus* (Berlin: Reprodukt, 2001 [2000]); an original charcoal drawing (2014) with the corresponding reproduction from *Genossin Kuckuck: Ein deutsches Tier im deutschen Wald* (Berlin: Reprodukt, 2023), 436; two original drawings in red India ink (2013) with the corresponding reproductions from *Genossin Kuckuck*, 60, 67. Photograph by Marina Rauchenbacher.

Figure 8.6. Anke Feuchtenberger, *Genossin Kuckuck: Ein deutsches Tier im deutschen Wald* (Berlin: Reprodukt, 2023), 436.

as in several of her other pieces—also those exhibited at the Sigmund Freud Museum—Feuchtenberger addresses sexualized and gender-based violence. *Genossin Kuckuck* explores childhood in the GDR, friendship, adolescence, family, social policy, power, and violence. In the postscript, Feuchtenberger returns to one of her central themes: the rape of German women by Russian soldiers at the end of the Second World War and the transgenerational transmission of these traumatic experiences. For the exhibition, Feuchtenberger lent us a charcoal drawing from 2014 that illustrates this theme. This drawing—like all drawings from the postscript—was originally published in an edition of Heinrich von Kleist's novella *The Marquise of O*, which first appeared in 1808.[33] In this story, Kleist's eponymous marquise is raped by a Russian officer during the War of the Second Coalition (1799–1802). The resulting pregnancy leads to the marquise being ostracized—until her innocence is proven. In *Genossin Kuckuck*, Feuchtenberger's drawings for Kleist's novella are recontextualized (figs. 8.5 and 8.6), once again narrating violence against women—this time in the GDR, after World War II. The publication history of the exhibited drawing sheds light on the difference between the original and the corresponding image in *Genossin Kuckuck*, even as it demonstrates the universal relevance of the topic. The gaze of the depicted women is cast down; they are speechless and do not attempt to make eye contact: words cannot express the suffering they have experienced, nor the shame associated with it. The newly added text in *Genossin Kuckuck* (fig. 8.6)—"But what did we have to tell anyway? We had experienced it ourselves. Or watched it" (my translation)— reinforces the tropes of speechlessness and looking.

On Display: Violence in Comics—Spotlights

In developing a concept for the exhibition, it was crucial to me that experiences of violence were represented in multifaceted and diverse ways. Thus, the exhibits and object texts addressed a variety of different forms of violence, ranging from concrete manifestations, such as physical, psychological, sexualized, and gender-based violence, to abstract forms, which are theoretically described, for example, as structural and epistemic violence. In doing so, the exhibition sought to highlight mutual dependencies among the various forms of violence. Building on these reflections, I took into account structural and (intersecting) identity categories, such as gender, race, ethnicity, disability, class, or age, as well as power

---

33   Heinrich von Kleist, *Michael Kohlhaas: Zeichnungen von Johannes Grützke; Die Marquise von O…: Zeichnungen von Anke Feuchtenberger; Der Findling: Zeichnungen von Martin Grobecker* (Frankfurt am Main: Büchergilde, 2014).

hierarchies, grief, and trauma.[34] As comics consistently reflect on their own narrative strategies through the medium's structural overdetermination, recipients are challenged to engage with these reflections and to consider their emotional and ethical implications.[35]

Comics inherently demonstrate the vulnerability of bodies,[36] as bodies in comics are "confined" within panels, often cut off or cropped by the panel's edges.[37] Consequently, comic bodies are much more than mere graphical representations of characters; they serve as spaces for the visualization of emotions, suffering, and abstract processes, for what El Refaie refers to as "pictorial embodiment."[38] In this way, comic bodies undergo continuous defamiliarization, abstraction, or redefinition through overdrawing and exaggeration, a process that underlines their aesthetic condition as embodiments, which is itself of vital importance to a comic exhibition and its pedagogical aim.

Among others, Lust's *Heute ist der letzte Tag vom Rest deines Lebens* exemplifies the function of the comic body as a space for embodying and reflecting on emotions and pain. The autobiographical avatar Ulli repeatedly experiences sexualized and gender-based violence, culminating in rape. In the excerpt discussed above (figs. 8.1–8.4), Ulli burns down to a skeleton after a sexual assault. This metaphoric dimension of the drawn body, which visualizes traumatization and pain, is contrasted with the external perspective of a man who flirts with Ulli. While readers learn of his intentions through his speech bubbles, Ulli's perspective is narrated on both a graphic and textual level. Since her body remains a skeleton, the man's gaze has no graphic equivalent, subversively depriving sexist objectification and sexualized violence of its visual object.

During guided tours, I highlighted to the audience—many of whom were engaging with the comics medium for the first time—the critical difference between content and form. Notably, an excerpt from Aline Kominsky-Crumb's *Love That Bunch* (1990) provided a platform for discussing explicitly drawn physical violence enacted by the autobiographical avatar's father, including the mother's rape, juxtaposed with the grotesquely exaggerated graphical depictions of bodies.[39] This particular

---

34 Rauchenbacher, "Gewalt. Eine begriffliche Annäherung / Violence. Approaching a Definition."

35 Kate Polak, *Ethics in the Gutter: Empathy and Historical Fiction in Comics* (Columbus: Ohio State University Press, 2011), 2.

36 Eszter Szép, *Comics and the Body: Drawing, Reading, and Vulnerability* (Columbus: Ohio State University Press, 2020).

37 Klar, "Wir sind alle Superhelden!"

38 Elisabeth El Refaie, *Autobiographical Comics: Life Writing in Pictures* (Jackson: University Press of Mississippi, 2012), 51.

39 Aline Kominsky-Crumb, *Love That Bunch* (Seattle, WA: Fantagraphics Books, 1990).

excerpt facilitated a conversation about aesthetic distance, challenging the notion of authenticity and pointing towards the deliberate construction of the comic.

During my tours, I also always explored the diversity of perspectives, aesthetics, and aims within the Shoah section, thus pointing to the diversity that informed the exhibition as such.[40] The section's introductory text featured a page from Horst Rosenthal's *Mickey aux Camp de Gurs* (1942)[41] and referred to Al Feldstein and Bernard Krigstein's *Master Race* (1955). The section then opened with three excerpts from Art Spiegelman's *MAUS—A Survivor's Tale* (1986 and 1991),[42] followed by Sid Jacobson and Ernie Colón's didactic work *Anne Frank* (2010).[43] Thus, from the outset, diverse approaches were evident, spanning from the (auto)biographical to the didactically enhanced biographical-historical comic. Jacobson and Colon's work was followed by three excerpts from Regina Hofer and Leopold Maurer's *Insekten* (Insects, 2019), which again presents an (auto)biographical and aesthetically challenging position.[44] Hofer and Maurer took turns in creating this comic, recounting Maurer's grandfather's involvement with the "Waffen SS." In drawings that transition between figural and abstract forms, Hofer comments on the grandfather's relativizing and Hitler-worshipping statements expressed in interviews conducted by the authors (fig. 8.7).[45] Maurer's chapters reflect an attempt to gain a deeper understanding of the grandfather that breaks through the layers of relativization instated and maintained by the family. For instance, in an autobiographical recreation, Maurer recalls his perspective on the grandfather when he was a child, incorporating various

---

40 A groundbreaking comic exhibition on the Shoah, titled *Holocaust im Comic*, was on display at various locations in Germany between 2001 and 2017; for more information, see Ralf Palandt, "'Ich bin schwer beeindruckt ...' Die Wanderausstellung 'Holocaust im Comic,'" in *Ran an die Wand, rein in die Vitrine?!*, ed. Loffredo and Eggert, 64–76.

41 Horst Rosenthal, "Mickey au Camp de Gurs," in *Mickey à Gurs: Les carnets de dessins de Horst Rosenthal*, ed. Joël Kotek and Didier Pasamonik (Paris: Calmann-Lévy, 2014), 1–6. Rosenthal created at least three notebooks detailing his experience in the French internment Camp de Gurs before being deported to Auschwitz-Birkenau, where he was murdered.

42 Art Spiegelman, *The Complete MAUS: A Survivor's Tale* (London: Penguin Books, 2003).

43 Sid Jacobson and Ernie Colón, *Anne Frank: The Anne Frank House Authorized Graphic Biography* (New York: Hill & Wang, 2010).

44 Regina Hofer and Leopold Maurer, *Insekten* (Vienna: Luftschacht, 2019). This comic has not yet been translated into English.

45 The text translates as: "and he never stops glorifying his Hitler ... / what a highly intelligent person Hitler was. / Those blue eyes ... / mesmerizing" (my translation).

Figure 8.7

Figure 8.8

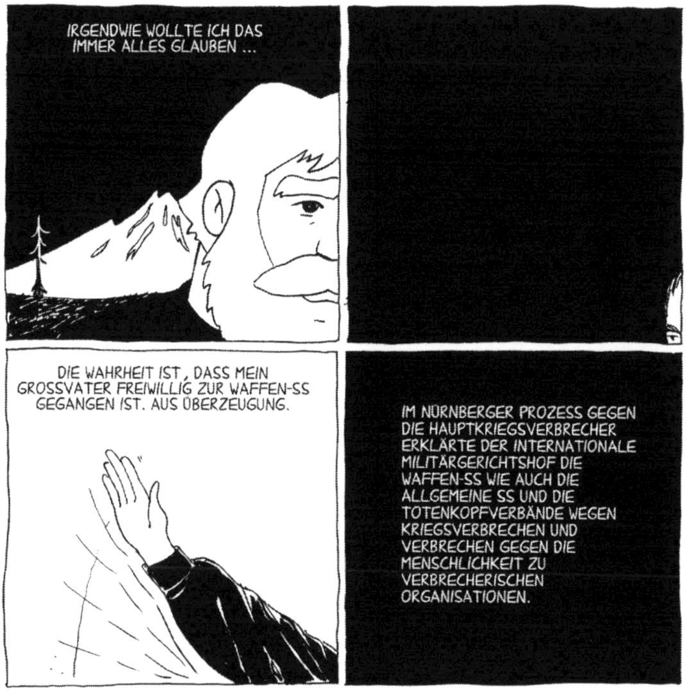

Figures 8.7 and 8.8. Regina Hofer and Leopold Maurer, *Insekten* (Vienna: Luftschacht, 2019), 12 and 235.

iconographic references, such as the grandfather from the well-known *Heidi* anime, in his poignant cognitive process (fig. 8.8).[46]

Comics on the Shoah speak to the medium's role in knowledge transfer, remembrance work, witnessing, the transmission of stories of survival, and the task of raising awareness. Such comics contribute to the diverse voices and images of the Shoah. They are increasingly utilized in teaching and education,[47] and they are a fundamental part of research/artistic projects. Following *Insekten*, the exhibition displayed an excerpt from Barbara Yelin's *But I Live* (2022), which was published in an eponymous anthology[48] as part of Charlotte Schallié's project *Narrative Art & Visual Storytelling in Holocaust & Human Rights Education*.[49] In the context of this project, Yelin interviewed survivor Emmie Arbel, who was detained at Ravensbrück concentration camp as a child. The last exhibit in this section was part of the project *Redrawing Stories from the Past*, directed by artist and comic theorist Ole Frahm and comic artist Sascha Hommer. It focused, in one of the two parts, on victims of National Socialism.[50] In the comic *Tamgout, Buchenwald, Paris* (2015), Nino Bulling used archival material to recount the stories of two marginalized victims of National Socialism, namely the Algerian Mohamed Kaci and Ahmed Somia, originally from Tunisia.[51] Thus, this section develops what Hillary Chute emphasizes as a central function of comics: comics are particularly adept at narrating traumas and at the repetitive and reconstructive portrayal of lived experiences to generate alternative concepts.[52] This is all the more

---

46   The text translates as: "Somehow, I always wanted to believe all that … / The truth is that my grandfather volunteered for the Waffen SS. Out of conviction. / At the Nuremberg trial of the principal war criminals, the International Military Tribunal declared the Waffen SS, the Allgemeine SS, and the Totenkopfverbände belligerent organizations responsible for war crimes and crimes against humanity" (my translation).

47   Dennis Bock and Christine Gundermann, eds., *Comics in Gedenkstätten*, special issue of *Geschichte in Wissenschaft und Unterricht* 74, no. 5/6 (2023).

48   Barbara Yelin, "But I Live," in *But I Live: Three Stories of Child Survivors of the Holocaust*, ed. Charlotte Schallié (Toronto: New Jewish Press, 2022). After the exhibition had been fully conceptualized, Yelin published a separate, more extensive comic on this topic: *Emmie Arbel: Die Farbe der Erinnerung*, ed. Charlotte Schallié and Alexander Korb (Berlin: Reprodukt, 2023).

49   https://holocaustgraphicnovels.org/educational-resources, accessed January 15, 2024.

50   https://redrawingstoriesfromthepast.com/project/forgotten-victims, accessed September 16, 2024.

51   Nino Bulling, "Tamgout, Buchenwald, Paris," https://drawingthetimes.com/story/tamgout-buchenwald-paris/, accessed September 27, 2024.

52   Hillary L. Chute, *Disaster Drawn: Visual Witness, Comics, and Documentary Form* (Cambridge, MA and London: The Belknap Press of Harvard University Press, 2016), 4.

important in the context of the Shoah, especially considering the small number of surviving witnesses.

Conclusion

The exhibition *Narrating Violence: A Comic Exhibition* was conceived along complex considerations, oriented towards the specifics of the comic medium itself and towards the sensitivity of the theme. To meet these dual interests, the exhibition followed a comprehensive concept based on the guiding principles of "diversity", that is, taking into account a variety of perspectives, themes, aesthetics, and styles, "contextualization" (to avoid a voyeuristic effect), and "self-reflection" with regard to the concept of the exhibition and the structure of the comics medium. Based on these principles, the exhibition concept offers a number of starting points for a comprehensive examination of how violence in public space can be critically addressed. Through its multitude of displayed perspectives, stories, and aesthetics—in a relatively small space—the exhibition allowed for a polylogue in space, offering an experiential dimension for visitors. Also, in the specific spatial arrangement, narratives about violence, pain, and trauma intertwined and interacted within the reception context. As one moved through the exhibition, one could perceive the interplay between the clarity of the structure and the simultaneous intensity of the exhibits. Visitors, many of whom were engaging with comics for the first time and often had associated the term "comic" primarily with mainstream comics, were surprised by the themes and aesthetics and often emphasized how affected they were by what they had seen and read—in fact experiencing productive unease by experiencing the creativity of the comics medium.

9: Disrupting the Counterculture: An Analysis of Rolf Dieter Brinkmann's Sampling of Comics

John D. Benjamin

WHEN CONSIDERING THE relationship of comics to social justice, textual meaning can be understood in two interconnected ways.[1] First, new comics contribute to an ongoing tradition of graphic narratives reaching back over a century, documenting and supporting normative views of dominant groups, revolutionary social change from the margins, and everything in between. Second, their authors and readers engage with comics as formally malleable multimodal texts with unique affordances for representation.[2] Given their communicative capacity through both content and form, comics' ability to address representational injustice and other oppression that can lead to trauma requires that we effectively understand *what* as well as *how* they communicate.

To investigate the complexity of this interplay and how it relates to injustice and trauma, this chapter considers how Rolf Dieter Brinkmann (1940–75) samples comics in his *Popliteratur* work. In two poetry volumes created in dialogue with 1960s American counterculture, *Die Piloten* (The Pilots, 1968) and *ACID: Neue amerikanische Szene* (ACID: New American Scene, 1969), Brinkmann samples comics for his aesthetic goals—to interrupt normativity and preclude any attempt at literary analysis.[3] This chapter focuses on the playful form and countercultural con-

---

1   The views expressed in this chapter are those of the author and do not necessarily reflect the official policy or position of the Department of the Army, DoD, or the US Government.

2   Multimodality refers to the interaction of modes of meaning. A mode is a potential for meaning with affordances interacting with other modes in multimodal texts. Examples of modes include volume, texture, space, timbre, and color. See Günther Kress and Theo Van Leeuwen, *Reading Images: The Grammar of Visual Design* (London: Routledge, 2006); and Frank Serafini, *Reading the Visual: An Introduction to Teaching Multimodal Literacy* (New York: Teachers College, 2014).

3   Rolf Dieter Brinkmann, *Die Piloten: Neue Gedichte* (Cologne: Kiepenhauer & Witsch, 1968); Rolf Dieter Brinkmann and Ralf-Rainer Rygulla, eds., *ACID:*

tent—sampled from the American Beat and hippie movements—in the comics Brinkmann selects. It considers how their formal innovations ultimately fail to undermine certain content norms, specifically heteronormativity and hypermasculinity. Thus, through the results of considering their multimodal form and content separately, I point to the shortcomings in Brinkmann's project of using samples to break norms and—by extension—promote social justice.

Following a discussion of how the comics form can be mobilized to support—or harm—social justice, I detail Brinkmann's aesthetics within the postmodernist movement of *Popliteratur* and consider how his comics samples function in terms of both form—as structurally disruptive—and content—by adopting the views of 1960s American counterculture in an attack on the conservative mainstream. I then problematize Brinkmann's separation of form and content, especially his purportedly contentless *bricolage*, before turning to feminist and queer theory to better characterize his aesthetics in relation to consumer capitalism and note its ineffectiveness against normativity.[4] Finally, I evaluate his comics sampling in *Die Piloten* and *ACID* and conclude that considering form and content together in comics studies may better serve social justice ends.

Social Justice and Representation in Comics

To locate this chapter within ongoing discussions of how comics relate to social justice, I follow German comics scholar Elizabeth Nijdam's introduction to the fall 2020 special issue of *Seminar* by looking to Social Justice Education (SJE).[5] SJE helps learners and readers develop "the critical analytical tools necessary to understand the structural features of oppression and their own socialization within oppressive systems."[6] This process aims at ending inequities that are "created when differences are sorted and ranked in a hierarchy that unequally confers power, social and economic advantages, and institutional and cultural validity to social groups based on their location in that hierarchy."[7] The goal of SJE is to identify problems

---

Neue amerikanische Szene (Frankfurt am Main: März bei Zweitausendeins, 1975).

4   Here, I look to Susan Bordo, *Unbearable Weight: Feminism, Western Culture, and the Body* (Berkeley: University of California Press, 1993).

5   Elizabeth Nijdam, "Introduction: The Social Justice Work of German Comics and Graphic Literature," in "The Social Justice Work of German Comics and Graphic Literature," ed. Elizabeth Nijdam and Charlotte Schallié, special issue of *Seminar* 56, nos. 3–4 (2020): 191–211.

6   Lee Anne Bell, "Theoretical Foundations for Social Justice Education," in *Teaching for Diversity and Social Justice*, ed. Maurianne Adams, Lee Anne Bell, Diane J. Goodman, Dave Shlasko, Rachel R. Briggs, and Romina Pacheco (New York: Routledge, 2023), 3–25, here 4.

7   Bell, "Theoretical Foundations," 4.

pertaining to social justice through scholarship and instruction in a range of contexts and texts. This chapter presents an example of this process through the analysis of Brinkmann's sampling of comics.

Comics have often worked in opposition to social justice. Dominant social groups have long used comics to bolster oppression by perpetuating ideologically defined differences, tropes, and stereotypes—including binaries in race, gender, and sexual identity.[8] Yet this relationship is not inherent to the comics form, whose affordances lie in the myriad interactions of its modes. In reference to graphic medicine and its ability to depict trauma, for example, Donovan and Ustundag note how comics can "capture the nuances of an embodied experience that are often invisible and hard to articulate through words alone."[9] And the representational strength of the comics form results from more than the addition of the visual to the verbal; comics signify through the interaction of a variety of multimodal conventions ranging from panel composition to speech bubbles to the gutters separating panels. Meaning is thus constructed by comics readers in the spaces between image and text, in the gutter, from page to page, across the individual but often connected strips and issues that constitute a given comics title, and even in their relationships with other artistic forms such as literature and film through adaptation and intertextuality. The result is an expansive potential for meaning that allows a great deal of nuance in what comics depict, including difficult topics, such as trauma.[10] It comes thus as no surprise when, in reference to what constitutes accepted proof in normative legal contexts, Donovan and Ustundag argue that comics' enhanced representational ability empowers the suppressed voices of minoritized populations to speak about otherwise underrepresented issues.[11]

In view of their representational capacity, this chapter considers what happens when these formal affordances are instead used to reify existing norms. In line with SJE, my analysis aims, in the words of Elizabeth Nijdam, "to draw attention to the representational injustices of the past and reveal how the comics form is equally capable of accomplishing the goals of social justice."[12] Comics studies and SJE can thus address these types of oppression both by showing the potentiality of the comics form for representation and by shedding light on the presence of representational injustice in individual texts. In this chapter, I discuss

---

8 Nijdam, "Introduction," 191. Here, Nijdam also provides a history of comics representation.
9 Courtney Donovan and Ebru Ustundag, "Graphic Narratives, Trauma & Social Justice," *Studies in Social Justice* 11, no. 2 (2017): 221–37, here 229.
10 Donovan and Ustundag, "Graphic Narratives," 223.
11 Donovan and Ustundag, "Graphic Narratives," 222–23.
12 Nijdam, "Introduction," 193.

how Brinkmann's *Popliteratur* sampling employs comics to undermine normativity through form and deconstruct binaries that oppress, but nonetheless ends up perpetuating potentially trauma-inducing cycles of violence through the heteronormative and hypermasculine representations of women and women's bodies. These issues in Brinkmann thus open up important questions for German comics studies and scholarship on postmodernist *Popliteratur* while also representing an example of SJE scholarship.

Comics, Sampling, and Bricolage in Brinkmann

Popliteratur arose in a West German cultural landscape shaped by two factions. The first, indebted to the Frankfurt School, viewed popular culture as passive and normative. Horkheimer and Adorno, for example, note that "Donald Duck in den Cartoons wie die Unglücklichen in der Realität … ihre Prügel [erhalten], damit die Zuschauer sich an die eigenen gewöhnen" (Donald Duck in the cartoons and the unfortunate victims in real life receive their beatings so that the spectators can accustom themselves to theirs).[13] The second looked longingly across the Atlantic at the Beats, San Francisco psychedelia, and New York pop art. Exemplifying this view, Marshall McLuhan positively understands a more participatory pop as "the clown reminding us of all the life and faculty that we have omitted from our daily routines."[14] Its opponents saw pop as repetitive empty fun salving the pain of reality and reinforcing norms. To its proponents, it was a radical shift away from a detached modernist criticism toward a more immediate and inclusive performative authorship with agency.

At Freiburg Universität in 1968, American literary critic Leslie Fiedler called for an end to "the period of early 20th-century modernism … in which criticism first invaded the novel, verse and drama and ultimately threatened to swallow up all other forms of literature."[15] Here, Fiedler is arguing against the decreasing distance between authors and critics and the related excessive theorization of and formalism in literature. The result was an exclusionary and growing cleft between literary

---

13 Max Horkheimer and Theodor Adorno, *Dialektik der Aufklärung* (Amsterdam: Querido Verlag, 1947), 166. Translation: Max Horkheimer and Theodor Adorno, *Dialectic of Enlightenment: Philosophical Fragments*, ed. Gunzelin Schmid Noerr, trans. Edmund Jephcott (Stanford, CA: Stanford University Press, 2002), 110.

14 Marshall McLuhan, *Understanding Media* (New York: McGraw-Hill, 1964), 167.

15 Leslie A. Fiedler, "Cross the Border, Close the Gap," in *Looking Ahead: The Vision of Science Fiction*, ed. Dick Allen and Lori Allen (New York: Harcourt Brace Jovanovich, 1975), 335–51, here 336.

producers and popular culture. Thus, Fiedler desired a reduction of the distance between author and audience to undermine the binary of high and low art and weaken what he saw as a range of oppressive hierarchies. Later that year, Brinkmann reacted with "Angriff aufs Monopol: Ich hasse alle Dichter" (Attack on the Monopoly: I Hate All Writers),[16] in which he called for such a literature in German, which came to be known as *Popliteratur*. In its antipathy to the high-low culture divide of modernism, its proximity to and embrace of mass culture, and its opposition to normative forms, *Popliteratur* can be understood as German literary postmodernism.

Popliteratur's avant-garde, from the 1960s to the 1980s, centered around Brinkmann, Hubert Fichte, and Rainald Goetz. Later *Popliteratur* authors include Thomas Meinecke, Benjamin von Stuckrad-Barre, Andreas Neumeister, Christian Kracht, and Thomas Brussig. This later group's work resembles that of like-minded authors abroad, including Bret Easton Ellis, Irvine Welsh, and Nick Hornby. While the latter generation focuses on popular culture—for example, the protagonists in Stuckrad-Barre's *Soloalbum* (1998) and Hornby's *High Fidelity* (1995) both discuss lost love in terms of their music fandom—the earlier group actively mimics and samples forms. For example, Rainald Goetz uses caesurae and repetition to perform techno music in *Rave*.[17]

These *Popliteratur* authors became archivists, frantic samplers of the high, low, and in-between. In his explanation of the movement's appeal, Goetz refers to the same opposition to analysis Fiedler desired: "Pops Glück ist, daß Pop kein Problem hat. Deshalb kann man Pop nicht denken, nicht kritisieren, nicht analytisch schreiben, sondern Pop ist Pop leben, fasziniert betrachten, besessen studieren, maximal materialreich erzählen, feiern" (The joy of pop is that pop has no problem. Therefore, you cannot think, criticize, or write pop analytically. Rather, pop is living pop, observing it in fascination, studying it obsessively, narrating it with as much material as possible, celebrating it).[18] While Goetz's claim here performs *Popliteratur's* immediacy, Brinkmann also theorizes pop aesthetics and its commitment to ending hierarchies and norms. Throughout his writings, he discusses pop's preference for *Oberflächenbeschreibungen*[19]—a

---

16   Originally published in 1968, it is cited here from Rolf Dieter Brinkmann, "Angriff aufs Monopol. Ich hasse alle Dichter," in *Roman oder Leben: Postmoderne in der deutschen Literatur*, ed. Uwe Wittstock (Leipzig: Reclam, 1994), 65–78.

17   Rainald Goetz, *Rave* (Frankfurt am Main: Suhrkamp, 1998).

18   Rainald Goetz, *Hirn* (Frankfurt am Main: Suhrkamp, 1986), 188. This translation and all following are mine.

19   Rolf Dieter Brinkmann, "Der Film in Worten," in *ACID*, ed. Brinkmann and Rygulla, 389. For more on Brinkmann's surface aesthetics, see Gerd Gemünden, "The Depth of the Surface, or, What Rolf Dieter Brinkmann Learned from

poetics of the surface with no room for analysis—and its commitment to *sampling* and *archiving*. *Sampling* is the citation of cultural artifacts and their reintroduction into new contexts in often disorienting ways. As Thomas Ernst notes in his monograph on *Popliteratur*, "Durchgängiges Motiv war, dass die Literatur ein subversives Spiel mit vorhandenen Zeichen und Texten sein müsse, eine Collage aus Zitaten, ein Sampling aus Vorhandenem, vergleichbar der aufkommenden DJ-Culture" (a consistent theme was that literature was to be a subversive game with available symbols and texts, a collage of citations, samples on hand, similar to emerging DJ culture).[20] *Archiving* is the process of gathering as much material as possible to document and produce the immediacy of pop without normative organizing principles. Moritz Baßler describes pop thus as the "Ergebnis einer Tauschhandlung zwischen anerkannter Kultur und der Welt des Profanen" (result of bartering between canonical culture and the world of the profane) and thus "als Medium des Neuen, zuallererst eine Archivierungs- und Re-Kanonisierungsmaschine" (as a medium of the new, first and foremost an archiving and re-canonizing machine).[21] Finally, *the surface*, the central aesthetic metaphor for *Popliteratur*—and for postmodernism more broadly—is the fleeting ideal space precluding analysis where authors and readers collectively and constantly seek to remain. In its striving to confound the calcification of forms for analysis, *Popliteratur* thus reflects Brinkmann and his contemporaries' belief—just as in SJE work against injustice—in the damaging nature of norms.

Brinkmann aims to undermine norms with samples reintroduced into multimodal textual environments.[22] He intends for his samples to disrupt formally rather than shock through content. His goal is a "zeitadäquate Form, die heterogenstes Material zu einem Thema sammeln und miteinander verbinden kann, [die] sich nur erst vereinzelt andeutet—collagenhaft, mit erzählerischen Einschüben, voller Erfindungen, Bild—also Oberflächenbeschreibungen, unlinear, diskontinuierlich … ein Raum, in dem herumzuspazieren einfach wieder Spaß macht" (form adequate to the times that can gather the most heterogeneous material on

---

Andy Warhol," *German Quarterly* 68, no. 3 (1995): 235–50; and Harry Louis Roddy Jr., "The 'Mass Ornament' at Play in Rolf Dieter Brinkmann's *Oberflächenbeschreibungen*," *South Atlantic Review* 75, no. 1 (2010): 45–65.

20 Thomas Ernst, *Popliteratur* (Hamburg: Rotbuch, 2001), 34. Sampling is prevalent in the musical genres/techniques of hip hop, dub, plunderphonics, and musique concrète.

21 Moritz Baßler, *Der deutsche Pop-Roman: Die neuen Archivisten* (Munich: C. H. Beck, 2002), 46.

22 See, e.g., Stephanie Schmitt, "'Ich möchte mehr Gegenwart!' Aspekte der Intermedialität in den Texten Rolf Dieter Brinkmanns," in *Medialität der Kunst: Rolf Dieter Brinkmann in der Moderne*, ed. Markus Fauser (Bielefeld: transcript, 2011), 175–92, here 178.

a theme and join it together, that initially becomes apparent only in isolated instances—like a collage with narrative insertions, full of inventions, image—an aesthetics of the surface, nonlinear, discontinuous ... a space in which walking around is fun again).[23]

This new literature, however, is not meaningless. In order to understand how an empty formalism creates meaning for *Popliteratur* readers, we can view the latter as what Dick Hebdige calls a *subculture*: "This is what distinguishes the visual ensembles of spectacular subcultures from those favoured in the surrounding culture(s). They are *obviously* fabricated. ... In this they go against the grain of a mainstream culture whose principle defining characteristic ... is a tendency to masquerade as nature."[24] Hebdige refers to these fabricated constellations of samples as *bricolage*—a process whereby the revaluation of objects through reorganization and juxtaposition results in collage-like texts—noting that these "magical systems of connection ... are capable of infinite extension because basic elements can be used in a variety of improvised combinations to generate new meanings within them."[25] Sampled concrete objects in bricolage are thus placed in "a symbolic ensemble which serve[s] to erase or subvert their original straight meaning."[26] The concept of bricolage allows us to characterize Brinkmann's surface as something more than a frenzied and meaningless site inundated with random pop-cultural samples.[27] Through bricolage, Brinkmann instead derives meaning from the multimodal interaction of the samples, deterritorializing normative forms through repeated interruption and precluding any reterritorializing analysis.

In its ability to signify through decontextualization, bricolage is the defining move of the postmodernist. Frederic Jameson notes that "what replaces these various depth models is ... a conception of practices, discourses and textual play ... here too depth is replaced by surface, or by multiple surfaces."[28] These undermined depth models rely on binaries including "essence and appearance," "latent and manifest,"

---

23 Brinkmann, "Der Film," 388–89.

24 Dick Hebdige, *Subculture: The Meaning of Style* (London: Methuen, 1979), 101–2. Though Hebdige's focus is punk, the connection between subculture and form also holds true for Brinkmann. Further, punk is present in *Popliteratur*, e.g., Goetz's *Hirn*.

25 Hebdige, *Subculture*, 103.

26 Hebdige, *Subculture*, 104.

27 For more on bricolage in Brinkmann's poetry, see Jan Röhnert, "Der Fächer mit der Aufschrift 'Kleiner Nordwind': Die Max-Jacob-Episode von Aragons *Anicet* in der Lesart Rolf Dieter Brinkmanns: Recycling oder Bricolage?," *Arcadia* 40, no. 1 (2005): 97–116.

28 Frederic Jameson, *Postmodernism, or, The Cultural Logic of Late Capitalism* (Durham, NC: Duke University Press, 1990), 62.

"authenticity and inauthenticity," and "signifier and signified." In agreement, Brinkmann clarifies that *Popliteratur* play breaks with all forms of normativity (or depth models), including the word-image binary: "Der 'Tod' der Literatur kann bloß durch Literatur selber erfolgen, indem Geschriebenes sich nicht mehr dem zuordnet. Also: aufhören über 'Literatur' zu reden ... als ob es noch darum ginge" (The "death" of literature can happen only through literature itself when writing no longer designates itself as such. So: stop talking about "literature" ... as if that was still the point).[29] And remaining written texts should break norms by attacking the high-low culture binary. For inspiration, Brinkmann looks beyond the postmodern cultural present, noting forbears in the literary innovations of Gottfried Benn and the class-marked prose of Louis-Ferdinand Céline[30] (perhaps only "sampling" the language of the Frenchman and thus undermining his virulent antisemitism and sympathy for Nazism), as well as in traditions beyond the written word including the Dadaism and conceptualism of Marcel Duchamp.[31]

Most importantly, though, Brinkmann attacks the literary modernism of Europe—"das *europäisch*-abendländische Kulturmonopol [ist] gebrochen" (the *European*-western cultural monopoly is broken)[32]—and mines the American counterculture of the 1960s for material.[33] These new American literary products, he believes, "polemisieren nicht einmal, sie sind einfach gemacht worden und 'da,' und daß sie das zuerst sind und sagen, mag ihre Provokation für den abendländischen Literaturgeschmack darstellen. Man kann sich herausnehmen, was einem gefällt ... 'Literatur' von der Leine lassen, sie nicht mehr als Kettenhund ansehen, ihr langsames Eingehen an der leeren Forderung nach 'objektiver' Bedeutsamkeit überspringen" (do not even polemicize, they are simply created and "there," and the fact that they are like this—first and foremost—and that they say as much constitutes their provocativeness for western literary taste. Take from this whatever you like ... let "literature" off the leash, don't view it anymore as a chained dog, skip right past its slow dying from the empty demand for "objective" meaning).[34] He looks specifically to Beat poetry and the New York School, including Frank O'Hara, William S.

---

29 Brinkmann, "Der Film," 391.
30 Brinkmann, "Angriff aufs Monopol," 75.
31 For Brinkmann's work in the context of visual poetry, see Roddy, "Mass Ornament." On the relationship between bricolage, Dadaism, and Surrealism, see Hebdige, *Subculture*, 105. Finally, for Brinkmann on Duchamp, see Brinkmann, "Angriff aufs Monopol," 75.
32 Brinkmann, "Angriff aufs Monopol," 65. Emphasis mine.
33 On Beat poetry and other American literature in the 1960s in this context, see Jonathan Woolley, "Beyond the Beats: An Ethics of Spontaneity in the Poetry of Rolf Dieter Brinkmann," *College Literature* 30, no. 4 (2003): 1–31.
34 Brinkmann, "Der Film," 399.

Burroughs, Michael McClure, and Charles Bukowski; pop art by Andy Warhol; music, especially The Doors and Frank Zappa; and underground comix.

Brinkmann celebrates this American cultural production for its frantic bricolage nature, which he ties to the rapid technological shifts of the 1960s: "Der konkreten Erfahrung eines miesen Vermitteltseins wird somit heute direkt und unverstellt Ausdruck gegeben in der Literatur der jungen Amerikaner" (Today, the concrete experience of a pathetic mediatedness is expressed directly and without disguise in the literature of the young Americans).[35] The technologized counterculture of New York and San Francisco pop environments represents for Brinkmann the new, formally unstable postmodern, ripe for sampling, in contrast to normative European modernism. Accordingly, Brinkmann's artifacts are taken from the present, the "technisierte Umwelt" (mechanized environment) of the 1960s: "Kinoplakate, Filmbilder, die täglichen Schlagzeilen, Apparate, Autounfälle, Comics, Schlager, vorliegende Romane, Illustriertenberichte" (film posters and images, daily headlines, gadgets, car accidents, comics, hits, available novels, magazine reports).[36] For Brinkmann as *bricoleur*, American popular culture represents innovation specifically with respect to form.

Comics are central for Brinkmann because they enable significant formal and multimodal play, most notably in the unstable and shifting distinctions between verbal and visual modes of communication. Their complicated network of formal conventions, from speech and thought bubbles to panel-panel relations and from color, time, and depth to page layout, offers authors and readers much to manipulate when creating meaning. Comics theorist Thierry Groensteen has argued using his term *arthrology*—the way panels and pages interrelate rhizomatically—that the comics form is a complex generative language asking readers to do much of the productive work.[37] Further, intertextuality has long been central to comics, which often integrate elements of storylines that play out from a variety of perspectives across multiple titles. It is this malleability and resulting formal play that allows comics to both represent the otherwise unrepresentable—as discussed above in their affordances for social justice—and confound and interrupt, thus enabling a postmodernist surface aesthetics.

As an initial example of Brinkmann's use of comics and comics sampling for formal destabilization, let us consider the cover of his *Die Piloten* (fig. 9.1). This bricolage work juxtaposes comics characters with

---

35 Brinkmann, "Angriff aufs Monopol," 73.
36 Brinkmann, "Angriff aufs Monopol," 71–72.
37 Thierry Groensteen, *The System of Comics*, trans. Bart Beaty and Nick Nguyen (Jackson: University Press of Mississippi, 2007), 2.

Figure 9.1. Multimedia collage cover of Brinkmann, *Die Piloten: Neue Gedichte* (Cologne: Kiepenheuer & Witsch, 1968).

photographs, speech bubbles, and other drawings. The front cover contains the title, author, and publisher as an onomatopoetic comics sound bubble, while the back contains five speech bubbles. Four feature text in English, German, and an East Slavic language,[38] and the final one contains an exclamation in an undetermined language. These speech and sound bubbles and an additional onomatopoetic "WHAAM!" are the only verbal text on the cover other than Brinkmann's name on the binding. Beyond this text from diverse languages and sources, the cover is dominated by a wide variety of photographs and drawings, most of which portray people. Of these, most are women, many unclothed.

This cover is a clear example of Brinkmann's use of ostensibly decontextualizing bricolage, sampling, and popular culture, with comics central in formally destabilizing play. However, it is also an initial hint that

---

38 While the word "хлибожлер" likely means something insulting like "bread eater" or glutton, it is perhaps spelled wrong (consider Ukrainian "хлібожер" or Russian "хлебожор"). It is sampled from an American comic, where its meaning is unclear: Michael O'Donoghue and Frank Springer, *The Adventures of Phoebe Zeitgeist* (New York: A Grove Press, 1968), 67.

formal play cannot effectively subvert these samples' original meaning for all readers equally. It is clear that comics and images here are not, as Brinkmann suggested, "simply created and 'there'" for everyone.[39] Instead, comics and sexualized bodies create meaning for specific audiences by drawing on their countercultural origins but ultimately reinforce oppressive norms. In the following section, I consider how the creators and readers exercise power in different ways through the consumption of this content and thus the performance of oppression. Identifying the role of power in these samples is an initial step in the performance of SJE in the present chapter.

Representations of (Hetero-)Normativity in Brinkmann

Brinkmann views the transgressive meaning of his comics samples as resulting not as much from the content of the texts themselves but more from what consumers of *Popliteratur* do with them as forms, that is, as Hebdige's states, through "the signifying practices which represent … objects and render them meaningful."[40] Reading these comics in their reintroduced contexts is meant to destabilize the predominance of the written word and genre distinctions and thus produce immediacy and the surface. This move is intended to occur in two complementary ways, through (1) the intentional defamiliarization of forms through juxtaposition and (2) the immediate recognition of comics artifacts among other pop-cultural examples. Only the seemingly familiar can be destabilized. These methods are not meant to deceive; readers are in on the game. By subverting formal norms and enabling the specific signifying practices of comics, pop becomes exciting.[41] Nevertheless, the second method

---

39 Brinkmann, "Der Film," 399.

40 Hebdige, *Subculture*, 127. Elsewhere, as an example of repurposing and recontextualizing symbols, Hebdige references the punk usage of the swastika to generate anger rather than express Nazi views. See Hebdige, *Subculture*, 116–17.

41 An example of this excitement—through both shock and recognition—came during a 1983 television broadcast, during which Goetz sliced his forehead with a blade and bled on the text he was reading about doing exactly that: "Ihr könnts mein Hirn haben. Ich schneide ein Loch in meinen Kopf, in die Stirne schneide ich das Loch. Mit meinem Blut soll mir mein Hirn auslaufen. Ich brauche kein Hirn nicht mehr, weil es eine solche Folter ist in meinem Kopf. Ihr folterts mich, ihr Schweine, derweil ich doch bloß eines wissen möchte, wo oben, wo unten ist und wie das Scheißleben geht. Wie geht das Scheißleben?" (You can have my brain. I cut a hole in my head, in my forehead I cut the hole. With my blood my brain will flow out. I don't need a brain anymore because it's such torture in my head. You're torturing me, you pigs, while I want to know just one thing, which way is up, which down, and how this shitty life works. How does this

for producing immediacy already contains a limitation. Brinkman relies on an exclusionary technique: only those whom the content in question addresses can find the texts subversive. His selection of a specific genre, underground comix, for his sampling was thus not a neutral choice, but rather one that reinscribed existing norms of consumption and undermined their intended use as contentless vehicles for formal play.

Underground comix arose in the hippie countercultures of San Francisco, Austin, and New York.[42] Notable authors include Robert Crumb, Aline Kominsky-Crumb, and Gilbert Shelton. Beyond their formal innovations, these comix were also a reaction to the Comics Code (1954–2011),[43] which prohibited depictions of or positive references to sex, drug use, and queer stories. The comix Brinkmann selected portray hypodermic needles, disrespected policemen, and, most relevant to this chapter, naked female bodies. Klaus Rümmele suggests that such pornographic elements are meant to disrupt normalcy and provide a caricature of the "sauberen Amerikaner" (clean American).[44] Underground comix thus acted as more than formal interruptions in Brinkmann's bricolage: they also attacked the content norms of the Comics Code.

Brinkmann's selection of inherently meaningful content may not appear problematic for his goals. Even if the comics were chosen for their formal qualities, their content might still play a useful role. And if the subversion of meaning through bricolage was undermined by the ideological content, it nonetheless would seem appropriate for comics to attack cultural norms via their content. But if content then functions as a signifying

---

shitty life work?). Rainald Goetz, "Subito," in *Klagenfurter Texte zum Ingeborg-Bachmann Preis 1983*, ed. Humbert Fink, Marcel Reich-Ranicki, and Ernst Willner (Munich: List, 1983), 65–77, here 75.

42 Santiago García, *On the Graphic Novel*, trans. Bruce Campbell (Jackson: University Press of Mississippi, 2015), 103. On underground comix and German (comics) culture, see Andreas Knigge's monographs, *Fortsetzung folgt: Comic Kultur in Deutschland* (Frankfurt am Main: Ullstein, 1986) and *Comics: Vom Massenblatt ins multimediale Abenteuer* (Reinbek bei Hamburg: Rowohlt, 1996).

43 The Comics Code was a set of regulations self-imposed by major comics publishers intended to preempt government intervention following the anti-comics debates and congressional hearings associated with Fredric Wertham's book *The Seduction of the Innocent* (New York: Rinehart, 1954). Wertham's book argued that reading comics would make children violent. See Hillary Chute, *Why Comics? From Underground to Everywhere* (New York: Harper, 2007), 114. On the anti-comics debates, see *Pulp Demons: International Dimensions of the Postwar Anticomics Campaigns,* ed. John A. Lent (Madison, WI: Fairleigh Dickinson University Press, 1999).

44 Klaus Rümmele, *Zeichensprache: Text und Bild bei Rolf Dieter Brinkmann und Pop-Autoren der Gegenwart* (Karlsruhe: Universität Karlsruhe Universitätsbibliothek, 2012), 55.

practice in his norm-breaking project, Brinkmann also allows its meaning to be analyzed on its own.

A striking example of comix' content is seen in the abovementioned cover of *Die Piloten* (fig. 9.1), in which the naked bodies he uses to disrupt are overwhelmingly female. In reproducing comics and images depicting sexualized female bodies, Brinkmann defines the female body as a static object or site for cultural inscription by others, thus establishing and performing his power as a male subject.[45] While underground comix were designed to oppose the norms upheld by the Comics Code, including prohibitions on nudity, "illicit sex," "sexual abnormalities," and "sex perversion or any inference to same," most underground comix artists were upholding the discourse of heteronormativity while performing the hypermasculine.[46]

Consider here Robert Crumb, perhaps the first major underground comix artist to depict explicit sexual acts.[47] Shortly after the appearance of the first few issues of his seminal *Zap Comics* (1968–2014), Crumb focused more directly on explicit sex—including violent and demeaning scenes of rape and incest—in titles including *Snatch Comics*, *Big Ass Comics*, and *Jiz Comics*[48]—and divided his audiences. Though his popularity increased overall, many, especially female comics creators, viewed this turn as sexist and misogynistic,[49] objecting specifically to the visual representation and the culture surrounding it. Trina Robbins, who helped publish the first all-female comic *It Ain't Me Babe* (1970), remembers that she "objected from the very beginning to all the sexism, to the incredible misogyny" that was not just about "making fun of women" but rather "representations of rape and mutilation, and murder that involved women, as something funny," and that she was excluded as a result. She

---

45   On the female body as performatively generated and externally defined, see Judith Butler, *Gender Trouble* (New York: Routledge, 1999), 163–80.

46   On the production of discourses on sex, consider "The Incitement to Discourse" in Michel Foucault, *The History of Sexuality: Volume 1, An Introduction*, trans. Robert Hurley (New York: Pantheon Books, 1978), 17–35. On heteronormativity, see Adrienne Rich, "Compulsory Heterosexuality and Lesbian Experience," *Journal of Women's History* 15, no. 3 (2003): 11–48. See also Hillary Chute on comics as queer code in *Why Comics?*, 349–50. On the relationship of comics, especially underground comix, to gender, sex, sexuality, and norms, see the discussions in Chute's chapters "Why Sex?" (103–40) and "Why Queer?" (349–88). See also García, *On the Graphic Novel*, 105–7. And on the performativity of gender, Butler notes "the signifying gestures through which gender itself is established" as an identity that has its causes in "institutions, practices, discourses" (Butler, *Gender Trouble*, xxviii–xxix).

47   Chute, *Why Comics?*, 105, 114.

48   Chute, *Why Comics?*, 89.

49   Chute, *Why Comics?*, 124, 127.

concluded: "I objected to that, so they objected to me."[50] Even Crumb himself described his content as "all this craziness, the sexual stuff, the hostility toward women."[51]

This type of sexualization of female bodies—in popular culture more broadly, in comix contexts often promoting or depicting violence, and in Brinkmann's work—reinforce norms not only through their very presence, but also in their assumed availability for consumption by an audience. In her 1993 monograph on the body and feminism, Bordo connects the postmodern to the "amoral and ceaseless proliferation of products and images" resulting from "the progress of consumer capitalism,"[52] which "depends on the continual production of novelty, of fresh images to stimulate desire."[53] Novelties themselves, Brinkmann's comics samples are read, interpreted, and consumed. The immediacy Brinkmann seeks in American underground comix subculture can thus be interpreted in terms of a hypercapitalist rush to consume the female body, which thus distracts from the aesthetics of the surface.

In *Popliteratur*, pop culture references can thus reproduce existing power relations in society, a problem often omitted from analyses of the genre. Margaret McCarthy criticizes scholarship that presents pop culture's value in *Popliteratur* as being "available to everyone, a position which bends over backwards to correct the wide divide between the 'haves' with access to high culture and the 'have nots' who must make do with mass culture and improvise an empowering relationship to it."[54] Though Brinkmann's sampled comics may disrupt readers through formal innovation, their content does not address, represent, or empower all readers equally, and not all norms and binaries are undermined. When heteronormativity and hypermasculinity are repeatedly performed, female readers and creators are excluded and shunned as passive observers.

Brinkmann thus uses comics in two distinct and often antagonistic ways. Comics formally disrupt hierarchies through multimodality, play, and pop-cultural immediacy. But as content, they also represent a normative popular culture and thus address a specific and exclusive audience.

---

50 Quoted in Patrick Rosenkranz, *Rebel Vision: The Underground Comix Revolution 1963–1975* (Seattle, WA: Fantagraphics Books, 2002), 155. Following Robbins's *It Ain't Me Babe*, underground comix became far more open to women authors, especially with *Wimmen's Comix* (1972–1992)—initially coproduced by and including content from Aline Kominsky, the later wife of Robert Crumb. These titles, however, arrive years after the content sampled by Brinkmann in question in this chapter. For more, see Chute, *Why Comics?*, 120–30.
51 Quoted in Rosenkranz, *Rebel Vision*, 137.
52 Bordo, *Unbearable Weight*, 277–78.
53 Bordo, *Unbearable Weight*, 25.
54 Margaret McCarthy, "Introduction," in *German Pop Literature: An Introduction*, ed. Margaret McCarthy (Berlin: DeGruyter, 2015), 1–29, here 10.

Brinkmann wants to shock readers with rapid formal shifts within and between comics and other texts and defamiliarize conventions within each of these forms. In selecting comix, he seeks to disrupt normativity more broadly, both in form *and* in content. And while these comix stand in defiance of the norms represented in the Comics Code, they do not oppose certain cultural norms of Brinkmann's time, most notably hypermasculine attitudes toward gender and sexuality. This problematic back-and-forth haunts the sampling of comics throughout his work.

Die Piloten (1968)

Beyond its cover, *Die Piloten* is relatively reserved in its use of formal play. Inside, it contains few comics and images. Its poems are primarily made up of written text, printed mostly in one font and arranged largely in free verse. The content, however, clearly focuses on popular culture, with references to comics and other narratives from the United States, from Buffalo Bill and Mary Poppins to Elizabeth Taylor and Humphrey Bogart. This initial focus on content points to Brinkmann's reliance on popular culture beyond form.

Brinkmann makes limited use of formal play in the verbal text of the poems. Play in page layout makes the poem "Einfach Sonne" (Simply Sun) more immediate as each use of the deictic "hier" (here) refers to its unique physical location on the page. In "Das Verschwinden eines Flugzeugs" (The Disappearance of a Plane) vertically orientated text alters the meaning of a reference to Coca-Cola. Bolded and enlarged text makes further mention of Coke stand out alongside a reference to the US in "Gedicht auf einen Lieferwagen u. a." (Poem to a Delivery Truck Among Other Things). Finally, an all-caps, enlarged, and bold "ENDE" (THE END) closes "Alle Gedichte" (All Poems), the last poem in the volume, as if the final shot in a film.

Comics references appear in the poems verbally, further blurring the distinction between form and content. Mention of speech bubbles, references to characters including Batman, Superman, and Tarzan (all hypermasculine characters), and comics onomatopoeia are sprinkled throughout the poems. "Populäres Gedicht Nr. 17" (Popular Poem No. 17) contains repeated references to America—"Mr. Amerika" (Mr. America), "made in U.S.A.," "des großen amerikanischen Hau" (of the great American blow); allusions to superheroes—"feuerfest" (fireproof), "Muskel" (muscles), "Kryptonit" (kryptonite), and "super-super"; and sound effects and exclamations—"POW" and "WOW."

Finally, the cover, discussed above (fig. 1), undermines formal norms through multimodal play. But it also signals through its numerous naked female bodies available for consumption that it will disrupt the sexual norms of the Comics Code but not those of the heteronormative counterculture. Further examples of gender binaries abound. The first page of the volume presents a comic in the form of an advertisement addressed to men and boys. The book's three sections begin with comics criticizing American bourgeois culture and canonicity in comics while Nancy, from the eponymous comic strip by Ernie Bushmiller, literally loses her mind as her brain, labeled as "Verstand" (reason), falls out of her skull.[55] Finally, Brinkmann ends the volume with a series of disconnected single-panel comics by Edwin Demby and Joe Brainard arranged as a unified comic but each individually declaring "the end." In this final comic, a male soldier is valorized, likely ironically, through his shiny lieutenant's bars, while a lovestruck woman is shown crying, emotional.

Die Piloten thus both disrupts and reinforces normativity, relying on formally unstable bricolage as well as signifying content. The experiments with typeface and page layout as well as the bricolage cover, the advertisement, and the comics references all serve to interrupt and address the reader on the surface. At the same time, the comics' content blunts this interruption by reducing women to emotional and sexualized bodies available for consumption by the hypermasculine men the volume overtly addresses.

ACID: Neue amerikanische Szene (1969)

A year after *Die Piloten* appeared, Brinkmann and Ralf-Rainer Rygulla published *ACID: Neue amerikanische Szene*, consisting primarily of American Beat poems and essays collected and translated into German. In contrast to *Die Piloten*, not only the comics but also most of the texts in *ACID* are sampled from works by other authors, then cut up and rearranged. Pertinent to the discussion of gender and addressivity, while female comics artists, poets, and cultural critics are not absent from *ACID*, of the approximately ninety-five longer texts featured, only seven are by women.

Like the cover of *Die Piloten*, *ACID* is strikingly visual throughout: photographs, advertisements, and comics appear between, under, and within poems. Beyond the poetry by authors including Burroughs, McClure, and Bukowski, *ACID* contains interviews with and essays by Zappa, Warhol, and McLuhan. The volume begins with "The New Mutants," an essay by Fiedler describing 1960s American counterculture. It ends with Brinkmann's own "Der Film in Worten." Far more than in *Die Piloten*, comics—taken from underground comix artists including

---

55 Feminist and queer theories have drawn attention to the gendering of reason and irrationality. Consider, for example, Bordo's discussion of how the gendered mind-body duality views women as separated from reason (*Unbearable Weight*, 2–11).

Robert Crumb, Joe Brainard, Tom Veitch, and Tuli Kupferberg—play a central role. The individual poems, interviews, images, and advertisements are not meant to be read separately; instead, they are to be taken together as "materials"[56]—as bricolage.

Among the many instances of comics play in *ACID* performing Brinkmann's surface aesthetics, three contrasting examples serve to illustrate how the work as a whole fails to effectively undermine norms. The first, "Eine Buchkritik" (A Book Review, fig. 9.2) by Ron Padgett, comes closest to Brinkmann's desired aesthetics; it gives the reader no opportunity for depth by using formal play with little content.

"Eine Buchkritik" appears between two vignettes or short stories, one containing flow charts and the other punctuated by comics. The work tells us that Padgett likes a book by Edward Gorey and flouts several comics conventions. A single image—or perhaps unbound comics panel—depicting a rhinoceros in front of a mountain appears nine times; only the speech bubbles and the text change. Four panels contain speech bubbles enclosing a single typed word in one font. Another contains the number "15," the reviewed book's title, handwritten and larger. In three other panels, the bubble contains only part of the word—the remainder extends to the left or right. The final panel contains two handwritten words and no speech bubble.

A reader may well question whether this is a comic. Its form, combining speech bubbles, unchanging serial images, and declarative text creates doubt as to its composition. It resists attempts at narrativizing or, in Groensteen's terms, *vectorizing*[57] it as a comic rather than as a playful arrangement of images and text. Ultimately, its non-normative form and lack of analyzable content enabled through formal play exemplify Brinkmann's desired absence of ostensible meaning.

The second example, interspersed in an interview with Frank Zappa titled "Mutationsblues" (Mutation Blues), proves less successful at subverting content.[58] Zappa speaks positively of the purchasing power of consumer youth culture to break established forms. Accompanying the interview are four images, illustrations, or comics (fig. 9.3).

It is difficult to define these formally. The first, an image of a gorilla in front of what may be an American flag, follows Zappa's discussion of fashion trends. The second, interrupting Zappa's attack on organized groups, including Vietnam War protestors, is a photograph of an angry, shirtless man holding a lump of coal or maybe feces. The third, a grainy image of

---

56   Brinkmann and Rygulla refer to *ACID* as a "Materialsammlung mit Lesebuchcharakter." *ACID*, 417.

57   Thierry Groensteen, *Comics and Narration*, trans. Ann Miller (Jackson: University Press of Mississippi, 2013), 13.

58   Brinkmann and Rygulla, *ACID*, 286–93.

Figure 9.2: Toward the surface in Ron Padgett, "Eine Buchkritik," in Brinkmann and Rygulla, *ACID: Amerikanische Szene* (Frankfurt am Main: März bei Zweitausendeins, 1969), 181.

Figure 9.3: Images accompanying an interview with Frank Zappa, in Brinkmann and Rygulla, *ACID: Neue amerikanische Szene* (Frankfurt am Main: März bei Zweitausendeins, 1969). Main: März bei Zweitausendeins, 1969), 287–88, 292–93.

a toilet, accompanies Zappa's expression of distaste for psychiatrists. The fourth, a single-panel comic, references a description of totalitarianism from Orwell's *Nineteen Eighty-Four* (1949): a man's face getting stamped by a boot as he utters "MUSIC" through a speech bubble.[59] Here, Zappa complains about the emptiness of countercultural music, an acknowledgment that not even pop's own aesthetic is sacred. In each instance, Zappa argues that normalized form limits meaning, echoing Brinkmann's opposition to normative analysis. And the sampling of the visual media, such that it is unclear which are photographs or drawings, or whether the speech bubble marks the last image as a comic, attempts to subvert its presented content.

Despite the jarring interplay of images and forms, the context of their use within Zappa's interview nonetheless renders them meaningful. Further, the presence of Zappa himself carries significant meaning for Brinkmann and his readers, as the former's music and persona affect the interpretation of his interview answers. Like *Popliteratur*, Zappa's musical oeuvre is simultaneously rife with formal play and extreme hypermasculinity. A particularly instructive example is his song "Harry, You're a Beast" from the 1968 The Mothers of Invention album *We're Only in It for the Money*. This eighty-two-second song features a Romantic-period piano introduction partly accompanied by a drum set, interrupted by a psychedelic rock song, itself interrupted by a musique concrète bricolage sample containing edited tape. The song's lyrics and narration denigrate American women and describe sexual assault and rape while a traumatized woman cries in the background. Excerpts include: "You paint your head, your mind is dead / You don't even know what I just said / That's you, American womanhood!" and "You're phony on top, you're phony underneath / You lay in bed and grit your teeth." [60] Here, a "phony" or *constructed* female body is available for consumption through sexual violence.[61] What in this song appears to be an attack on form quickly becomes real content, specifically trauma depicted aurally, resulting from

---

59   George Orwell, *Nineteen Eighty-four* (New York: Harcourt, Brace, 1949), 271: "If you want a picture of the future, imagine a boot stamping on a human face—forever."

60   The Mothers of Invention, "Harry, You're a Beast," in *We're Only in It for the Money* (Verve Records, 1968).

61   In her chapter on the construction of the body in postmodernism, Bordo suggests that, "gradually and surely, a technology that was first aimed at the replacement of malfunctioning parts has generated an industry and an ideology fueled by fantasies of rearranging, transforming, and correcting, an ideology of limitless improvement and change, defying the historicity, the mortality, and, indeed, the very materiality of the body." "'Material Girl': The Effacements of Postmodern Culture," in Bordo, *Unbearable Weight*, 245–75, here 245.

Figure 9.4: Formal play in Kenward Elmslie and Joe Brainard, "Jellied Salads: Shrimp and Cole Slaw," in Brinkmann and Rygulla, *ACID: Neue amerikanische Szene* (Frankfurt am Main: März bei Zweitausendeins, 1969), 107.

the perpetuation of cycles of violence casually accepted within the connected discourses of heteronormativity and hypermasculinity.

The final example, "Jellied Salads: Shrimp and Cole Slaw," by Kenward Elmslie and Joe Brainard (fig. 9.4), is the clearest instance in *ACID* of a comics text simultaneously subverting form through bricolage while reinforcing heteronormativity.

The comic interrupts another text by Elmslie, "Heimisches Eingeweide" (Domestic Entrails),[62] a short story containing a list of

62   Brinkmann and Rygulla, *ACID*, 107.

planned events and meals. The comic shows a woman crying in front of the panels considering a strange recipe that explodes during preparation. Questions regarding its nature as a comic, a recipe, a part of the story it interrupts, or how the panels and temporality work are unanswerable. While there appears to be no way to spatially, temporally, or formally pin down the text, its misogynistic content provides the reader a clear starting point for analysis. A woman in shock is once again reduced to hysterical tears, this time following a traumatic setback *in the kitchen*. As in similar moments in *Die Piloten* and the Zappa song discussed above, the woman here performs her gender as defined by the audience Brinkmann addresses.

Subversive Form and Representational Injustice

Brinkmann attempts to disorient the reader using sampled texts, mobilizing multimodal formal play to preclude analysis and destabilize genre norms. The comics form, complex and playful, appears ideal for his aesthetic project. However, the comics' shock value here does not stem from formal disruption alone. Brinkmann attempts to show formal but also cultural norms as *fabricated* (Hebdige) or *culturally constructed* (Butler)[63] through the specific underground comix he samples. The interruption of the values of the Comics Code through sexually explicit images and content relies on Brinkmann's performance of the hypermasculine—sustaining gender norms—and reveals a gap in his overall undermining of normativity. The formally disruptive force of comics is thus blunted by their content. Brinkmann's comics samples lose their subversive potential by upholding the dominance of an oppressive popular culture dominated by heteronormativity and the consumption of female bodies.

While it is certainly worthwhile to characterize Brinkmann's work with its preponderance of sexualized bodies as an example of representational injustice, to best identify how oppression functions in these texts we must go further by refusing to separate the heteronormative content he samples from his formal innovations. To best serve social justice goals, this chapter thus considers the connections between Brinkmann's larger postmodernist aims and his reinscription of (hetero-)normativity and problematizes the strict separation of form and content, a heuristic held in this chapter to show a weakness in his postmodernist *Popliteratur* project. By "draw[ing] attention to the representational injustices" inherent in Brinkmann's claims, as Nijdam advocates,[64] we can better demonstrate how dividing content from form entails weaknesses broader than heteronormativity. Such an approach serves SJE—by effectively addressing

63 Hebdige, *Subculture*, 102; Butler, *Gender Trouble*, 10.
64 Nijdam, "Introduction," 193.

representational injustice potentially resulting in trauma as well as normativity more broadly—better than a mere attack on Brinkmann's reinscribed norms. It leads us to ask whether the poetic work of Brinkmann, if not of *Popliteratur* or even postmodernism, is actually "fun" after all. Perhaps it is closer to Horkheimer and Adorno's Donald Duck than one might think.

Notes on Contributors

Aylin Bademsoy is Assistant Professor of Germanic Languages and Literature at Washington University in Saint Louis. Bademsoy earned her doctoral degree from the University of California, Davis, and her first book project examines the entwinement of processes of modernization and racialization in German and Turkish cultural discourse. Bademsoy has also contributed essays on gendered violence in capitalist patriarchies and *völkisch* racism in the colonial context, and co-edited with Marco Abel and Jaimey Fisher a volume of translated interviews of the Berlin school filmmaker Christian Petzold. Most recently, she wrote an essay for the CLCWEB Special Issue on *Value and Culture* on the theory of value-dissociation vis-à-vis Adorno's *Aesthetic Theory*, which is forthcoming in 2025.

John D. Benjamin is Assistant Professor of German in the Department of English & World Languages at the United States Military Academy at West Point. He earned his PhD in 2019 in Germanic Studies from the University of Texas at Austin. His scholarship focuses on L2 reading, applied linguistics, and multimodality; German comics; and the role of cultural form in identity and nationalism. His publications have appeared in *Die Unterrichtspraxis*, *The German Quarterly*, and *Second Language Research & Practice*, as well as in edited volumes on applied linguistics and visual culture.

Katja Herges is a physician, literary scholar, and educator. In addition to her medical degree, she earned a PhD in German and Feminist Theory and Research at the University of California, Davis. She has held various positions in neuroscience, mental health care, and in the medical humanities. Based on her interdisciplinary background, her research and teaching are situated at the intersection of German cultural studies, medicine, visual culture, and gender studies. Specifically, she is interested in how contemporary autobiographies of chronic illness (re)shape how we are sick and how we think of illness and dying. Katja has published in venues such as *Literature and Medicine*, *BMJ Medical Humanities*, *Seminar: A Journal of Germanic Studies*, and *Gender, Women and Research*, among others.

Christina Kraenzle is Associate Professor of German at York University, Toronto, Canada. Her teaching and research focus on modern and contemporary German-language cultural studies, with a concentration on issues of mobility, transnationalism, and cultural memory. She has published articles on contemporary German-language comics in *The Journal of Graphic Novels and Comics*, *Seminar*, and in the edited volume *Anxious Journeys: Contemporary German Travel Literature*. Along with Julia Ludewig, she co-edited a special issue on *Transnationalism in German Comics* in the *Journal of Graphic Novels and Comics* (2020). She is also the co-editor (with Maria Mayr) of *Seminar: A Journal of Germanic Studies*.

Priscilla Layne is Professor of German and Adjunct Associate Professor of African Diaspora Studies at the University of North Carolina at Chapel Hill. Her book *White Rebels in Black: German Appropriation of Black Popular Culture* was published in 2018 by the University of Michigan Press. She has also published essays on Turkish German Culture, translation, punk, and film. She translated Olivia Wenzel's debut novel *1000 Serpentinenangst*, which was published in June 2022. Her two most recent books, *Out of This World: Afro-German Afrofuturism* (Northwestern University Press) and a critical guide to Fassbinder's *The Marriage of Maria Braun* (Camden House), both appeared in 2024.

Miriam Libicki is an award-winning creator of comics and graphic narratives. Her short comics have been featured in publications such as *The Nib* and the *Journal of Jewish Identities*. She has published with presses such as Abrams and Rutgers University Press. Her graphic essay collection, *Toward a Hot Jew*, received the Vine Award for Canadian Jewish Literature in 2017, and her painted essay "Who Gets Called an Unfit Mother" was nominated for a Best Short Story Eisner Award in 2020. Libicki also received the Inkpot Award and served as Writer in Residence at the Vancouver Public Library in 2017. She currently teaches Humanities and Illustration at Emily Carr University in Vancouver, Canada.

Elizabeth "Biz" Nijdam is an Assistant Professor and settler scholar in the Department of Central, Eastern, and Northern European Studies at the University of British Columbia in Vancouver, Canada, where she works, learns, and lives on the traditional, ancestral, and unceded territories of Musqueam, Squamish, and Tsleil-Waututh Nations. She is currently completing her book manuscript *Graphic Historiography: History & Memory through Comics and Graphic Novels* (Ohio State University Press). Biz's research and teaching include the representation of history in comics, comics and new media on forced migration, intersections between Indigenous studies and German, European, and migration studies, digital and analog game studies, and feminist methodologies in the graphic arts. Biz sits on the Executive Committee of the International Comic Arts Forum, is the Director of the Comics Studies Cluster in UBC's Public Humanities Hub, and is Co-Director of the Popular Media for Social Change Research Excellence Cluster.

Evelyn Preuss teaches at the University of Oklahoma while finishing her PhD on DEFA cinema at Yale University. She has published articles and anthology chapters on DEFA's aesthetics and narrative structures, the intersection of architecture and film, as well as the diverging historiographies in post-1990 East and West European film and their political impetus. She also co-edited the anthology *The GDR Tomorrow: Rethinking the East German Legacy* (2024), which outlines research trends among a new generation of East German Studies scholars.

Marina Rauchenbacher is affiliated with the International Research Center Gender and Performativity at the University of Music and Performing Arts Vienna, where she worked on the research project "Visualities of Gender in German-language Comics." She also teaches German literature and comics at the University of Vienna. Her research focuses on German-language literature, comics, visual culture studies, gender and queer studies, intersectionality, and environmental humanities. Marina is a board member and founding member of the Austrian Association for Comics and a board member of Arbeitskreis Kulturanalyse.

Charlotte Schallié is Professor of Germanic Studies at the University of Victoria (Canada) and the editor of the multi-award-winning anthology *But I Live: Three Stories of Child Survivors of the Holocaust*. Her teaching and research interests include memory studies, visual culture studies & graphic narratives, teaching and learning about the Holocaust, genocide and human rights education, community-engaged participatory research, care ethics, and arts-based action research. Together with Andrea Webb (UBC), she is the project co-director of a seven-year SSHRC-funded Partnership Grant entitled "Survivor-Centred Visual Narratives" (www.visualnarratives.org).

Gilad Seliktar is a graphic novelist, illustrator, and lecturer in illustration. He has written and illustrated three graphic novels, focusing on documentary and autobiographical themes. These works include *Tsav 8* (2014), *The Demons of Mongols* (2008), and *Who Are You Anyway* (2005). His latest book, *Arad 95*, won the 2024 Navon Award for Best Graphic Novel in Israel. His collaborative work *Farm 54* (2009), written by his sister Galit Seliktar and which he illustrated, earned a place in the official selection of the Angoulême Festival and was named one of *Publisher's Weekly*'s top ten graphic novels of 2011. In 2018, Seliktar received an honorable mention in the Israel Museum's Ben-Yitzhak Award competition for children's book illustration. Seliktar currently teaches at the Bezalel Academy of Art and Design and lives in Pardes Hanna-Karkur, Israel.

Heather I. Sullivan is Professor of German and Comparative Literature at Trinity University in Texas, USA. She has published widely in North America and Europe on ecocriticism and the Anthropocene, Goethe, German Romanticism, petro-texts, the "dark green," fairy tales, and critical plant studies and is currently working on a manuscript titled *The Dark Green: Plants, People, Power.* Sullivan is co-editor of *German Ecocriticism in the Anthropocene* (2017); and of *The Early History of Embodied Cognition from 1740–1920* (2016)*;* author of *The Intercontextuality of Self and Nature in Ludwig Tieck's Early Works* (1997), and co-editor of special journal issues on ecocriticism in the *New German Critique* (2016), *Colloquia Germanica* (2014), and *Interdisciplinary Studies in Literature and the Environment* (2012). She is currently the President of the North American Goethe Society, Associate Editor of the European Ecocriticism Journal *Ecozon@*, and co-editor of the new De Gruyter series, "Ecocriticism Unbound."

Birgit Weyhe was born in Munich in 1969. She spent her childhood in East Africa and studied literature and history in Konstanz and Hamburg. After graduating from art school, Weyhe has been working as a comics artist in Hamburg. Her graphic novels have been nominated for several prizes in Germany, France, and Japan. *Madgermanes* received the Berthold Leibinger Stiftung Comic Book Prize in 2015 and the Max und Moritz Prize in 2016 as the best German-language comic. In 2022 she was awarded the Lessing scholarship of the city of Hamburg. Her book, *Rude Girl*, was shortlisted for the Hamburg Literature Prize as "Book of the Year" and was the first comic ever to be nominated for the Leipzig Book Fair Prize in 2023.

Barbara Yelin, born in Munich in 1977, is an accomplished graphic novelist and illustrator who studied illustration at the Hamburg University of Applied Sciences. With a career spanning work for newspapers and international anthologies, Yelin is known for her focus on research-based historical and biographical graphic novels. Much of Yelin's work to date has focused on women's stories. In 2014, she published the award-winning graphic novel titled *Irmina*. Yelin's long-term collaboration with Holocaust child survivor Emmie Arbel resulted in the 2023 graphic novel *Emmie Arbel: The Colour of Memory*, edited by Charlotte Schallié and Alexander Korb and published by Reprodukt. In recognition of this work, Yelin received the Gustav Heinemann Peace Prize for Children's and Youth Literature in 2024.

Index

Aarons, Victoria, 9, 13
Adorno, Theodor, 86–87, 88n18, 100, 185
aesthetic distance: content and form in *Narrating Violence* exhibits, 177–78
aesthetic traditions in *Madgermanes*, 31, 33
affect: ocean and landscape representations of trauma, 37
affiliative postmemory, 89–92
Agamben, Giorgio, 43–44
agency: open landscape in *Endzeit*, 54; plant life in *Endzeit*, 64, 68–69; the reader's control, 10
alternative comics: *Narrating Violence* exhibition, 165. *See also* underground comix
American Beat movement, 183; Brinkmann and Rygulla's *ACID*, 197–202
American cultural production, Brinkmann sampling, 189–90
American Indian Movement (AIM), 55n36
Amin, Idi, 104
"Angriff aufs Monopol: Ich hasse alle Dichter" (Brinkmann), 186
animals, 24; bird motif in *Madgermanes*, 26–28; connecting affective memories in *Hat man erst angefangen zu reden*, 37–38; domestic violence in *Kiesgrubennacht*, 153; *Endzeit* imagery, 61–62; the healing effects of birds and, 37–39n55; hybridization in *Endzeit*, 71–72; ironic authenticity in *Kiesgrubennacht*, 157–58; mythology connections, 27–28n20;
Reiche's Nazi metaphors, 146–47; sexualized- and gender-based violence in *Narrating Violence* exhibits, 172, 176; traumatic memories in *Madgermanes*, 30–32
anthropomorphic masks: *Maus*, 82, 93–94
Antigone (Vieweg), 57–59, 57n43
antisemitism: *Kiesgrubennacht*, 154. *See also But I Live;* Holocaust trauma
Antoinette kehrt zurück (Antoinette Returns) (Vieweg), 41, 58
Anzaldúa, Gloria, 30
Arbel, Emmie, 122–23, 125, 127, 133, 135–36, *139*, 180, 180n48
archiving *Popliteratur*, 186–87
art, Black German, 111
art form, comics as, 1–2
arthrology, 190
Arts of Living on a Damaged Planet (Tsing, Swanson, Gan, Bubandt), 73–74
Assman, Aleida, 90
atrocities, 140–41, 146
authenticity: of childhood memories, 35–36; comics about making comics, 113–14; content and form in *Narrating Violence* exhibits, 177–78; factual accuracy in comics, 12; *Popliteratur*, 188–89; racial identity in modern discourse, 93
autobiography, 1–2; autobiographical narratives of trauma, 4–5; diversity of media in the *Narrating Violence* exhibition, 178–79; Lust's *Heute is der letzte Tag*, 172; Reiche's earlier prototype material, 142–48; relational and transnational, 21–23. *See also Belonging; But I Live*

banned books, 91–92
Baßler, Moritz, 187
Bauman, Zygmunt, 49n23
Beat poetry, 189–90
Beauvoir, Simone de, 86
Bechdel, Alison, 88
Becher, Christina, 64
Becoming Unbecoming (Una), 170
Beeler, Permin, 33–40
Belonging: A German Reckons with History and Home (Krug), 91, 100–101; biologistic and social paradigms, 84; generational trauma, 84–85; inherited guilt, 94–99; multimodality, 82; visual strategies of *Maus* and, 98–99
Berlin Wall, 45
binaries: comics' potential for undermining normativity, 184–89, 195–97; *Endzeit*, 45–53
Binky Brown Meets the Holy Virgin Mary (Green), 172n27
biological reductionism, 81–83
biologism, 83–84; biological nature of memory, 30–31; collective guilt in *Belonging*, 95–98; *Maus* and *Belonging*, 84–85; *Maus* resisting and unmasking, 93–94; quantifying traumatic wounds, 88–89; racial identity and, 93; social paradigms, 85–88
birds. *See* animals
Black by Design (Black), 116
Blackness: criticism of *Madgermanes*, 102–3; origins of *Rude Girl*, 106–7; Weyhe's representation of, 108–9
bleeding (comics technique), 9
Bordo, Susan, 195, 197n54, 200n61
Braiding Sweetgrass (Kimmerer), 65–66, 75
Brainard, Joe, *201*, 201–2
Breakdowns (Spiegelman), 141–44, 143n7, 144–45, 145n10
bricolage, Brinkmann's use of, 188–92, 196–98
Brinkmann, Rolf Dieter: *ACID*, 197–202; comics, sampling, and bricolage, 185–92; *Die Piloten*, 190–91, *191*, 192–97; explicit representations challenging normalcy, 192–96; representational injustice, 202–3; representations of heteronormativity, 192–96; sampling American cultural production, 189–90
Buchenwald Memorial Site, 47n19
Bulling, Nino, 180
Burdock, Maureen, 24
But I Live: Three Stories of Child Survivors of the Holocaust, 180n48; collaborating during the Covid-19 pandemic, 129–31; comics exhibition, 180; cover pages, 136–39; documenting the artistic practice, 119–20; the drawing process, 131–33; meeting the survivors, 124–27; responsibility for telling the truth, 122–23; story creation and composition, 127–29; survivor biographies, 134–35; working across languages, 133–34

capitalism: biologism in, 83–84; *Maus* as the commodification of trauma, 93–94. *See also* neoliberalism
Caribbean women's literature, gardens in, 29–30
Caruth, Cathy, 5–6, 9n20, 23, 56, 88–89, 91
causes of trauma, 4
censorship: Comics Code, 193, 193n43, 194, 196–97, 202
Ceremony (Silko), 34–35
chameleons: Weyhe's early formative memories, 104–5
Chaney, Michael, 12, 24
children and childhood: appeal of *Rude Girl*, 112–13; authenticity of memories, 35–36; cover pages of *But I Live,* 136–39, *138*; creation and composition of *But I Live*, 128, 131, 133; filming for *But I Live,* 124–25; intergenerational trauma transmission, 83–84; juxtaposing adult and child selves

in *Madgermanes*, 32; questions of memory in *Kiesgrubennacht*, 156–57; Reiche's "Ein Tag in meinem Leben," 142–43; sexualized and gender-based violence in *Narrating Violence*, 176; talking about Holocaust trauma, 126–27; violence in *Kiesgrubennacht*, 149–55, 159–62; Weyhe's nomadic life, 103–5
Chute, Hillary, 1, 8–10, 24, 36–37, 62–63, 92, 180–81
class, social: ocean and landscape images, 37
climate change: subfields of comics, 21. *See also Endzeit*
Coccia, Emanuele, 68–69
Cole, Tim, 131
collaborative works. *See But I Live: Three Stories of Child Survivors of the Holocaust; Rude Girl*
collective guilt, 96–98
color: creating *But I Live*, 131–33; imagery of vegetation and heat in *Endzeit*, 61–62, 71–72; Lust's *Heute ist der letzte Tag*, 172; violence in *Kiesgrubennacht*, 162
Comics, Trauma, and the New Art of War (Earle), 3
Comics Code, 193, 193n43, 194, 196–97, 202
comics form: *Kiesgrubennacht*, 155–58
coming of age: *Narrating Violence* exhibition, 164–65
commodification of trauma, 13, 93–94
community trauma, 34–35
consubstantial fatherhood, 88–89n20
contextualization: bricolage in *Popliteratur* sampling, 188–89; curating the *Narrating Violence* exhibition, 167
A Contract with God and Other Tenement Stories (Eisner), 1
control: arrangement of *Narrative Violence* media, 171; creating the drawings for *But I Live*, 132–33
counterculture, American: Brinkmann and Rygulla's *ACID*, 197–98; Brinkmann's sampling, 189–91;

Die Piloten, 196–97; underground comix, 191–92
courage: talking about Holocaust trauma, 126
cover pages: Brinkmann's *Die Piloten*, 191, 194, 196–97; *But I Live*, 136–39; family tree in *Belonging*, 95; *Kiesgrubennacht*, 149–51
Covid-19 pandemic and lockdown: collaboration on *But I Live*, 127, 129–31
cross-species infection in *Endzeit*, 61–62, 69–71
Crumb, Robert, 193–95
cultural appropriation, 22–23, 23n5, 26n17, 107–8
cultural construction of norms, 202–3

Das Haus (Feuchtenberger), *174*
Das Lachen der Medusa (Feuchtenberger), *174*
De Angelis, Richard, 31–32
dehumanization: Holocaust survivor experiences, 135
Der SS-Staat (Kogon), 155
dialectical method and positivism, 98–99
dialogue: comics as narrative drawing, 62–63
Die Piloten (Brinkmann), 190–91, *191*, 192–97
digital drawing: creating *But I Live*, 132
Digital Humanities, 81, 87n15
Diplomarbeit (Vieweg), 61
Disaster Drawn: Visual Witness, Comics, and Documentary Form (Chute), 92
disease in *Endzeit*: cross-species infection, 61–62, 70–71; trauma as infection, 44
disenfranchisement: East Germany, 43–44, 57–59
diversity: curating the *Narrating Violence* exhibition, 166–67, 178
DNA testing, 81–83, 81n2, 83
domestic violence in *Kiesgrubennacht*, 140–42, *144*, 149–55, 161

Donald Duck, 158, 185
Donovan, Courtney, 24
dream sequences: fantastical animals in *Madgermanes,* 32–33; Freud's interpretations, 56–57n40; Reiche's *Kiesgrubennacht,* 155; Reiche's "Über *Breakdowns,*" 144–45, 147, *148,* 162–63
dystopian future: *Endzeit,* 56

Eakin, Paul John, 25
East Germany: the consequences of neoliberalism, 41–44, 57–59. *See also Endzeit*
ecocriticism, 64, 66–67
eco-feminist thinking, 67
"Ein Tag in meinem Leben" (Reiche), 142–43, *144*
"Eine Buchkritik" (Padgett), 198, *199*
Eisner, Will, 1, 9–10, 11n39
Elmslie, Kenward, *201,* 201–2
embodied experience, 89–90
embodiment: Bordo on the materiality of, 200n61; drawings for *But I Live,* 132; graphic medicine, 184; *Narrating Violence* media, 170, 177
emotional response: curating the *Narrating Violence* exhibition, 166; *Heute ist der letzte Tag* embodying, 177
Endzeit (Vieweg), 2, 41; cross-species infection, 60–62, 61n3, 69–71; defining trauma, 50–51; emphasizing hybrid transformation, 74–76; establishing and transcending binaries, 45–53; the function of strawberries, 69–71; open ending, 53–57; persistence and transformation of conflict, 55–57; strategies for resisting zombies, 67–68; *The Strawberry Statement* and the East-West continuum, 48–49; visualizing plant power, 62–64; visualizing the monstrous nature of human lives, 73–74

entanglements, 13–14; multi-species entanglements in *Endzeit,* 15, 64–65, 72–73
Environmental Culture (Plumwood), 69
Ernst, Thomas, 187
Erwachsenen-Comics aus deutschen Landen (Adult Comics from German Lands) (Reiche), 151
ethics: comics facilitating engagement with Other, 14; the ethics of testimony in comics, 1; representational politics in contemporary culture, 23; testimony collection for *But I Live,* 121–22
ethnic conflict, 37
ethnicity. *See* race and ethnicity
ethnography, *Maus* as, 91n30
exhibitions, comics, 178n40. *See also Narrating Violence*
Exit Wounds (Rutu), 169–70
Extremities: Trauma, Testimony, and Community (Miller and Tougaw), 3
eyes: symbolism and importance in *Kiesgrubennacht,* 153

fabrication of norms, 202–3
familial postmemory, 88–92, 141–42
family: Adorno on the ambivalent situatedness of, 88n18; causes of trauma, 4; childhood of violence in *Kiesgrubennacht,* 149–55; the drawings for *But I Live,* 132; family, race, and mask in *Maus,* 91–95; fostering a sense of belonging, 91; group effort for *But I Live,* 124–25; Holocaust survivors, 134–35; inherited guilt in *Belonging,* 95; lineage and genealogy in trauma narratives, 82; memories and narratives in *But I Live,* 124–26; multiple perspectives in *Madgermanes,* 28; postmemory in *Kiesgrubennacht,* 141–42; quantifying traumatic wounds, 88–89; questions of memory

in *Kiesgrubennacht*, 155–56;
transnational family trauma, 22;
zombies in *Endzeit*, 51–52. *See also*
transmission of trauma
family trees, 82, 95–96
fathers: *Kiesgrubennacht*, 140, 143, 146, 152–55, 157, 159, 161–63; *Maus*, 149; sexual violence in *Love That Bunch*, 177–78; spiritual and consubstantial fatherhood, 88; SS involvement, 178. *See also* domestic violence
Faulkner, William, 46–47
fear: creating the cover pages of *But I Live*, 136
feminist philosophies: knowledge of plants, 67
fences as metaphor: *Endzeit*, 46–47, 49–54, 61, 67–69
Feuchtenberger, Anke, 172, 172n32, *174*, *175*, 176
Fiedler, Leslie, 185–86
film: fictionalizing a life, 106–7; imagery in *Endzeit*, 48–50
Finzi, Daniela, 164
flashbulb memories, 9
fleeing: *Narrating Violence* exhibition, 169–70
form and content: *Die Piloten*'s poetry, 196–97; *Narrating Violence*, 177–78
formal play, Brinkmann's use of, 190, 193, 196–98, 200, *201*, 202
Foucault, Michel, 99, 99n41
fragmented nature of comics, 8–13
Frahm, Ole, 180
frame narrative: in *Hat man erst angefangen zu reden*, 34; *Kiesgrubennacht*, 156
Frank, Anne, 131
Frankfurt School, 185
Freiburg Universität, 185–86
Freud, Sigmund, 6, 56–57n40, 84n9, 89, 91–92
Friedrich, Caspar David, 39, 95, 98
front covers. *See* cover pages
Fun Home: A Family Tragicomic (Bechdel), 24, 88

fungi: cross-species infection, 60–61, 61n3

Gardener, Jared, 156–57
the Gardener *(Endzeit)*, 69–72, 74–75
gardens, 28–29; symbols of power in *Madgermanes*, 29–30
gender: storm narratives and gendered injustices, 37
gender binaries: Brinkmann and Rygulla's *ACID*, 197; *Die Piloten*, 196–97; gendering reason and irrationality, 197n54
gender-based violence: *Narrating Violence* exhibition, 164–65, 169, 172. *See also* sexualized violence
generational trauma, 147–48. *See also* family; transmission of trauma
genocide: collective guilt in *Belonging*, 97; generational trauma, 84; increasing depiction in comics, 140–41; Reiche's *Kiesgrubennacht*, 142. *See also* Holocaust
Genossin Kuckuck: Ein deutsches Tier im deutschen Wald (Feuchtenberger), 172, 172n32, *174*, *175*, 176
George, Jessica, 64
German Calendar No December (Weyhe), 108–9
Gobineau, Arthur de, 87
Goethe, Johann Wolfgang von, 63
Goetz, Rainald, 186, 192–93n41
Gonçalves, Michelle, 114
Gonzales, Susana Vega, 26–27
graphic medicine, 21, 110–11, 184
Gravel Pit Night, 140
Green, Justin, 172n27
Greenspan, Henry, 120
Groensteen, Thierry, 190
group memory, 90
guilt: *Belonging*, 85, 94–99; *Kiesgrubennacht*, 140–42, 154–55; responsibility for racial trauma, 134; "Über *Breakdowns*," 148; working though familial and racial trauma, 100–101
Gunderman, Gerhard, 43–44, 55–56

gutters, use of: aptness for representing trauma, 8–10; constructing meaning between image and text, 184; facilitating closure, 33; materialization of trauma and history, 92; *Narrating Violence* exhibition, 167–68; thematic connections in *Narrating Violence*, 170

Hall, Matthew, 75
Hamburg, Germany, 105–6
Hansaplast patch, 95–96, 98
haptic interaction: *Narrating Violence* exhibition, 168–69
Haraway, Donna, 64
Hat man erst angefangen zu reden (Beeler), 33–40
Hatfield, Charles, 10, 157
healing: comics counteracting trauma, 11, 25
health: subfields of comics, 21
Hebdige, Dick, 188, 188n24, 192, 192n40
Heimat/homeland: coming home in *Endzeit*, 53; East Germany's post-1990s loss, 57–59; inherited and collective guilt in *Belonging*, 94–98; the loss of homeland in Vieweg's trilogy, 42–45; Weyhe's formative memories, 105
"Heimisches Eingeweide" (Domestic Entrails) (Elmslie), 201–2
Henry, Onyx Camille, 114
Hensel, Jana, 43
Hergé, 11
Herman, Judith, 7
heteronormativity, 183; "Jellied Salads," *201*, 201–2; representations in Brinkmann's work, 192–96
Heute ist der letzte Tag vom Rest deines Lebens (Today is the Last Day of the Rest of Your Life) (Lust), 2, 172, *173*, 177
hierarchies, racial, 87
High Fidelity (Hornby), 186

hippie movement, 183
Hirsch, Marianne, 88–89, 100, 146–47
historical comics, perception of, 157
historical trauma narratives, 99–100
Hofer, Regina, 178–79, *179*
Holocaust im Comic exhibition, 178n40
Holocaust trauma: Buchenwald Memorial Site, 47n19; family and trauma, 92; increasing depiction in comics, 140–41; *Narrating Violence* exhibition, 164–65, 179–80; Reiche's "Über *Breakdowns*," 146–48; suffering and trauma in *Belonging*, 96; unspeakability of trauma, 23–24; Weimar's history and landmarks, 47–48. *See also But I Live*; *Maus*
homeland. *See* Heimat/homeland
Hommer, Sascha, 180
Homo Sacer: Sovereign Power and Bare Life (Agamben), 44
Hopi prayer: *Endzeit*, 54–55n35, 54–56
Horkheimer, Max, 185
Horn, Tammy, 62
Hornby, Nick, 186
horror genre: plant growth and activity, 64–65
Huck Finn (Vieweg), 41, 58
humor: composition of *But I Live*, 129
hybrid nature of comics, 171–72
hypermasculinity, 183, 185, 194–97, 200–203

I Contain Multitudes: The Microbes Within Us and a Grander View of Life (Yong), 72–73
Ich weiß (Weyhe), 28n20, 32, 109
identity, ethnic and racial: biological reductionism, 81–83; inherited guilt in *Belonging*, 94–95; migrant experience defining East Germany's, 43–44
ideology: biological reductionism, 81–83

implicated subject, Reiche as, 142
inclusion/exclusion binary in *Endzeit*, 49–51
Indiana Jones movies, 106, 115
indigenous knowledge: human-plant hierarchies, 65–67
inherited trauma, inherited guilt and, 94–99
insects: cross-species infection, 60–61
Insekten (Maurer and Hofer), 178–79, *179*
intergenerational trauma, 82–84
Interpretation of Dreams (Freud), 56–57n40
intersectional question: curating the *Narrating Violence* exhibition, 166
intertextuality of comics, 190–91
intimacy, comics creating a sense of, 10
Irmina (Yelin), 82n3, 91n28
ironic authentication, 157
It Ain't Me Babe comic, 194–95

Jameson, Frederic, 188–89
"Jellied Salads" (Elmslie and Brainard), *201*, 201–2
Jews: themes of guilt in *Belonging*, 95, 97. *See also But I Live*
Jurassic Park (film), 70, 75

Kabalek, Kobi, 131
Kaffeetrinken (afternoon meal), 49–50
Kamp, Nico, 119, 122–26, 131–33, 135–36, 138, *138*
Kamp, Rolf, 119, 122–26, 131–36, 138, *138*
Keetley, Dawn, 63–64
Kenya: Weyhe's early formative memories, 105
Kesper-Biermann, Sylvia, 157
Kiesgrubennacht (Reiche): childhood of violence, 149–55; cover art, 149, *150*, 151; Reiche's earlier material, 142–43; representations of violence, 159–62; use of the comics form, 155–58; *Zebra* and "Über Breakdowns," 141
Kimmerer, Robin Wall, 65–66, 75

Kindheitsmuster (Patterns of Childhood) (Wolf), 46–47
kitschification of pain, 13
Kleist, Heinrich von, 176
Knigge, Andreas C., 160–61
Kogon, Eugen, 155
Kominsky-Crumb, Aline, 177–78, 195n49
Koné, Christophe, 113
König, Ralf, 160–61
Korb, Alex, 131
Kraenzle, Christina, 22–23, 31
Kramer, Anke, 66
Krug, Nora: familial transmission of memory, 90–91. *See also Belonging: A German Reckons with History and Home*
Krüger-Fürhoff, Irmela Marei, 11
Kunka, Andrew, 1, 91n30, 99–100
Kurdish landscape, 34

La Gerusalemme Liberata (Tasso), 88–89
labor migration, 21–22
LaCapra, Dominick, 3, 10–11
land: imagery in *Hat man erst angefangen zu reden*, 37
Land vor unserer Zeit (Land before our Time) (Vieweg), 57–58, 57n43
landscape, 24; coming home in *Endzeit*, 53; connection with Germandom in *Belonging*, 95–96; cultural trauma of oppressed communities, 34–35; gardens in *Madgermanes*, 29–30; in *Hat man erst angefangen zu reden*, 33–40; the open future in *Endzeit*, 53–57; relational and transnational, 39; scale framing in *Madgermanes*, 27–28; Vieweg's *Antoinette*, 41–42
language: collaborative creation of *But I Live*, 133–34; cover of Brinkmann's *Die Piloten*, 191; *Narrating Violence* exhibition, 165n3
The Language of Plants: Science, Philosophy, Literature (Gagliano, Ryan, and Viera), 68

The Last of Us video game, 60–61
Layne, Priscilla: co-creation of *Rude Girl*, 103; cultural appropriation in *Madgermanes*, 23; interview with Weyhe, 105–6; lived experience and fiction, 109–10; melding the text and graphics, 113–15; motivation for *Rude Girl* collaboration, 106–7; politics, racism, and symbolism in *Rude Girl*, 111; representing skin color in comics, 109; TED talk, 115–16; Weyhe's representation of Blackness, 108–9
Lebenslinien comics (Weyhe), 106, 109
Lederman, Marsha, 124
Libicki, Miriam, 122–31, 133–36, *137*
Liebe: Ein Männer-Emanzo-Comic (Love: A Men's Emancipation Comic) (Reiche), 145–46, 151, 151n15
The Life of Plants (Coccia), 68–69
Lila (Robinson), 39–40
Literaturen und Kulturen des Vegetabilen (Literatures and Cultures of the Vegetable), 66
Little Nemo in Slumberland (McCay), 147
Love That Bunch (Kominsky-Crumb), 177–78
Lust, Ulli, 2, 172, *173*, 177

Madgermanes (Weyhe), 2, 25–33, 114; bird metaphors, 39; documenting migrant experiences, 21–22; representation of Blackness, 102–3; representing skin color in comics, 109; Weyhe's memories and characters, 105
Magritte, René, 99, 99n41
Marder, Michael, 66–67
The Marquise of O (Kleist), 176
masks: African-style masks in *Madgermanes*, 26, 26n17, 27; race as a mask in *Maus*, 15, 82, 84, 91–95
mass murders: Reiche's *Kiesgrubennacht*, 152, 154–55
materiality of comics, 89, 170
Maurer, Leopold, 178–79, *179*
Maus (Spiegelman): animals as metaphor, 24, 31–32; biologistic and social paradigms, 84; factual accuracy, 12; family, race, and mask, 91–95; generational trauma, 84–85; growth of Shoah theme in comics, 140–41; language translation, 134; multimodality, 82; *Narrating Violence* exhibition, 178; Reiche's "Über *Breakdowns*," 146–47; resolving racial trauma, 100–101; trauma in graphic novel form, 1; visual strategies of *Belonging* and, 98
McCarthy, Margaret, 195
McCay, Winsor, 147
McCloud, Scott, 63, 92
McFall-Ngai, Margaret, 73–74
McLuhan, Marshall, 185
Means, Russell, 55n36
media: creating the cover pages for *But I Live*, 136–39
memoir: *But I Live*, 119–39; origins of *Rude Girl*, 106–8; Reiche's *Kiesgrubennacht*, 140
memory: autobiographical narratives of trauma, 4–5; biological nature of, 30–31; biological trauma transmission, 83–84; conditions of traumatic memories, 5; cultural memory through objects, 85, 96; interviews for *But I Live* narratives, 124–26; *Madgermanes* as relational autobiography, 25–33; oceanic waves expressing emotional waves, 35–36; questions of memory in *Kiesgrubennacht*, 155–57; Weyhe's early formative memories, 104
mental health: subfields in comics, 21–22
Mickey aux Camp de Gurs (Rosenthal), 178, 178n41
Mickey Mouse, 109, 178, 178n41
microbial life, 72–73
Middle East conflict, 1; *Narrative Violence* exhibition, 169–70

migration: comics capturing migrant experiences, 21; in *Hat man erst angefangen zu reden*, 34–40; inherited guilt in *Belonging*, 94–95; migrant experience defining East Germany's identity, 43–44; migratory birds motif in *Madgermanes*, 26–28; *Narrating Violence* exhibition, 164–65, 169–70
mindfulness training, 37–38
misogyny: explicit sex in underground comix, 194–95
Modan, Rutu, 169–70, 170n21
modes of meaning, 182n2
Morrison, Toni, 27
mothers: composition of *But I Live*, 131; depiction in *Kiesgrubennacht*, 153–55, 161
mother-son relationships, 33–34
Mozambique, 25–26, 30, 105
multimodality: Brinkmann's *Die Piloten*, 196–97; Brinkmann's sampling of multimodal play, 183, 189–91; comics addressing social injustice, 182; comics disrupting hierarchies and norms, 195–96; defining, 182n2; effectiveness of graphic novels, 10; *Maus* and *Belonging*, 82; undermining norms through sampling *Popliteratur*, 187–88
multispecies kinships, 64
music, 199, 200–201; *Endzeit*, 53–54, 76–77n37; Gunderman's "Ossi-Reservation," 43–44, 55–56; Weyhe's use of, 113–15
"Mutationsblues," 198, 200–201
myths: symbolism of birds, 27–28n20; trauma transmission, 83n6

Narrating Violence: curating and staging the museum exhibit, 165–68; exhibition of reproductions and originals, 171–76; multifaceted representations of violence, 176–81; the spatial arrangement, 168–71
narrative strategies and style: duality of memories in *Kiesgrubennacht*, 149; frame narrative in *Kiesgrubennacht*, 151, 156–57; representations of violence in *Kiesgrubennacht*, 162–63; representations of violence in *Narrating Violence*, 176–77
Native American thinkers, 54–55n35, 54–56, 65–66
Nazi ideology, 49n23, 134; generational trauma, 95; Hofer and Maurer's narration of violence, 178–79, *179*; inherited guilt in *Belonging*, 95–96; Krug's sense of belonging, 91; metaphorical reading of animals, 31–32x; Reiche's father, 161–62; Reiche's *Kiesgrubennacht*, 140–42, 152–54; Reiche's metaphorical use of animals, 146–47; resonances in *Endzeit*, 47–48
neocolonialism: Othering reinforcing colonial power relations, 22–23
neoliberalism: East German trauma in *Endzeit*, 42–44; political and social consequences for East Germany, 41–42; post-1990s trauma, 57–59; statelessness ensuing from, 14, 42–45
Neo-Nazis, fantastical animals symbolizing, 31–33
New York School of poetry, 189–90
Nichols, Bill, 157–58
Nijdam, Elizabeth "Biz": Satrapi's *Persepolis*, 141n2; social justice in comics, 183–85, 202–3; Weyhe interview, 105–6, 108–16
Nineteen Eighty-four (Orwell), 200, 200n59
Nömaier, Peter, 164
normative behavior: *ACID* failing to undermine, 198–99; Brinkmann mining American counterculture, 189–90; comics' potential for undermining, 184–89, 195–97; cultural construction, 202–3; *Die Piloten* disrupting sexual norms, 196–97; Zappa interview and *ACID* visualization, 200
Novelle (Goethe), 63

oceanic waves: imagery in *Hat man erst angefangen zu reden,* 35–37
Oedipus complex, 91–92
O'Hara, Frank, 189–90
On Photography (Sontag), 99n41
"On the Inequality of Races" (Gobineau), 87
Oreo (Ross), 116
Orwell, George, 200n59
"Ossi-Reservation" (Gunderman), 43–44, 55–56
Other: animals as metaphor, 24–25; inherited attributes of personality, 83; modal complexity in *Madgermanes,* 33; physical barriers in *Endzeit,* 45–46, 50–51; transnational trauma, 22–23

Padgett, Ron, 198, *199*
paintings: wound culture, 159–60
Palestine (Sacco), 169–70
panels: composition of *But I Live,* 129, 131–32; German victimhood and suffering in *Belonging,* 97; *Narrating Violence* exhibition, 167–68; narrative strategies in *Narrating Violence,* 177; thematic connections in *Narrating Violence,* 170; unconventional use in "Eine Buchkritik," 198
Paronnaud, Vincent, 166, 169
Parque municipal Belo Horizonte, Brazil, 28–29, 29n24
patriarchy: womanhood as a social construct, 86
performativity: biological grounding of, 100; Holocaust survivors' stories and memories, 125–26
perpetrator trauma, 42n4; conflating suffering and victimization, 13; in *Kiesgrubennacht,* 140–42, 154–55; Reiche's "Über *Breakdowns,*" 146–48; Vieweg's trilogy, 42
Persepolis (animation), 24, 166, 169
personal trauma narratives, 99–100
Pessler, Monika, 164
photographs: collaboration on *But I Live,* 130; "reading," 99n41

pictorial embodiment, 177
pictorial encoding, 8–13
Plant Horror: Approaches to the Monstrous Vegetal in Fiction and Film (Keetley), 63–64
Plant Thinking: A Philosophy of Vegetal Life (Marder), 66–67
plants, 24; color palette in *Endzeit,* 71–72; connecting past, present, and future, 68–69; cross-species infection in *Endzeit,* 61–62, 69–72; the family tree in *Belonging,* 95–96; graphic images in *But I Live,* 124; hereditary transmission, 85–86; motifs in *Madgermanes,* 26, 28–29; post-apocalyptic growth, 60–61; the power and agency of, 64, 68–69; pushing the limits of knowledge, 63–64; status in *Endzeit,* 72–73
Plants as Persons: A Philosophical Botany (Hall), 75
Plants in Science Fiction (George), 64, 75–76
Plumwood, Val, 69
poetry: *Die Piloten,* 196–97; Nazi sympathizers, 161–62
Popliteratur: explicit representation of sexualized bodies, 192–96; the issues with sampling, 186–87; power relations, 195; representational injustice in Brinkmann's work, 202–3; reproducing power relations, 195; sampling and archiving, 186–88
Popper, Karl, 86–87
popular culture: comics disrupting hierarchies and norms, 195–96; form and content in *Die Piloten,* 196–97; representations of violence in *Kiesgrubennacht,* 159–62; West German and American visions of, 185–86; Weyhe's lack of cultural knowledge, 108
pornographic elements: challenging and disrupting normalcy, 193–94; voyeurism and images of pain, 10–11. *See also* sexualized violence

positivism, 99–101; biological reconstruction of race, 85–86; biological reductionism, 81–83, 86–87; visual strategies of *Belonging* and *Maus*, 98
Positivismusstreit (positivism controversy), 86–87
post-apocalyptic age, 60
postmemory, 89–92, 147–48
postmodernism, *Popliteratur* as, 186
post-racial era: representing skin color in comics, 109
power relations: Othering reinforcing colonial power relations, 22–23; pop culture references in *Popliteratur*, 195; powerlessness defining trauma, 7
protest: post-1990 East Germany, 41–42, 44–45; *The Strawberry Statement*, 48–50
psychic unity, 8
psychoanalysis: *Endzeit*, 67; *Narrating Violence* exhibition, 164, 168–69, 172, 176
psychological disorders, 54n34; *Endzeit*, 51; mindfulness training, 37–38; neoliberalism in East Germany, 41; storm as metaphor in *Hat man erst angefangen zu reden*, 36–37; therapeutic benefit of animals and birds, 37–39n55
punk, 113–14, 188n23, 192n40

race and ethnicity: biological determinism, 85–86; biological reductionism, 81–83; criticism of *Madgermanes*, 102–3; fostering a sense of belonging, 91; *Maus* unmasking, 92–94; ocean and landscape images, 37; origins of *Rude Girl*, 106–7; representations of violence in *Narrating Violence*, 176–77; as a social construction, 100–101; trauma transmission, 84; white privilege in *Madgermanes*, 26
racism: comics inflicting trauma on the reader, 11; migration in *Madgermanes*, 28; representing skin color in comics, 109

rape. *See* sexualized violence
Rave (Goetz), 186
ravens, 27–28n20
Ravensbrück Memorial site, 125, 180
reason and irrationality, gendering, 197n55
recursivity in pictorial representations, 9
Redrawing Stories from the Past (Frahm and Hommer), 180
Reiche, Volker: earlier autobiographical prototype material, 142–48; response to Spiegelman's *Breakdowns*, 144–45; "Über *Breakdowns*," 145. *See also Kiesgrubennacht;* "Über *Breakdowns*"
relational autobiography, 22–23; *Madgermanes*, 25–33
relational memory: *But I Live*, 120–21
reportage, comics and, 169–70
representation: comics empowering minoritized populations, 184–85; criticism of *Madgermanes*, 102–3; multifaceted representations of violence in *Narrating Violence*, 176–81
representational injustice, 17–18, 182, 184–85, 202–3
responsibility: *Kiesgrubennacht*, 154–55; Reiche's "Über *Breakdowns*," 148
restoring justice, 7–8
rhythm, 128–29; collaborative creation on *But I Live*, 128–30
Robbins, Trina, 11n40, 194–95, 195n50
Robinson, Marilynne, 39–40
Rosenthal, Horst, 178n41
Rothberg, Michael, 7–8
Rothe, Anne, 1n1, 13
Rude Girl (Weyhe), 23n5, 103; audience for and reception of, 112–13; co-creation of, 106–7, 109–15; explaining the title, 116; origins and expansion of, 105–107; physical representation of Blackness, 108–9; teaching, 110–11
Rygulla, Ralf-Rainer, 197–202

Sacco, Joe, 153, 169–70, 170n21
sampling *Popliteratur,* 187, 187n20, 190–92, *191,* 197–202
Sanyal, Mithu, 91n29
Satrapi, Marjane, 1–2, 141n2, 166, 169
Satterlee, Michelle, 34–35
savages: East German identity in *Endzeit,* 42–44; zombies in *Endzeit,* 46
scale framing, 27, 30
Schaffer, David, 124, 128, 131–36, *137*
Schallié, Charlotte, 133, 180
Schmid, Johannes C.P., 28
scripting: creating *But I Live,* 132
The Second Sex (Beauvoir), 86
secrecy: defying the unspeakability of trauma, 7–8
The Seduction of the Innocent (Wertham), 193n43
selective memory, 4–5
self, disintegration of, 5–6
self-portrait, *Kiesgrubennacht* as, 154–55
self-reflectivity, comics promoting, 10
Seliktar, Gilad, 122–28, 130–36, *138*
Seminar magazine, 183–84
Sendak, Maurice, 32
sensationalism in comics, 10–11, 11n38
sexual acts in comics: *Die Piloten* disrupting sexual norms, 196–97; inflicting trauma on the reader, 11; representational injustice in Brinkmann's work, 202–3; underground comix, 194–95
sexual liberation movements: Reiche's *Liebe,* 145–46
sexualized violence: content and form in *Narrating Violence* exhibits, 177–78; Crumb's underground comix, 194–95; designing and assembling the *Narrating Violence* exhibition, 164–65, 169–71; Feuchtenberger's work in *Narrating Violence,* 173, 176; Lust's *Heute ist der letzte Tag,* 172, 177; ocean and landscape images, 37
Shoah. *See* Holocaust
Sigmund Freud Museum, Vienna, Austria, 164
Silko, Leslie Marmon, 34–35
slapstick comedy: representations of violence in comics, 159, 161, 164–65n2; Spiegelman's *Breakdowns,* 144
social activism, Reiche's, 151
social construction: ethnicity as, 91; family and family trees, 82, 87–88, 91; family and racial trauma in *Maus* and *Belonging,* 100–101; trauma transmission, 15; womanhood as, 86
social justice: Brinkmann's postmodernist aims, 202–3; causes of trauma, 4; comics working in opposition to, 184; complexity of textual meaning, 182–83; creation of *Rude Girl,* 109; representational injustice in Brinkmann's work, 202–3; trauma in graphic narratives providing representation and empowerment, 12–13, 18, 24, 40
Social Justice Education (SJE), 183–85, 187, 202–3
social paradigms, biological determinism and, 15, 84–88
socio-political trauma, 42
Soloalbum (Stuckrad-Barre), 186
Sontag, Susan, 99n41
Spiegel, David, 5
Spiegelman, Art: *Breakdowns,* 143–44, 143n7, 144–45; factual accuracy in comics, 12; *Narrating Violence* exhibition, 178; Reiche's *Kiesgrubennacht,* 162–63; Reiche's "Über *Breakdowns,*" 145–47, 151
spiritual fatherhood, 88–89n20
Squier, Susan Merrill, 11, 27
statelessness: East Germany, 44–45, 52–53
Staying with the Trouble: Making Kin with the Chthulucene (Haraway), 64
Stobbe, Urte, 66

storyboard: creating *But I Live,* 131–32
strawberries: symbolism and function in *Endzeit,* 48–50, 67, 70–72, 74
The Strawberry Statement (film), 48–50, 53
Strizz (Reiche), 140fn, 144–45, 151, 157–61
structural characteristics: thematic connections in *Narrating Violence,* 170–71. *See also* cover pages; gutters, use of; panels
structural overdetermination: *Narrating Violence* exhibition, 167–68
Stuckrad-Barre, Benjamin von, 186
subculture, *Popliteratur* as, 188
subfields of comics, 21
subjectivity: of childhood memories, 35–36
substance, human, 88–89n20
subversive form, 202–3
suicide: *Endzeit,* 67–68
superhero genre, 11, 11n40; cover of *Die Piloten,* 196; history of violence in comics medium, 161, 164–65n2; representing hypermasculinity, 11
Sutcliffe, Peter William, 170–71
swastika, 192n40
Swiss landscape, 34

't Veld, Laurike in, 141, 153
Tamgout, Buchenwald, Paris (Bulling), 180
Tasso, Torquato, 88–89
teaching: *Rude Girl,* 110–11
TED talks, 115–16
testimony, comics as, 1
testimony collection practices: *But I Live,* 120–22
text-image contrast: alterations in *Narrative Violence* media, 172; cover of Brinkmann's *Die Piloten,* 190–92, *191*; curating the *Narrating Violence* exhibition, 167–68; "Eine Buchkritik"'s unconventional panels, 198; enabling transmediation in *Endzeit,* 62; factual accuracy in comics, 12; gutters constructing meaning, 184; panels of *Die Piloten,* 196–97; the power of plants in *Endzeit,* 64; the role of race in *Maus,* 92; role of the Gardener in *Endzeit,* 71; visual strategies of *Belonging* and *Maus,* 98–99
Ther, Philip, 44
time: comics shifting the linear progression of, 9–10; effects of trauma on the perception of, 6
Tintin in the Congo (Hergé), 11
translation: *Narrating Violence* exhibition, 165n3; working across languages in *But I Live,* 133–34
transmediation, 62
transmission of trauma, 83n5; lineage and genealogy in narratives, 82; postmemory, 89–92; prevalence of biologism, 83–84; Reiche's "Über Breakdowns," 146–47; sexualized and gender-based violence in *Narrating Violence,* 176
transnational contexts of trauma, 21–23; *Madgermanes,* 25–26
trauma, defining, 3–8, 50
trauma, recent scholarship on, 8–13
trauma theory, 82; entwinement of family and trauma, 91–92; ignoring bystanders, 84n9; quantifying traumatic wounds, 88–89; recovering from trauma, 42; social and biological presuppositions, 86–88
Trezise, Thomas, 7, 7n20, 23
trust: talking about Holocaust trauma, 126
truth-telling: *But I Live* testimony collection, 122–23
Tsing, Anna, 75–76
Turkey: *Hat man erst angefangen zu reden,* 34

"Über *Breakdowns*" (Reiche), *145, 148; Kiesgrubennacht* and, 151, 162–63; postmemory, 147–48; Spiegelman's *Breakdowns* and, 144–45

Uganda, 25–26, 104–5
Uhu glue, 95–96, 98
Ukraine: *Narrating Violence* exhibition, 166–67, 170n21
Una, 170–71
underground comix, 172n27; Brinkmann and Rygulla's *ACID*, 197–98; Brinkmann's *Die Piloten*, 190–91, *191*, 194; Brinkmann's exclusionary technique, 191–92; explicit sexual acts and sexualized violence, 192–96; gender-diverse perspectives, 195n50; *Narrating Violence* exhibition, 165; use of formal play, 196–97
Understanding Comics (McCloud), 63, 92
Ustundag, Ebru, 24

Väterliteratur, 140–41
vectorizing, 198
vegetation. *See* plants
victimization: *But I Live* cover page, 136; childhood trauma in *Kiesgrubennacht*, 16–17; commodification of and habituation to trauma, 13; effect of trauma on readers, 11; *Endzeit*'s zombies, 51–53; intergenerational trauma, 84, 84n8; perpetrator trauma, 42n4, 51, 141–42, 148; the power of storytelling, 8; recovery from, 42; refusal to become victims in *Endzeit*, 52–53; resistance to representation, 5–7, 7n20; self-victimization in *Belonging*, 95–98. *See also But I Live*
victim-witness dynamic, 7–8
video games: violence in *Kiesgrubennacht*, 160
Vieweg, Olivia. *See Endzeit*
violence: anti-comics debate, 193n43; creation and composition of *But I Live*, 127–28; fantastical animal metaphors, 32; history in comics medium, 164–65n2; Kurdish unrest, 34; *Narrating Violence* exhibition, 164–65; perpetration and consumption of, 142; representations of violence in *Kiesgrubennacht*, 159–62; state and family violence in *Kiesgrubennacht*, 152. *See also* domestic violence; *Narrating Violence;* sexualized violence
Visser, Irene, 23
visual encoding, 8–13
visual strategies: *Maus* unmasking race, 92
Volk: positivistic construction of race, 85–86; suffering in *Belonging*, 96; trope of German victimhood, 96–98
voyeurism, comics lessening the tendency towards, 10–11, 13

Waffen SS, family involvement with, 178, 180n46
The Wanderer above the Sea of Fog (Friedrich), 39, 95, 98
Wanning, Berbeli, 66
war: familial transmission of memory, 90–92; generational trauma, 84; increasing depiction in comics, 140–41; *Narrating Violence* exhibition, 164–65, 169–70; occupation in conflict zones, 1–2; representations of violence in *Kiesgrubennacht*, 159–62; sexual violence in *Narrating Violence*, 176. *See also* Holocaust
war crimes, 47
War of the Second Coalition (1799–1802), 176
watercolor: creating the drawings for *But I Live*, 132–33, 136
webcomics: curating the *Narrating Violence* exhibition, 166–67; haptic interaction in *Narrating Violence*, 169
Wertham, Frederic, 193n43
Western philosophy: human-plant hierarchies, 65–67
Weyhe, Birgit: audience for and reception of *Rude Girl*, 112–13;

collaborative process for *Rude Girl*, 114–16; cultural knowledge, 108; interpretation of Layne's narrative, 110–11; representing skin color in comics, 109; struggling with the storytelling, 107
Where the Wild Things Are (Sendak), 32
white privilege, 26
Why Comics (Chute), 62–63
Wilhelm Busch und die Folgen (König and Knigge), 160–61
Wimmen's Comix, 195n50
witches, 67
Witnessing Witnessing: On the Reception of Holocaust Survivor Testimony (Trezise), 9n20
Wolf, Christa, 46–47
women: children's perspective of narration, 36; comics readership, 11n40; conveying trauma-related challenges, 24; effect of biological determinism, 85–86; explicit sex in underground comix, 194–95. *See also* sexualized violence
World War II: familial transmission of memory, 90–92. *See also* Holocaust; war
wound culture, 159–60
wounds, traumatic, 88–90

Wulz, Janine, 122

xenophobia: inherited guilt in *Belonging,* 95; zombies in *Endzeit,* 46

Yelin, Barbara: *But I Live* interviews and artwork, 122–23, 125–31, 133–36, *139,* 180, 180n48; resolving inherited trauma, 91n28
Yong, Ed, 72–73
Yorkshire Ripper, 170–71

Zap Comics (Crumb), 194
Zappa, Frank, 198, *199,* 200–201
Zebra (Reiche), 142–43
zombies in *Endzeit,* 44n10, 70–71; cross-species infection, 61–62, 61n3, 69–71; East German identity, 42–44; establishing and transcending binaries, 46; the Gardener in *Endzeit,* 69–70; Hopi prayer, 55–56; learning resistance strategies, 67–68; as metaphor for humanity, 51; the monstrous nature of human lives, 73–74; politics of inclusion and exclusion, 48–49; symbolism of strawberries, 48–50

Printed in the United States
by Baker & Taylor Publisher Services